One Day

One Day

The Extraordinary Story of
an Ordinary 24 Hours
in America

Gene Weingarten

BLUE RIDER PRESS
New York

blue
rider
press

An imprint of Penguin Random House LLC
penguinrandomhouse.com

LIBRARY OF CONGRESS CATALOGING-IN-PUBLICATION DATA

Names: Weingarten, Gene, author.
Title: One day : the extraordinary story of an ordinary 24 hours
in America / Gene Weingarten.
Description: New York : Blue Rider Press, 2019.
Identifiers: LCCN 2019001936 | ISBN 9780399166662 (hardback) |
ISBN 9780698135598 (ebook)
Subjects: LCSH: United States—Social conditions—Anecdotes. |
United States—Social life and customs—Anecdotes. | United States—
Biography—Anecdotes. | BISAC: HISTORY / United States / General. |
SOCIAL SCIENCE / Sociology / Urban. | POLITICAL SCIENCE /
Public Policy / General.
Classification: LCC E185.86.W4355 2019 | DDC 973—dc23
LC record available at https://lccn.loc.gov/2019001936

Printed in Canada
1   3   5   7   9   10   8   6   4   2

BOOK DESIGN BY KATY RIEGEL

To Max

One Day

Introduction

To see a World in a Grain of Sand,
And a Heaven in a Wild Flower,
Hold Infinity in the palm of your hand
And Eternity in an hour
—WILLIAM BLAKE, *"Auguries of Innocence"*

A t 2:05 P.M. on Thursday, December 13, 2012, I sent an email to Tom Shroder, my friend and editor. It said, in its entirety: "I wonder what happened on May 17, 1957."

The phone rang. It was Tom. "That's a good idea," he said.

If it doesn't sound like an idea to you, much less a good one, it's because you lack context. Tom and I were forever bouncing off each other ambitious concepts for our next book. We usually trashed them, for kindness' sake.

Between us, Tom and I had written seven books, only two of which—one apiece—had even approached commercial success. The business model for the book publishing industry resembles the business model for nineteenth-century oil-well wildcatters—that is to say, it is an economy of informed guesswork. Most books are financial failures, but the rare hit becomes a gusher and underwrites all the dry holes. This may keep the publishing industry afloat, but it wreaks hell on writers' egos. With book ideas, friends don't let friends get too enthusiastic.

But Tom liked this idea and understood it implicitly. Select an ordinary day at random, report it deeply, then tell it like it happened—from midnight to midnight, the most basic, irreducible unit of human experience. Ideally, the more you'd learn, the more firmly you'd establish that in life, there's no such thing as "ordinary." Also, that in the events of a single day—in that telltale grain of sand—you would find embedded in microcosm all of the grand themes in what hacks and academics tend to call The Human Experience.

It was a stunt, at its heart. But I *like* stunts, particularly if they can illuminate unexpected truths. The magazine story for which I am best known involved placing Joshua Bell, the renowned violinist, outside a Metro stop in downtown Washington, D.C., at rush hour, incognito. In jeans, a polo shirt, and a baseball cap, for three-quarters of an hour on his priceless Stradivarius, Bell played timeless music, masterpieces by Bach and Schubert and Massenet, with a violin case at his feet, open for handouts, seeded with petty change. Would anyone notice the extraordinary beauty that was happening twenty feet away?

Few did. Most people hurried by, as if the fiddler in the subway were a nuisance to be avoided. What happened that day became a story not about our taste and sophistication but about our priorities: Have we so overprogrammed our lives that it is impossible to experience unscheduled awe? How many other worthy things are we racing past?

The stunt of reporting an ordinary day would also test a journalistic conceit I embrace: That if you have the patience to find it and the skill to tell it, there's a story behind everyone and everything—that although great matters make for strong narratives, power also can lurk in the latent and mundane.

As the Sunday features editor at *The Washington Post*, I once assigned five writers to each hammer a nail into the phone book and do a profile of whomever the nail stopped at. It was a wild stab, literally, and it hit a vital organ—we got five compelling stories. One Christmas I summoned four of the best writers at the *Post* and sent them off in different directions—one north, one south, one east, one west, with instructions to walk no farther than seven blocks and bring me back a good Christmas story. If you don't find one, I said, you may as well not return. They all came back, and collectively they pulled off a Christmas miracle.

The most important book of my teenaged years, the one that really changed the way I thought about things, was *Flatland*, an obscure 1884 work of science fiction and social satire written by an unassuming English schoolmaster and theologian named Edwin Abbott Abbott. The man with the eccentric name wrote what may well be the most eccentric book of his generation, a slender, crudely illustrated novella set in a two-dimensional world inhabited by sentient geometric figures.

The narrator, a square, is visited one day by a sphere. Initially, the square sees this three-dimensional being only as a circle of rapidly changing diameter. This is because a sphere, arriving from above and descending into and through the two-dimensional plane in which the square lives, would fluctuate in circumference depending on the diameter of the portion of the sphere that happens to be intersecting the flat plane, as a circle, at any particular moment. (There will be no more math.)

The sphere is received as something of a deity. He has selected the square to be his disciple and prophet. He would show the square the existence of a third dimension, and then send him back to his land to spread the news as gospel. Thus the sphere elevates the square above Flatland into Spaceland, so he can look down and see his circumscribed, unlovely world with disturbing new clarity—a despotic, socially rigid, class-obsessed aristocracy—even further diminished by the startling knowledge of an entirely new, seemingly limitless dimension of existence.

Back in Flatland, the square's excited vision of Spaceland seemed to others not like science but like faith, since such a thing could not be demonstrated or even adequately explained within the context of a two-dimensional world. In the end, the square was punished for his insights because they challenged accepted dogma. He was Galileo, but he did not bend. He became a martyr for truth.

It's a charming little book and considerably deeper than it seems. It anticipates relativity and quantum physics. It explores the self-protective hypocrisy of organized religion, the suppression of inconvenient thought, and the ugliness of class oppression. But to my teenaged eyes it was mostly about the possibility of heightened perception through heightened perspective—thinking outside the box.

Our ordinary understanding of the world is myopic, limited not only by our imperfect senses and flawed powers of analysis but also by the capricious nature of the news narrative we are presented with, day to day and year to year. Fame is transient and shallow, and even the more reflective storytelling of historians tends to shine arbitrary spotlights; significant events and meaningful connections go undiscovered.

Hence *One Day*. But it would be one day presented both microscopically and panoramically, from deep within but also high above, able to see forward and backward in time—applying the added, illuminating benefit of that fourth dimension.

WHAT REMAINED WAS selection of the day, and it had to be completely random. That is how Tom Shroder and I came to be at the Old Ebbitt Grill, a stately Washington, D.C., oyster house, at lunchtime on New Year's Day, 2013. We brought an old green fedora.

Tom had suggested a dart thrown at a sheet of numbers, but I demurred. You can aim a dart; even blindfolded and with the best of intentions, there'd be a feel of manipulation. So we went with the hat, into which we would crumple sixty-four slips of paper in three separate drawings. First, the twelve months of the year, then the thirty-one days of the month, and last, the twenty-one years to which we'd decided to limit the field: 1969 through 1989. (We wanted a date far enough in the past to feel like "history" and have a future to explore, but not so far back that living witnesses would be hard to find.) We'd left ourselves with 7,670 possible dates.

The first draw was made by Oscar Southwell, age eleven, who was dining with his parents at a nearby table. Oscar pulled December. His sister, Willow, eight, drew the twenty-eighth. Not wishing to incite sibling squabblery for rights to the final dip, Tom and I returned to our table and asked the waitress to pick the year.

December 28, 1986, would be our day, for better or worse. A quick calendar check revealed it to have been a Sunday.

Tom and I spent the following few minutes in silence, consuming mollusks and contemplating, separately and sourly, our grotesque bad luck.

Any journalist can tell you that Sunday is the slowest news day of the week, and what little news there is often goes underreported by skeleton newsroom staffs. That's why, particularly in the journalistically flush 1980s, the local newspaper that would on all other days thud onto your driveway like a sack of wet succotash, would, on Mondays, settle like a leaf.

Also, any journalist can tell you that the softest news week of the year is the sleepy one between Christmas and New Year's. So we had the worst day of the week in the worst week of the year. Nineteen eighty-six didn't ring any particular big-news bells, either.

Obviously, there could be no do-overs. *Randomly* is built into the DNA of the book; it is its central swagger, and a mulligan would dismantle that claim. (If, in a weak moment, either Tom or I considered timidly suggesting a secret waiver of that central principle in the face of the problematic date, neither of us has yet admitted it to the other.)

I got home to an email from Tom. "John D. MacDonald died on The Day," he said. It was our first solid fact, a top hit when you search the date. It also provided the first strange reverberation in a project that would end up with many more. This echo was serpentine, and personal, and weird, and it reached a half century into the past. It will take some explaining.

John D. MacDonald was a prolific writer of hard-boiled detective thrillers and the creator of Travis McGee, the emotionally callused but philosophically articulate "salvage consultant" who lived on a houseboat in Florida and hired himself out to recover items that had been lost by victims of larceny, swindle, or assorted other unscrupulousnesses. These stolen things could be as concrete as a car or as abstract as a reputation. I'd read some Travis McGee and liked it.

MacDonald's death in a Milwaukee hospital on December 28, 1986, was not eventful, as ends of lives go. He'd uttered no dramatic last words—indeed, no last words at all. Three months before, at seventy, he'd walked into that hospital on his own steam for scheduled heart bypass surgery, but afterward, things quickly went bad. His lungs filled with fluid faster than a dipso broad at an open bar. By December 1, he was in a coma, and two weeks later his brain was cheese. Death sucker-punched John D. MacDonald, sapped him from behind like the gutless punk it is.

Actually, MacDonald wrote nothing like that. His tough talk was graceful and his insights profound. In the thirty years before his death, he had almost single-handedly rescued the hard-boiled detective novel from a generation of Raymond Chandler imitators. MacDonald had taken the manhandled genre, shook off the cliché, reinstated the intelligence, and added a social conscience.

By the time of his death on December 28, 1986, his novels were widely accepted as literature, but there was a time when this hardly seemed likely. In the 1950s, he was essentially a pulp writer, cerebrally experimenting with the form, but very much a part of it.

MacDonald had become an adjunct member of a small literary colony in Sarasota, Florida, mostly men like MacDonald in reverent orbit around the dean of Florida writers, the dapper master of historical novels and short stories, MacKinlay Kantor. Kantor had turned his formidable skills as a storyteller into great fame, and for a time, considerable fortune. He won a Pulitzer for his masterwork, *Andersonville.* Drove a big brassy yellow Lincoln. Visited his friend Hemingway in Cuba.

Kantor would become a deeply influential force in MacDonald's life. But like many of Kantor's protégés, the ones he really cared about, MacDonald would pay a price for the older man's attention. Filled with himself, Kantor was disdainful of MacDonald's hard-boiled oeuvre and would turn that screw whenever it pleased him.

I am holding in my hand a letter from John D. MacDonald to MacKinlay Kantor. It is dated Monday, December 12, 1960, the night that MacDonald decided he would take it no more. It begins:

> Dear Mack—Here in a windy sobriety of midnight I foist upon you a windy letter, partly as an explanation of myself to you, and partly as a therapeutic self-analysis . . .

The letter goes on for three dense pages, at times deferential, at other times acrid and scolding. MacDonald did not yet know exactly who he was as a writer, nor precisely where he was going, but he knew he was not the unambitious hack in training that Kantor apparently saw. The letter shows the anarchy of spacing and variations in boldness typical of the old Remingtons and Smith Coronas, when you could slam or caress the keyboard according to your mood, and you'd see it on the page. On this night, clearly, the machine took a beating.

It has been your habit (over the years I have known you) to make snide remarks about the work I do which is of importance to me. They have stung. I have been unable to laugh. You speak of "that mystery stuff" with a slurring indifference . . .

Kantor had evidently poked fun at the jaundiced, misanthropic tone that is at the heart of hard-boil—tales narrated by emotionally closeted private ops who live in a seamy world of compromised morals. To this, MacDonald launches a fierce but nuanced defense of the genre not as a lesser form of literature but as a fully worthy form, a vessel into which a gifted writer can pour his heart, can seek truth, expose duplicity, skewer sanctimony, and develop characters of no less complexity than those in Kantor's works.

I believe the appraisals I make are more severe, more uncompromising, than yours. Yet we are both, in essence, moralists. We are both prying, searching, scrabbling for The Good. I seem to see it in the human animal less often than you do, but that does not mean the quest is less pressing, nor does it mean that I bleed less when I don't find it, or feel less glory when I do.

At forty-four, MacDonald was an angry, brilliant, insecure, largely unknown writer, and the letter crackles with amusing arrogance; he dismisses some of the most acclaimed writers of the day—James Michener, John Hersey, Leon Uris—as tiresome. John O'Hara is a diarist "of upper income fornication." He calls his own magazine stories—written for quick money—"meretricious."

But he unequivocally defends the integrity of his books, into which, he says, he has poured everything he has.

Kantor had made his fame by writing of the past and had urged MacDonald in the same direction, because he felt historical novels confer gravitas to a writer. MacDonald explains how he would not—*could* not—do that and remain true to his conscience:

> Damn it, I have to put my people against a current tapestry—one which I feel to be monolithic, onanistic, escapist and, in large degree, shameful. This IS a new time, unparalleled. These are the days when the world is filling up, and the significance of the individual is being muted by the hard logic of there being so many of him. We are all keeping our heads down, more than we should. And the greatest evil in the world is the sin of non-involvement . . .

This indignant letter from protégé to mentor is as eloquent a defense of any artistic genre as you are likely to encounter anywhere, delivered by a master of the form so early in his career that it is essentially a passionate mission statement. I did not find it in any book or scholarly work or in the papers of John D. MacDonald. It was given to me by Tom Shroder, who had it in a file cabinet.

MacKinlay Kantor was Tom Shroder's grandfather.

Tom remembers MacDonald from his childhood. The novelist would come to visit Mack Kantor from time to time; the two men had remained friends, despite lingering resentments never quite resolved.

On those visits, MacDonald would bring Travis McGee–themed trinkets for the grandkids—pencils and other promotional knickknacks. The books were huge by then, and MacDonald was rolling in dough. But by then MacKinlay Kantor had begun a decline; his ornamented writing style was fast going out of fashion.

But Kantor couldn't give up his perception of himself as a famous writer, one who could mint money on the onionskin paper he fed through his typewriter. In his view, shortages were always temporary, so he continued his grand style of picking up checks at fancy restaurants and booking first-class cabins on cruises to Europe, eventually mortgaging his house on ten acres of beachfront so he could keep up the show. Then his body, abused by drink, began to give way. His publishers stopped returning calls. MacDonald helped him out with some cash and tried, unsuccessfully, to get him writing gigs.

When MacKinlay Kantor died on October 11, 1977, he was deeply in debt and largely forgotten. When John D. MacDonald died on December 28, 1986, his obit was atop the network news.

What does it mean that a man who died on The Day knew the child who would become the man who would help pick the day? Nothing but coincidence, obviously, except in the way it speaks to degrees of separation, and our common suspicion that the deeper you drill into anything, the more eerily intertwined things become. We are more connected—to one another, and perhaps even to any single point in time—than we know.

In the course of reporting this book, I spoke to one man—the son of the drummer of the Grateful Dead—about Jerry Garcia, whose experience on the day was significant. When we were done with the interview, we compared times and places and realized that he and his dad and Garcia, when they were in Washington, D.C., had often stayed in the house of a friend of theirs, and that it happened to be the man from whom, years later, I bought my house. Same house. I looked around in awe. Jerry slept here.

FOR THIS BOOK, not much has gone as easily as I'd hoped. Some people I needed to talk to are dead. Some who are alive expressed no wish to relive the things that happened to them on December 28, 1986. Some promising newspaper stories from The Day have proven, upon further review, to have been 97 percent wrong.

At the perigee of my reporting, in desperation for reliable detail, however humble, I reached three of the people featured in a *60 Minutes* report about HSAM, or Highly Superior Autobiographical Memory. They are said to have in their minds virtual blueprints of their entire lives, day to day, hour to hour, available for instant upload; their feats of memory, on camera, were eye-popping. On the phone with me, about December 28, 1986, all three basically drew a blank.

There have been good developments, too, and some extraordinary surprises.

Researching The Day, I have so far seen and done things I never could have imagined. I exchanged emails with a famous man, not knowing he was in the hospital, neither of us suspecting he would be dead within days. I watched a man in a mask hold in his hands a beating human heart. I watched as a man with one eye, no hands, and a face that has terrified children in the streets—a man who almost died on The Day at the age of one—somehow type thirty-five words a minute with his stumps. One story line that was to be about hatred and savagery became, with deeper research, an epic narrative about love and forgiveness.

There were unexpected gifts of reporting, large and small.

In inner-city Washington, D.C., less than a mile from the U.S. Capitol, there is a barbershop called Brice's. On the window glass is painted, with great flourish if dubious grammar, *It Pays to Look Well*. Brice's Barber Shop is where I get my hair cut because I like the prices and I like the ambiance—Bibles *and* free condoms in the waiting room—and because I like the barber, whose name is Sheila Knox.

Sheila wears her own hair in a crew cut, under a baseball cap. She has more opinions than anyone else in the room and she is generous in sharing them, which works out well because her opinions are righteous and mighty. She is not big on homeschooling, or male Geminis, who are "needy and clingy." She disdains husbands who take for granted doormat wives. ("If you come home late, you should have ate.") She's got no patience for handsome but indolent men. ("I'll get me a good baby, then send him on his way.") She is deeply suspicious of authority, convinced the Illuminati run the world, along with the Bushes and the Rockefellers.

She talks like she was brought up hard, but you sense an underlying tenderness. And she's simply great with hair. At Brice's there are two barbers, sometimes three, but even with empty chairs, customers often wait for Sheila. I do.

Brice's oozes funk. The chairs are fifties-era green metal with orange leather seats. On the wall is *Dogs Playing Poker*, and a gauzy velvet American eagle shedding a tear over 9/11, and yellowed, sepia pictures of amusingly vintage hairstyles. Think Angela Davis, circa 1968.

One day I mentioned the book I was working on, and when I told Sheila the exact date, she stilled her scissors for a moment, squinted into a mirror. and said triumphantly, "I know exactly where I was that day."

Where?

"In prison."

Ah.

Sheila asked if the twenty-eighth was a Sunday, and when I confirmed it was, she smiled and said she also knew what had happened to her on that day because it had, in a small but important way, changed her attitude toward life.

On that day she'd just passed her twenty-second birthday as an inmate at the women's correctional facility at Jessup, Maryland. She was serving five to fifteen after having been caught with some extremely unsavory individuals in a stolen rental car with guns in the trunk. The takedown came in the parking lot of a suburban shopping mall, outside a Hecht's: weapons drawn, orders shouted, handcuffed facedown on the asphalt. Sheila might have avoided jail time—they got her only on conspiracy because she was just a ride-along—but she skipped her court date and fled to Atlanta. That added a fugitive warrant, and also pissed off The Man, and that meant time.

From the age of pigtails, Sheila Knox had been in hot water, a smart little girl who did well in school but thirsted for mischief. At eight, she broke into a locked room and stole money from a church. At eleven she stole her mama's car. At twelve she got a juvie record when, at his wit's end, her dad turned her in for breaking into houses, stealing guns, and selling them.

On December 28, 1986, at Jessup, she was in solitary for giving lip to the guards. ("Pick that up, Sheila." "Do I hear a *please?*") At noon, they told her she had visitors. In the visiting room were her mother and her father's father and her mother's mother, all part of a loving support matrix for her son, Willie, who was five. Willie was there, too. (The little boy had been the result of a one-time thing with the friend of a friend. Even in romance, Sheila was reckless.)

Prison conversations with family in an antiseptic common room tend to have a familiar flavor and structure. It was no different with the Knoxes. On days like these, someone would ask Sheila whether she was ready to turn her life around, and Sheila would dish the most earnest I've-come-to-Jesus bullshit she could, and Mom would nod and Grandpa would roll his eyes, and sometimes there were silences when no one seemed to have anything to say.

On this Sunday, one of those silences got filled when Sheila's mom, Shirley, mentioned the peculiar thing that had happened on Christmas: A stranger had stopped by the house and dropped off two presents for Willie—a nice sweater and a toy racecar set.

Grandpa didn't like hearing this at all. He was a proud man, and he grumbled that the family doesn't need or want charity. But Sheila shushed him. She asked her mother to repeat what happened, because it was inconsistent with any reading of the world as Sheila Knox, twenty-two, understood it.

Yes, strangers at the door. Gifts for Willie.

Sheila remembered the two women who had come to the prison around Thanksgiving, saying they were a charity organization that arranged for kids to get Christmas presents. Sheila figured they had an angle—every stranger in her life had an angle, and most were acute—but she couldn't figure this one out, so she ponied up her son's name and her mother's address. That's when the ladies asked her something that made Sheila *sure* they were phonies. They asked if she had a favorite clothing designer—like they're gonna go *shopping* for a black woman in prison. "Ralph Lauren Polo," she said, with affected sophistication.

In the barbershop, Sheila laughs at the memory.

"I remember thinking, 'Yeah, whatever,' and forgetting about it right away. Nobody gonna do something for somebody for nothing."

But someone had. The organization turned out to be Angel Tree, a church-based prison ministry. They *had* gone shopping. And the sweater for Willie was, indeed, Ralph Lauren.

Sheila Knox remembers December 28, 1986, as the first day in her young, reprobate, passionately cynical life that she understood that even among strangers, and even through institutions, there can be such a thing as unconditional kindness.

It wasn't seismic; it was one of those "huh!" moments. They happen and you move on, maybe with a slight adjustment of attitude. When Sheila finally walked out of Jessup three and a half years later, she'd lost none of her iconoclasm, but her adolescent war on authority was over. She played mostly by the rules, which took her, by and by, to Brice's, where she remains the barber for whom men wait.

And Willie now volunteers for Angel Tree.

————

THE ONLY DEITY I believe in is the one I have always called the God of Journalism, to whom I attribute unanticipated gifts in reportage. You know He has shown up when facts align in unlikely ways to make a good story better or a great story perfect, or when you casually mention something to the lady cutting your hair, and a splendid little tale spools out (and then checks out).

The God of Journalism is just. He rewards effort. Time and again in my life He comes through for me, but only after I decide to conduct that last interview, the one I don't really think I need, or badger someone more than I'm entirely comfortable with, or stay at a scene longer than I'd planned, just to see what happens.

On this book I've encountered my god many times. But I have also known days and weeks of wretched, forlorn biblical doubt. I have had many disappointments, but I have also found funny things and poignant things and dramatic things, all of which originated in or culminated in or knifed through one particular 360-degree rotation of the third planet from a run-of-the-mill star.

Overall, it's been an oddly disorienting experience. In the writing, I have at times felt like that hapless Flatlander square, given knowledge but struggling to convey the almost inexplicable. In my case, it's about the concept of a day, the soul of it, something that is more feeling than fact. If I have succeeded half as well as Edwin Abbott Abbott, I'll be satisfied.

The Day

It is a Sunday, the 362nd day of the year of Chernobyl and *Challenger*, when preventable failures of technology humbled two superpowers.

The moon is a skinny slice. Before daybreak, its faintness will abet innumerable crimes, including a theft of extraordinary audacity and a murder of unfathomable brutality. Eighteen hours later, narrower still, it will lend an overhead wink to a lifelong romance getting off to its preposterous start.

At midnight on the East Coast, a team of doctors and nurses is hastily assembling to attempt something not one of them has ever done before, except in macabre rehearsals with corpses in the morgue. They've been waiting for weeks, to be summoned on a moment's notice. In the next few hours, they will try to save one life and help a family atone for the final unhinged act of another.

At midnight on the West Coast, a young woman's body lies undiscovered in a culvert beneath an abandoned highway overpass as her family crisscrosses the roads above in a frantic search to find her. They are on their own because police have refused to step in, on the grounds that in the life of a pretty blonde, being two hours late on a Saturday night is not late at all.

A little after two A.M. in Washington, D.C., a conservative political operative, known for his ruthless tactics, dies at thirty-six. Fulfilling a promise to his patient, the man's doctor publicly diagnoses congestive heart failure of unknown origin. But it is just the final lie of a successful, influential, cynical, hypocritical, self-delusional life.

Just past three A.M. in a small town in Nebraska, a sullen young man, a dedicated hell-raiser who has never done anything right, finally does, and it kills him.

Just before daybreak, in a suburb of Memphis at a sleepover with a friend, a precocious eleven-year-old girl from a strict Mormon family wakes up in a darkened house and starts on a video game she is not allowed to play at home. Five hours later, she will decide that December 28, 1986, is a date so memorable that she solemnly writes it down on a slip of paper, signs it, and puts it in a shoebox to keep forever. As it happens, she was on to something.

The bestselling nonfiction book in America, in its thirty-fourth week on the list, is Bill Cosby's *Fatherhood,* a slender, amusing, surprisingly sardonic take on being a dad. It is ghostwritten, but Cosby hasn't revealed that and has no plans to. Driven by the entertainer's wholesome popularity and salt-of-the-earth reputation, *Fatherhood* is becoming the fastest-selling hardcover in history.

Where it isn't unseasonably warm, it is unseasonably cold. Car radios play to saturation "Walk Like an Egyptian," a hypnotic, slickly stylized bit of silliness by the Bangles. The milestone will go unnoticed, but the group has just become the first all-female band to top the charts playing their own instruments. For women, it is a time of restive transition. On this day in a Native American village in New Mexico, a tribe's elders—all male—try but fail to negate the election of its first woman governor because custom forbids it. In dozens of Sunday newspapers, an Associated Press story matter-of-factly reports that men across the country, feeling threatened as heads of their households, are dissuading their wives from going back to school to get their GED degrees—sometimes under threats of violence. The story quotes sixteenth-century scholar Erasmus: "Just as a saddle is not suitable for an ox, so learning is unsuitable for a woman."

At 8:15 A.M., in Cedar Rapids, Iowa, a man with a big secret is awakened by his beaming wife on the morning of his thirtieth birthday. She has a present for him. The moment is utterly anodyne, sweet and ordinary, but to this man, who is vacillating over a paralyzing existential dilemma, it is a reminder of how strong and centered and fundamentally *good* his marriage is. And that, as it happens, is a big problem.

At 10:50 A.M. a fire breaks out in a little house outside of Dallas. No one is in the room except two babies. One dies. The other will become a modern-day Quasimodo, faced with the agonizing challenge of figuring out how to navigate the world as a monster.

The network news is chockablock with opportunistic automotive ads urging you to buy *now* because on January 1, under the Reagan administration's new, simplified tax code, you will no longer be able to deduct new-car sales tax on your returns. The pragmatic, unsentimental strategy will work better than the usual crowing about engineering and aesthetics: American car sales in 1986, hugely goosed in the fourth quarter, will be higher than any year before or since.

At 11:10 A.M. a car departs a psychiatric hospital in Washington, D.C., on a secret mission. Word of it has leaked—but not the destination—so news reporters are out front, in their vehicles, ready for pursuit. To elude them, the driver takes his car out a back exit, with U.S. Secret Service cars preceding and trailing it. Inside this middle car are a doctor, a nurse, and a pudgy, nondescript nebbish, the most notorious psychotic in the world. Doctors had decided that John Hinckley—1981 shooter of Jim Brady and the would-be assassin of Ronald Reagan—was largely cured of his febrile, erotic delusions and could be trusted in supervised visits with his family outside the institution. It was to be a precursor to eventual discharge. The meeting will go off without incident, but not long afterward, guards will discover hidden in Hinckley's room photos of Jodie Foster, a letter to a mail-order house requesting a nude drawing of the actress, and evidence of an ongoing pen-pal relationship with serial killer Ted Bundy and Manson family acolyte Squeaky Fromme. It will be another thirty years before Hinckley would get out for good.

Around noon, the flamboyant mayor of New York City, trying to defuse racial tensions after the death of a black man at the hands of a white mob, walks into a church in a working-class neighborhood in Queens. The mayor expects a warm welcome from these blue-collar white people, his most loyal constituency, the demographic that has voted him into office three times despite lingering mistrust among people of color. The reception he gets flabbergasts him, and will strip bare the maddening complexity of race relations in urban America.

Eyeglasses are all over TV, big and bold, on faces male and female, in news and sitcoms and commercials, making spectacles of themselves: huge goggle-like affairs, with enormous lenses suspended in what appeared to be face scaffolding. This will turn out to be a defiant final stand for eyewear, and one of those visual markers of an era: 1987 will be the year truly comfortable contact lenses become widely available.

The New York Times announces the upcoming nuptials of a "Miss Van Cleve" to a "John Van Doren." Decades tardy to the basic protocols of feminism, the Gray Lady's matrimonial pages are also notoriously elitist, biased toward America's blue-blooded white aristocracy. Eventually this will change, but not any time soon, nor will the newspaper's occasional willingness to make journalistically excruciating accommodations to assure that this important demographic remains sufficiently cosseted. On this day, the engagement story duly notes the pedigree of the groom's grandfather—a poet, critic, and literature professor who inspired Allen Ginsberg and Jack Kerouac—but about the groom's father, Charles Van Doren, it reports only that he is a former college professor and a writer. Discreetly not mentioned: Charles's international notoriety as the leading villain in the spectacular quiz show scandal of the 1950s.

At 2:35 P.M. in Washington, D.C., a London musical is making its pre-Broadway debut at the Kennedy Center Opera House. Thirty minutes into the matinee performance, action stops. Something is wrong. The $200,000 rotating stage has broken. The day's two productions are canceled. An eerily identical snafu had happened in Baltimore the year before, thirty minutes into the opening act of the pre-Broadway debut of the Ben Vereen musical, *Grind*. The moving stage froze, as did future ticket sales in that memorably sour box office flop. Will this snafu augur something similar? Nah. *Les Misérables* will do just fine.

At 4:25 P.M. in the Pacific Northwest, a couple of fishing buddies flying in a helicopter make an emergency landing in a lumberyard, to remove a door for better visibility in fog and rain. When they take off, a strut catches on some debris and the copter inverts, its rotor pulling it to the ground. The pilot's last thought before impact is "no one ever survives this."

At 6:10 P.M. in tiny Winslow, Indiana, the town's Pentecostal pastor answers the door to find two young parishioners standing there—a sixteen-year-old girl and her twenty-year-old boyfriend. They say they are worried because her parents have been missing for two days. In the kitchen, the pastor's wife overhears this and feels dread. They are dead, she thinks, and have been murdered, and I know who did it. She is right, and right, and right again. But her intuition takes her only so far. She never anticipates the penumbra of ugly small-town rumors that would, in time, engulf even her own home.

At 6:15 P.M., in a ceremony on a hotel veranda in Montego Bay, Jamaica, a very pregnant woman from Cherry Hill, New Jersey, marries her longtime boyfriend. In the ensuing years their love story will become a horror story, then a captivating adventure yarn, then a police procedural, and then a love story again—with a denouement so melodramatic that the plot would be laughed out of any Hollywood pitch meeting.

At 6:30 P.M. in Tempe, Arizona, busloads of large young men descend on a steak restaurant. They are the members of two college football teams that will be squaring off five days later in what will be the most watched college football game ever. The dinner was to be a fun time, a few hours of camaraderie before a few hours of busting one another's heads. Unfortunately, to lighten the moment, someone had a *very* bad idea.

At 7:45 P.M. in New York City, more than a dozen families have gathered at Kennedy Airport awaiting a flight to return to the Soviet Union, which they had left a few years before, never intending to return. The émigrés tell American reporters about their disappointment with life in the United States and nostalgia for their old country. The mass departure has been secretly orchestrated by the Soviet government as in-your-face propaganda, one of the last bits of gamesmanship in the shabby final days of the Cold War. But in this game the playing field is not level, and what will soon happen to these families will mirror, almost exactly, what will soon happen to much of Eastern Europe.

These are the final days of three-network TV, before channel surfing will further fragment the American attention span, so ABC, CBS, and NBC let their year-end wrap-ups run long and deep and dull. Here are some of the things that happened in 1986 that they saw fit to include: The death of Desi Arnaz, the man who Loved Lucy. The hundredth anniversary of the Statue of Liberty. Mandatory urine tests for federal job seekers. People linking hands in an earnest but imperfect effort to span the continental United States for fifteen minutes, as a symbolic act to fight poverty and homelessness. Here is something that happened in 1986 that none of the networks saw fit to include: A Seattle company named Microsoft took itself public.

Technology is advancing at such bewildering speed that even the visionaries can see only so far ahead. Just before eight P.M. the New York City alternative radio station WBAI airs its nerdy

Personal Computer Show, which on this day includes an interview with a thirty-one-year-old Bill Gates. Gates is charming, and he is prescient in many ways, predicting, among other things, eventual crises in cybersecurity. But in his twenty-seven minutes of airtime he underpredicts the technological future, envisioning only "a computer in every home." He does not predict the miniaturization of technology that will make access to information as portable as people. And he does not seem to foresee an innovation that is a mere nine years away and barreling toward us all: the mighty, inexhaustible, bottomless real-time interconnection of humans and ideas that we now call the Internet.

At 10:30 P.M. in Oakland, California, the Grateful Dead has taken the stage. It is the band's fifth performance since front man Jerry Garcia returned from a coma that had nearly killed him. His first four appearances were worrisomely listless. But on this day at this concert, onstage, something overpowering kicks in. And for once it is not pharmaceuticals.

It was a day unlike any other, 23 hours 56 minutes and 4.0916 seconds of a planet speeding around Earth's axis at the velocity of a bullet, occupying a spiral of space that will never be revisited.

12:01 A.M., Charlottesville, Virginia

A lan Speir hadn't had a drop to drink. The reason why was on the phone.

When the call came, Speir had just fallen asleep in the guest bedroom of his sister's home. He and his family were visiting for the Christmas holidays, and now his brother-in-law was waking him, phone in hand.

Speir didn't have to be told who the midnight caller was or why he was calling, or that the next few hours would be memorable. Okay, thrilling.

Speir wasn't famous in his field yet. A quarter century later, he'd be the man who would sew a new heart into Dick Cheney's chest. But in 1986 he was a reasonably obscure cardiovascular surgeon in a busy hospital in suburban Washington, D.C. His name had not been in the newspapers. That was about to change, for better or worse.

The midnight caller, as he'd assumed, was his surgical colleague Edward Lefrak. The terse message, as he expected, was that there was a donor. Speir was now fully awake. Within three-quarters of an hour he was dressed and in his car, beginning the two-hour drive north to Fairfax, Virginia, going through a heart surgeon's mental checklist, which included, somewhere around step five, keeping your own heart steady.

Lefrak had made a few more calls himself; others, he delegated. By three A.M., the whole team had assembled. There were four doctors, eleven nurses, a physician's assistant, and two medical instrument operators, gathered in two rooms.

In operating room 12 a body lay supine on the table, butterflied. This is an adjective no one who was there would have used—the terminology of transplantation is determinedly dignified—but that is what it was. A man of small to medium stature, well muscled, had been sliced open from the neck straight down to the crotch, and then cranked apart by retractors, for better access to the organs. There wasn't much talking. The loudest sound was the insistent *whoosh-gasp* of a ventilator.

The man's head was behind a vertical drape, not visible to the surgeons, which was just as well. A single .22 rifle had been fired point-blank into the center of the forehead, the bullet crossing the midline of the brain, tearing through both hemispheres. Such wounds—*insults* in the curiously mannered lexicon of medicine—are almost invariably fatal, as this one had been. But they sometimes leave the heart beating, as this one did, so paramedics in the ambulance had eased a tube down the dying man's trachea and hand-pumped a bag to keep the body breathing, which was why it was here, in operating room 12 in Fairfax Hospital in suburban Washington, D.C., butterflied.

An exposed, beating human heart looks frantic and angry. Clench and release, clench and release. Because it is sheathed in a protective layer of fat, it's more yellow than red. It's only the size of a big man's fist, but it will dominate any operating room. You can't look away.

A tall, rangy man with weary eyes and a surgeon's preternatural calm, Lefrak was there for that heart. If everything went right, it would go into the chest of a woman just down the hall in operating room 6. Alan Speir was there, opening her up.

This was to be both men's first heart transplant, and the very first in the immediate Washington area. In 1986, no one taught this procedure in a classroom. Lefrak had been training himself for two years, practicing on corpses in the morgue with a hand-picked team of doctors, nurses, and technicians, the same people who will surround him for the next few hours in what would be a significant gamble, both with Lefrak's career and his hospital's fortunes.

A second team—an abdominal surgeon and his assistant—was in the room as well, to harvest the kidneys. *Harvest* is another word that laymen use but transplant surgeons seldom do, because it sounds impersonal and opportunistic, which of course it is. Organs are precious and prized; organs from young, healthy bodies, especially so. The dead man on the table, whose name was Mark Willey, was just nineteen.

Sometimes surgeons with different organs to remove find themselves working in an awkward scrum, jostling for position like basketball players under the boards. That almost happened here. There was to have been a third surgical team to take the liver, but at the last minute the intended recipient became too sick to survive surgery, so the liver would be wasted—there was no time to find and qualify another patient. That's the way it goes with organ transplants—they are dependent on speed and timing, but also on factors you cannot control.

That this was happening in the early hours of a Sunday was unsurprising. Young, healthy people are most likely to do life-threatening things late at night on Fridays and Saturdays, so organ transplants often occur at one or two A.M. on Saturdays and Sundays. That's because it takes roughly twenty-four hours of lab work and paper-pushing to set everything up; felicitously, two A.M. also happens to be when operating rooms tend to be free of scheduled surgery.

The process also involves diplomacy, a task that had fallen to a fourth man in the room, standing away from the operating theater. James Cutler was the hospital's transplant coordinator, a meticulous man with the commiserating demeanor of a mortician, which was an occupational asset. Among Cutler's duties was to obtain consent from grieving next of kin, and this takes a subtle skill. He must be persuasive without seeming to persuade. The decision must be freely given, with no feel of pressure, even though, of course, at such times there is the extraordinary pressure of circumstance alone, the pressure of life and death.

Cutler had been the first in the hospital to learn of this death, from Fairfax police. As was his custom, he did not immediately alert the transplant team. Hospitals are careful about this; there must be no hint of collusion or ethical corner-cutting. A wall is maintained between the doctors who need the heart *now* and the team of people who must certify brain death (two opinions), test for blood-type compatibility, rule out certain diseases and blood-borne pathogens, and obtain unambiguous informed consent.

Usually Cutler approached this last task through a gentle appeal to a greater good: Let something positive emerge from this tragedy, and so forth. Sometimes he had an added tool, one that he deployed delicately but without apology. He'd used it here.

You must understand, he'd said to the stricken parents of the dead man, that because of the circumstances, the medical examiner will be involved. There will have to be an autopsy, anyway. The body will be opened and organs removed, anyway. You cannot spare your son from that, anyway.

"Because of the circumstances" was enough to get a yes. He didn't need to elaborate. What he meant was that there would be a police investigation, because the young man butterflied on the table had committed an abominable crime.

LATER, MUCH LATER, when she was going though her daughter's belongings, Ursula Ermert found the two letters. They were handwritten on loose-leaf paper, undated, from Mark Willey to Karen Ermert. They were love letters, of a sort. In hindsight, they were ominous. In hindsight, many things were ominous.

Mark and Karen, also nineteen, had been going out for almost two years—students from different high schools who had met the way suburban kids often met in the mid-eighties, at a mall. Karen was effervescent and effortlessly attractive, with a broad, intelligent face under feathered blond hair. (Her hairdresser once observed wryly that other clients paid extravagantly for what nature had casually dropped on Karen—multiple shades of blond in captivating layers.) She was conventionally hot, and a slight chipmunky overbite added a dose of adorable. In the high school band she played the girlie instruments—flute and piccolo—and she could be girl-bossy, like Lucy van Pelt. She was strong-willed, stubborn, mischievous, spontaneously funny. When she posed for a graduation photo beside her mother, she subverted the solemnity by dropping a stockinged leg into Ursula's hand, à la Harpo Marx.

There are two Polaroid photos in the murder file that are not from the crime scene; police apparently found them among Karen's effects and kept them, probably to spare Ursula from having to find them. They are from a funny moment in a cheap hotel room. They are both of Mark in stages of undress, and they appear to be taken after a prom. In one, Mark is wearing only the top of a tuxedo. He is natty from the waist up, naked from the waist down. In another, he is unflatteringly bare-assed. Karen was evidently snapping him in these undignified moments, a girlfriend's tease. But there is not a hint of humor in Mark's face. He looks awkward, even pained, as though this is something he is enduring, uncertain of whether he is being laughed at, unwilling to ask.

It is tempting to call Mark Willey a Lee Harvey Oswald type—insecure, nondescript, brooding. He worked as an auto mechanic and lived with his parents, in a sullen, silent standoff with an emotionally distant father. He was desperate for connection.

Ursula was in the high school bleachers with her daughter one day when she saw Mark walk onto the field below, his eyes searching the stands for Karen. Ursula remembers the exaggerated anxiety on his face, as though he felt existentially alone and hungered to belong. *A vulnerable person,* she thought.

Karen liked to fix things. Mark's vulnerability was appealing, at first.

In 1986, there was no term in the psychiatric lexicon for the infatuation with which Mark Willey would smother Karen Ermert. Today it would be known as obsessive love, and Mark checks every box in the clinical description. "Attracted"? Check. "Anxious"? Check. "Controlling"? Check. The final square is "Destructive."

Ursula Ermert was a 1960s German immigrant who had been widowed when Karen was twelve, which led to mother and daughter becoming exceptionally close, which meant they could too easily hurt each other. The years of teenaged rebellion had been particularly freighted for both. Once, at fifteen, Karen ginned up an argument over something trivial to undergird a foot-stampy, theatrical declaration that she was leaving home. Ursula was not about to loose a naive teenager on the streets. "If you find me so hard to live with," she told her daughter, "I will be the one to leave." And she did. She drove to the family's business, a dental lab, and slept on a mattress in a back room, amid the dentures and crowns. Eventually Karen figured where she must be and phoned in the middle of the night. Crying, she asked her mother to come home.

Ursula was crying, too. She said no, she would stay there until morning: "This has to hurt us both so much it will never happen again."

It didn't. Not that it would matter, in the end.

After high school, Karen went off to college in Shepherdstown, West Virginia, but soon dropped out because Mark Willey persuaded her to. He missed her too much, he'd said. When she got jobs—she was starting out as a clerk—Mark would show up at her workplaces, unannounced. He once crashed her office party. He didn't like these places in which she spent her days. They contained men.

It was all there in the notes, the ones Ursula found after it was too late. They were filled with incapacitating jealousy and lovesick histrionics, and in particular, a suffocating need for control. Mark had evidently been monitoring Karen's movements, day and night, and found them wanting. He'd left each note for her when she had not been precisely where he'd expected her to be precisely when he expected her to be there. The handwriting, corralled by blue horizontal lines, is neat but gallops to the right, as though he was racing to keep up with his emotions.

I took a shower and dressed up and did everything I could maybe to look halfway as nice as all the gorgeous guys you see every day. I would just kill to look as good as them and be able to catch your eye. Karen, I'm really hurting, in fact, I'm starting to cry . . . Where are you? Did you go out to eat? I feel like a fool that has been stood up. I love you so much. If words could be put on paper to describe how much there wouldn't be enough paper. I'm gonna call your house again. Karen, if you want to go out with some other guy, please tell me. It would hurt less if I found out that way. Love, Mark.

Karen, where are you? I am really worried. First thing I thought was that you stopped for dinner but I know you would have the courtesy to call me so I would not sit here and worry like this. I am always worried about you being in an accident because I would be the last to hear. God, if you aren't okay, I'll kill myself! You don't know what you mean to me.

ONE DAY NEAR THE END, Ursula drove her daughter to the emergency room to be treated for kidney stones. A nurse looked at Karen, did a double take, and asked, "Weren't you here two weeks ago with a head injury?"

Ursula waited for Karen to say the nurse must be confusing her with someone else. She didn't.

"Mark hit me," she said later. She had wanted to get out of the car, and Mark hadn't wanted her to. The explanation was unnervingly matter-of-fact.

Imagine the dilemma facing Ursula Ermert in 1986, trying to decide what to do with a headstrong daughter who at nineteen was living on her own and supporting herself because she treasured her independence. Karen would not be pushed to do things she did not want to do. In fact she might well stubbornly do the opposite, if nudged too hard. Should Ursula go to the police over Karen's objections? And what exactly would she tell them? What did she really even know?

Mother and daughter argued about it more than once. Once Ursula infuriated Karen by telephoning Mark's parents, telling them that if Mark ever hurt Karen again, she would hold them responsible. Mark, it turned out, was listening on an extension and told her to butt out. What followed was a letter from Karen to Ursula; it was typical Karen—firm, but affectionate. It said in effect: *Butt out. Stop complaining about my friends, and you and I can still love each other unconditionally.*

That was the dreadful state of affairs around Christmas 1986, when the tension lifted. Karen had decided she'd had enough. She told Ursula she was going to end the relationship, and she'd made the decision on her own. It wouldn't be a breakup so much as an escape. All that was left were logistics.

Mother and daughter conspired and came up with a plan. Karen would tell Mark a tactfully laundered version of the truth: She had just gotten a new job working at Dulles International Airport for the German military. That was true. She would tell Mark that she'd be so busy studying German that she would no longer have time for any dating at all. That wasn't exactly true— Karen was fluent in German. Mother and daughter reasoned that this story wouldn't seem so much like a personal rejection, and with luck, the "no dating" would keep Mark's jealousy at bay. But the answer would also have to seem final. For Christmas, he'd given her a table he had carpentered himself, and Karen was going to insist on returning it.

That was the plan. She was going to tell Mark on the phone on Friday, the night of the twenty-sixth.

Ursula waited by her phone. In early evening, Karen called.

"I did it," she said.

"How did he take it?"

"He said he'd kill me." Karen was giggling. She'd felt enormous relief, and it tickled her. It overwhelmed everything else, including caution.

"Come here now. Come stay with me."

But Karen said no. She hadn't taken Mark's threat literally. His love for her was septic, but still it was love—how could he kill her? She didn't expect to hear from him again that night, but if there were problems, Karen promised, she'd call. Ursula slept with the phone next to her head.

Midnight passed without a call, but the phone rang around two A.M., or at least Ursula thinks it did. Her sleep had been fitful, and to this day she knows she may have anxiety-dreamed that ringing phone. In any case, by the time she worked the receiver to her ear, there was only a dial tone. So she phoned Karen.

An unfamiliar man's voice answered hello.

"Who is this?" Ursula asked.

"Detective Lee."

She apologized for having dialed a wrong number, hung up, and called again.

"Detective Lee."

"This is Ursula Ermert. Are you in my daughter's apartment?"

"Yes."

"What happened?"

"I can't tell you over the phone."

So Ursula threw on clothes, ran to her car, and drove the fifteen minutes to Karen's apartment, trying to make no assumptions. The truth was, she didn't *know*. There were all *sorts* of scenarios, none of them benign but some less awful than others.

At the apartment, it fell to Detective Tommy Lee to confirm the worst.

Twenty-eight years later, Lee remembered the moment as the saddest thing he'd ever had to do as a police officer. He was thirty-nine. He had a sixteen-year-old daughter of his own at the time, and he was worried about the fast company she was keeping. Eventually he would lose her to a drug overdose. But on this day he was a just someone's father who had to break some terrible news to someone's mother.

Ursula whimpered, her knees buckled, and she collapsed into Lee's arms.

TWENTY-EIGHT YEARS LATER, sitting in her house, in the study that had once been her daughter's bedroom, with Karen's ashes in a box high on the top shelf, Ursula remembered what happened next.

She'd asked the detective, "How is Mark? Where is he?" Lee told her that Mark wouldn't survive, either.

It may have seemed like an oddly solicitous question, under the circumstances. It wasn't. If Mark was not dead, Ursula was going to see to it that he became dead, right then and there, whatever it took.

Ursula smiles. "If I had," this dainty woman says mildly, with a faintly Teutonic sibilance, "I would be getting out of prison right about now."

THE CALL HAD COME in as a shooting. Fairfax city patrol officer Ed Vaughan was among the first to arrive. He took Main Street toward Jermantown Road, alert for a car driving erratically, because that's sometimes how you catch the guy in the immediate frenetic aftermath of a domestic. But the streets were almost empty.

The address Vaughan was headed for, 11100 Gainsborough Court, was at the poor end of the city of Fairfax—a homely two-story, U-shaped apartment cluster surrounding an inner courtyard.

The front door was locked, so Vaughan went out back to find apartment 6, which was on the second floor. It had a balcony. He saw a downspout he could climb, and a tree. All seemed quiet.

Then Vaughan heard a single shot, and he flinched and looked for cover. He needn't have. As it turned out, it was the final shot, the suicide.

Ursula had hated that tree beside the balcony; she thought it provided an excellent hiding spot for a Peeping Tom or perfect access to someone intent on burglary or worse.

As police later reconstructed it, Mark Willey had shimmied up the tree with his rifle slung over his back. He'd stowed the weapon on the balcony and knocked to be let in. For reasons we will never know, Karen slid open the glass door. There was an argument. Voices were raised. Accusations were leveled. The finality of the breakup was confirmed. Mark stormed out. Seconds later, he was back, with the rifle.

That was the story line in the local newspapers on Sunday: Girlfriend breaks off relationship, returns Christmas present; enraged boyfriend commits murder and suicide.

But it turns out, there was an added dimension, another stratum of pain, one that Ursula Ermert had not known about, one that never got into print. It's there in the police report.

RICH LIEB IS NOW FIFTY-ONE. He had been casual friends with Mark Willey since elementary school. In 1985 and 1986, he'd double-dated with Mark and Karen a few times, until Lieb didn't have the stomach for it anymore. He didn't like what Mark became when he was liquored up, how he'd treated Karen.

Rich didn't know why such a feisty, self-possessed girl had accepted the abuse, but he had a theory. Early on, Karen had carried a few extra pounds, and maybe it affected her self-confidence. But by the end of 1986, she'd jettisoned the weight, looked great, and gained moxie.

In the era of the long phone call, Karen was a letter writer; she considered it an old-fashioned virtue. In November, she wrote a letter to Rich. It was just a friendly hello out of the blue, an old friend remembering the good times they'd spent together. Because he was a nineteen-year-old guy with the requisite lunkheaded cluelessness about such things, Rich didn't take the hint. He accepted the letter at face value and never responded. Weeks passed. Then, on Christmas evening 1986, Karen telephoned him to tell him she was lonely. Even a nineteen-year-old lunkhead could figure that one out.

They spent the night together. It was electric. Part was the new intimacy, and part was simply a natural rapport—they liked each other. Permeating it was a sense of elation and relief, as though Karen's eyes had just been opened to the possibilities of a relationship that didn't hurt.

Rich felt that it was the start of a romance that would last a lifetime. He and Karen spent the next day together at the house he lived in with his parents. He was to leave on a ski trip at three A.M., so a little after midnight, Karen left to return to her apartment.

What happened next is evident, if some of the details are not. Mark had somehow found out about Karen's new love. She may have told him when she broke up with him—she'd promised Rich Lieb that she was going to—or Mark may have discovered it on his own. But police are certain he knew, because before he arrived at Karen's apartment, he telephoned. Karen hadn't gotten home yet, but her roommate Christine was there, and Mark told the young woman of his anger, depression, and feeling of betrayal. Karen arrived during the call and talked to Mark as well.

After she hung up, Karen took a bath. After he hung up, Mark wrote a bitter suicide note and left it on his bed. (It's not in the police file, but Lee remembers the sick, sullen, self-pitying core of it: "She fucked my best friend.") Then Mark loaded his rifle and carried it to his car.

Madness, it is said, is a private religion—a set of values and beliefs that may seem irrational to others, but is perfectly manifest to the madman, consistent within his delusional world. Obsessive love is not formally classified as a mental illness, but it is a disordered mental state with some of the same rhythms. To Mark, all his dark suspicions were confirmed.

He *was* a paranoiac, but he *had* been betrayed. Beyond that bitter truth was blind rage, unmodulated by logic. It would not have occurred to him that his treatment of Karen had extinguished any right to demand or expect her loyalty; or for that matter, that killing her was a wildly disproportionate reaction to a predictable if painful development. He'd become unhinged, a lethal player in a dark psychodrama.

Rich Lieb didn't find out about the murder until he returned from his ski trip the following night to find his parents sitting up late, waiting for him, so he'd hear it from them first. For days afterward, Lieb couldn't drag himself out of bed.

He still lives in Virginia. He works in IT. He's divorced and single. Asked to write down his memories of Karen Ermert, he took some time. The intensity of his response may seem incongruous for a romance that lasted, strictly speaking, forty-eight hours. But Lieb trusts his feelings, infused as they may be by anger and guilt and loss and, above all, a bedeviling regret.

"She made me want to move mountains for her," he wrote, "and also made me feel like I could do it. She was everything I ever wanted and to this day is the standard against which I measure other women."

When Mark Willey walked back from the balcony into that apartment, he was firing, and firing with precision. Christine, who had witnessed the confrontation, ran.

Karen took five bullets, three to the head and neck. The crime scene photos are difficult to look at. There is a Christmas tree, and beside it, a wall with four Christmas stockings, three big ones for the roommates and a smaller one for the dog. On the floor is a once-beautiful young woman in a powder-blue bathrobe, a white patterned nightgown, and white underpants with cheerful pink leopard spots. Karen's hair is almost unmussed, but blood streams from her eyes and nose and mouth, soaking into a ratty rug and a dingy parquet-floored hallway near the dog's bowl.

In the police file, in plastic bags, are a half-dozen misshapen, sharp-edged pieces of bullet that had tumbled through the brain. So much tissue was destroyed that Karen's heart stopped.

Mark postponed the end as long as he dared, until there were cops in the courtyard and cops banging on the front door. He backed away from Karen's body, turned a corner, steadied the rifle against the floor, and reached a thumb for the trigger.

There's no way to shoot oneself multiple times in the center of the forehead. Mark Willey got one shot only, but aimed true, and that's why he died but his heart did not.

THE HEART DID NOT STOP for another twenty-six hours, at a few minutes after four A.M. on Sunday, December 28, 1986, when Dr. Lefrak stopped it. He placed a clamp on the aorta, signaled to anesthesiologist Mokie Shakoor to turn off the ventilator, and the room went quiet. The lungs deflated. Lefrak inserted a needle below the aortic clamp and injected two liters of a chilly cardioplegic solution. Within twenty seconds, he'd induced cardiac arrest.

Medically, the moment was of no significance: Mark Willey had long been officially dead. But when the heart stops beating and the lungs are suddenly still, the illusion of life is gone. Even among the experienced surgeons in the room, it was a gulp moment. Over surgical masks, eyes met eyes for an instant. And then everyone went to work.

If you've read about open-heart surgery or seen videos, you may have a mental image of what followed: hours of precise, delicate work on gossamer tissue and threadlike vessels, performed by beetle-browed people wearing those eyeglasses with little telescopes in them.

Discard everything but the furrowed foreheads and telescope glasses. Compared to other open-heart procedures in which Lefrak was already expert—say, coronary artery bypass—heart transplantation seems like butchery. The heart as a whole is a large, unsubtle organ, and those vessels feeding it that aren't the circumference of a D battery are still as fat as thumbs. Edward Lefrak removed Mark Willey's heart with a single tool: a pair of scissors not all that structurally different from what second graders use on colored paper. There were no nurses beside him handing him tools or mopping his brow.

First he separated the superior and inferior venae cavae, the two large vessels that return blood from the body into the right atrium, and severed them. Then he lifted the organ with his left hand and cut behind it with his right, one snip on each of the four pulmonary veins that run lung to heart. He lowered it back into the chest. Below the clamp, he cut through the aorta and finally the pulmonary artery, which runs heart to lung. The heart was now in the doctor's hands, free of the body. It felt cold, even through a latex glove.

Donor hearts, once removed, can typically last four hours or a little longer before their cells begin to degrade; sometimes, circumstances push that deadline harrowingly. Doctors bearing donor hearts have sprinted to charter airplanes, or sped long-distance on country roads, with police escorts.

In this case, the heart would travel all of ninety feet. Lefrak zipped it into a plastic bag, put that bag into a second, and then both into a third. This was to limit the possibility of contamination, since what was about to happen was not entirely sterile. Lefrak placed the tripled-bagged organ into a receptacle perfect for the purpose, if not designed specifically for it. It was a standard lunchbox cooler packed with ice. A human heart now was in a container labeled IGLOO.

The entire extraction had taken four and a half minutes.

———

BY 1986, HEART transplants were not yet completely routine, but they were at long last no longer completely irresponsible.

Pioneered in Cape Town, South Africa, in 1967 by the debonair heart surgeon Christiaan Barnard, the procedure was seen as a milestone human achievement, the medical equivalent of landing on the moon (which was still two years away). The celebration was somewhat disproportionate to the accomplishment; the operation was technically not all that difficult, except in the degree of nerve it took to attempt it. But the heart had always been a mystical organ, imbued in mythology and literature with powers and properties beyond the remarkable thing it already is—a mighty, indefatigable muscle, pumping two and a half billion times over a lifetime.

Being first to transplant a heart made Barnard, for a time, the most famous doctor on the planet. But the underlying truth was that in the early years, transplant results were too dismal to be clinically justified except for what they really were: learning experiences. Barnard's first patient, a fifty-four-year-old grocer, died eighteen days after his transplant. His second patient survived nineteen months, but suffered in poor health for most of those. In the month between Barnard's first two transplants, a New York surgeon named Adrian Kantrowitz tried a transplant on a newborn. The baby lived six hours. Though there were a few remarkable, sustained survivals, for a time during the early years the average survival rate was three hundred days. The whole enterprise was intoxicating and held vast promise, but to many it had a disturbing feel of human medical experimentation. Even worse, it seemed to be done mostly to massage the vanity of celebrity surgeons.

For another decade, as survival rates improved but remained largely disappointing, heart transplantation was attempted sparingly, and after a time, it stopped altogether. The principal problem was rejection, the process by which a body's immune system gangs up on what it perceives to be an intruder and tries to kill it. Drugs to mitigate this were unevenly effective. All of that changed with cyclosporine.

Isolated from a soil fungus found in Africa, cyclosporine was synthesized as an immunosuppressant by the pharmaceutical company Sandoz in 1980, and after wide testing, was released into the market in 1983. Its effectiveness was exponentially greater than anything that came before. The effect on transplantation was immediate and profound.

In 1986, Edward Lefrak, then forty-three, was already among the most highly regarded and lavishly remunerated surgeons on the East Coast. He had trained at Baylor College of Medicine in Houston under the famously demanding (and perpetually feuding) doctors Michael DeBakey and Denton Cooley, in what was then a crucible for cardiac surgeons, with a boot camp atmosphere. Lefrak missed the birth of his first child because DeBakey had him on a ninety-one-day tour in the cardiovascular intensive care unit, finding sleep when he could in the patient recovery rooms.

Baylor was a training ground for the next generation of heart surgeons, people with immense talents and corresponding egos. In that last sense, Lefrak was an outlier. He didn't swagger, he shuffled. He didn't bark orders, he mumbled them. He seemed to carry himself with an air of apology. He was a man you could underestimate, initially.

There was nothing tentative about Edward Lefrak in the operating room—or for that matter, in the way he approached the business of medicine. It was Lefrak who had pushed his hospital to move into heart transplantation, and to do so at enormous financial risk. The potential advantages may have been evident—in 1986, when it became known that a hospital did heart transplants, its reputation soared, and all departments benefited. The patients' thinking goes: If these guys can install a new heart, fixing my hernia must be a piece of cake.

But you cannot just declare yourself a heart transplantation center and expect a flood of referrals from local cardiologists with deathly ill patients. In 1986, they had other, if more distant, options at hospitals with a track record. What Fairfax Hospital needed was a track record, Lefrak argued, and there was only one way to get one. It had to make itself the last refuge of the desperate and the destitute.

Lefrak proposed that for the first handful of transplants—the first eight or ten—the hospital eat the cost: Offer them to the uninsured completely for free, with free lifetime follow-up care.

The hospital's administrator, Knox Singleton, was a grown-up with a grown-up job, a punctilious businessman with grave responsibilities. But Singleton had the soul of a gambler. He never did a detailed cost-benefit analysis on Lefrak's proposal, mostly because the results—each operation would amount to a $200,000 gift in 1986 dollars—might well require a fiscally prudent no. Singleton pushed all the chips in. Fairfax would be giving away millions of dollars in heart transplants with a free lifetime service contract. For the foreseeable future, no one would make money on any of it, including Lefrak.

All of that was theoretical, however. If Patient One did not survive the operation, Lefrak was not at all sure there'd be a Patient Two.

Another hurdle loomed. Getting the program medically certified by the state of Virginia would mean overcoming a widespread institutional bias against exactly what was being proposed. In 1986, the consensus in many medical communities was that envelope-pushing procedures were best reserved for the ivory tower—large teaching hospitals affiliated with medical schools, which were places with greater resources, underwritten by greater endowments. Two such places were within a couple of hours of Washington: Johns Hopkins University, in Baltimore, and the Medical College of Virginia, run by the Virginia Commonwealth University, in Richmond. Both had been doing heart transplants for a few years.

To get certified, Fairfax would have to submit to hearings before a Virginia medical tribunal. This was an adversarial proceeding with testimony pro and con, a political process masquerading as a medical process. Some doctors and institutions were openly aligned against Lefrak and Singleton, including the two hospitals that already did transplants and did not relish additional competition for both patient dollars and donor hearts.

The hearings were to be public; the media would attend. So Lefrak decided his side needed some oomph. Oomph, as it happens, was living in Oklahoma City.

Crippled by rheumatoid arthritis in his hands, Christiaan

Barnard had stopped doing surgery in 1983 and had become scientist in residence at the Oklahoma Transplant Institute of the Baptist Medical Center. He was still an international star. Lefrak went to visit. Might the doctor testify on Lefrak's behalf?

Barnard smiled. He was famously photogenic, with teeth that seemed to carry their own gleam. "You didn't have to come here," he told Lefrak; a phone call would have sufficed. It turned out Christiaan Barnard had strong feelings about the spread of heart transplant surgery, and he wasn't bashful about expressing them.

When the renowned surgeon arrived in Richmond, state health authorities treated him with giggly deference. *The Washington Post* described Barnard's arrival as having the feel of "Hank Aaron dropping by a neighborhood baseball sandlot."

Barnard, sixty-three, was in the company of a sultry young brunette. This was his girlfriend, Karin Setzkorn, twenty-two, a South African fashion model. (They would soon be married, and stay married for twelve years until the day Karin discovered in her seventy-seven-year-old husband's travel bag some Viagra pills and condoms. He'd been cheating on her with a still younger woman.)

This was not a man habitually given to caution or to judiciously qualified statements. Barnard's testimony surpassed anything Lefrak could have hoped for. Gesturing grandiloquently with his ruined hands—you couldn't miss the pathos—he informed the Virginia health establishment that given the lifesaving nature of the procedure, any bureaucratic process that denied a competent cardiac surgeon the right to perform transplants was "immoral."

Fairfax Hospital got its certificate.

———

FAIRFAX HOSPITAL, operating room 6, 4:15 A.M., December 28, 1986.

When Lefrak walked in, Alan Speir moved to the opposite side of the operating table. The younger doctor's principal job was over. In time Speir would become one of the most skilled surgeons in the country at heart transplants, but in 1986, he hadn't yet learned how to do them. His job had been to perform the median sternotomy on the recipient, sawing through the center of her breastbone, cranking it apart, cauterizing the bleeding vessels and oozing bone, slicing through the membrane that covers the heart, and then standing down. The rest would be Lefrak's show.

The exposed heart in room 6 was structurally the same organ as the one now in the cooler, but it looked entirely different. For one thing, it was huge—almost twice the mass of the donor heart, inflamed from whatever unknown microbe or whatever other unknown process was killing it. Also, it was barely beating—in medical terminology, it was hypokinetic—pumping at one-fifth the strength of a healthy heart, scarcely hard enough to keep the body's blood flowing.

Eva Baisey was a twenty-year-old single mother of two, an amiable nursing student from Anacostia, one of the capital city's poorest neighborhoods. Eva had been in good health until early October, when her breathing suddenly became labored and then deteriorated into a strangled wheeze.

Two steps, stop to catch her breath. Two steps, stop to catch her breath. The stops became longer until it would take her the better part of an hour to walk a block and a half. A flight of stairs seemed Himalayan.

She was in and out of the emergency room at D.C. General Hospital, where doctors found nothing wrong with her lungs. Eventually they referred her to a cardiologist, who did some tests, stared grimly at the results, then telephoned a man he'd met a few times, Ed Lefrak.

Baisey's diagnosis was idiopathic cardiomyopathy. That sounds bad, which it is, and also sounds definitive, which it isn't. It's weasel-word medicine—essentially a shrug. *Cardiomyopathy* means "something wrong with the muscles of the heart," and *idiopathic* means "of unknown origin," or more accurately, "we have no idea what's causing it." What Lefrak did know, for certain, is that Eva was dying, and dying short term. Also, she was poor and uninsured. Also, she was an admirable person.

That last fact was not of incidental importance. The qualifiers for transplantation do not end with ruling out diseases and confirming tissue compatibility. Also considered is the patient's overall health despite the failing organ, as well as his or her lifestyle. Organs are often denied to people who are mentally unstable, or chronically familiar to the police, or who have drug or alcohol addictions or other life-threatening habits. The lawless and rootless and feckless and helpless are not good gambles for too-scarce, meticulously rationed organs.

Eva Baisey lived clean. She was likable and ambitious, just a few credits away from becoming a nurse. Her will to survive was strong; she desperately wanted to be there for her two children, an eighteen-month-old son and an infant daughter. She had a healthy, self-deprecating sense of humor—about her appetite for junk food, her less than svelte waistline, even about her sudden, bewildering medical straits. Finally, she was self-reliant—she'd been living on her own since she was seventeen, when her parents moved from Washington, D.C., to North Carolina and left her behind in an apartment they subsidized.

Being unattached was bad for transplant protocols. Family support is the final qualifying criterion, an important one. Surviving this surgery is a life-changing ordeal. No one is stoic enough to go it alone. In the case of Eva Baisey, it was a potential deal-breaker—until it wasn't anymore.

Eva's mother, Barbara, had grown up unimaginably poor in the housing projects in Southeast D.C. Her family's poverty was almost cliché: All the children shared the same toothbrush. That sort of background can break your spirit, or it can do just the opposite.

There was nothing broken or even slightly bowed about Barbara Baisey. When Eva got sick, Barbara told her husband that they had to move back to D.C. He said no; he'd countenance weekend visits, but that was that. So she moved back on her own. Her daughter had been offered an astonishing gift, and Barbara felt her new purpose in life was to make it work, at whatever cost, including her marriage. She'd eventually get a divorce.

That was unimpeachable family support. Eva Baisey was approved as a recipient, and on December 4, 1986, she was transported from city to suburb, taken to Fairfax Hospital to await a donor.

Lefrak and his team might have been willing to relax some criteria to get that first transplant, but as it happens, in Baisey he had been handed a perfect patient. There was even a fortuitous intangible.

During the early years of heart transplantation—particularly in apartheid South Africa, but elsewhere, too—there was an undercurrent of controversy involving race. When Barnard's second transplant patient, a white South African dentist, received the heart of a mixed-race man, many grumbled about the unseemly precedent of an oppressed minority serving as an organ farm for the higher castes. It was an unfair charge—even early on, even in South Africa, some white organs went into black bodies—but it was understandable. In transplantation, racial concerns persist even today.

In 1986, in the majority black but still economically segregated Washington, D.C., there would be no such issues raised, either direct or whispered. Mark Willey was white. Eva Baisey was black.

At D.C. General, most of the patients and much of the staff had been African American, but when Eva arrived at the suburban Fairfax Hospital, she saw only alabaster. White patients, white doctors, white nurses, white orderlies. Eva was not conspiracy-minded, but when she initially got much sicker after her change of venue, she found herself wondering, almost amused, whether the staff was trying to do her in so a more ethnically suitable patient would arrive. What was really happening, of course, was by no one's design and to no one's desire: The patient was dying.

Then in the wee hours of the morning of December 28, the patient noticed an unusual number of people beginning to congregate in her room. She began to suspect something was up when nurses told her to soap herself really, really carefully. She was pretty sure something was up when they slathered her neck to belly with that iodine-smelly Betadine. She *knew* something was up when, at one A.M., her ma arrived.

It had taken more than three weeks, and a shattering tragedy, but Eva Baisey was about to get her new heart or die from the effort.

IN THE PRESENCE OF DEATH, the atmosphere in the donor room had been sepulchral. In the recipient room, with the possibility of a life restored, there was music.

Years later, no one could agree on what specifically was playing that night, except that it was twangy. Ed Lefrak was that extreme rarity: a devoutly liberal northeastern Jewish urban Yankees fan who happened to have a taste for country music. As was his custom, he'd brought a cassette tape, most likely Waylon Jennings or Emmylou Harris, or both. The music was just loud enough to provide a benign soundtrack that out-noised the respirator and other ambient distractions. It also discouraged talk. Some surgeons like chatter. Lefrak hated it.

He inserted cannulas—transparent silicon rubber tubes— into each of the vessels feeding and draining Eva Baisey's heart, and sewed them into place in the aorta and the two venae cavae. These tubes wove out of the body. The two venous lines met at a Y connector, turning into one. Baisey's circulation was now reduced to two tubes that fed out behind the surgeon and into a heart-lung machine.

Lefrak gave a nod to the perfusionist, Aaron Hill. The machine rumbled to life, and the tubes filled with blood—purplish dark coming from the body, then three shades lighter and a few degrees colder going back in. The machine was slowly cooling Eva down—eventually all the way down to 79 degrees, slowing her metabolism—but it was also breathing for her, oxygenating her blood. Her bad heart was now beside the point. Relieved of the burden that was grinding it to exhaustion, the organ shrank back almost to normal size, almost in an instant. It was dramatic. You could practically hear a *whew*.

Mary Dellinger, the scrub nurse to Lefrak's right, handed him scissors. What followed was not unlike what had happened in the donor room, with one principal exception: At the back of the organ, Lefrak left the pulmonary veins intact, slicing instead into the top of the damaged heart itself, leaving behind cuffs of tissue from Eva's left and right atria. To these, the new heart would be sewn. It was an odd counterintuitive procedure—why invite rejection by sewing heart tissue to heart tissue?

There was a good reason—pulmonary vessels are notoriously tricky to splice together, and this allows you to avoid it, retaining the recipient's own vessels. The technique had been pioneered a quarter of a century before by Stanford University cardiac surgeon Norman Shumway, while practicing on dogs.

More than anyone else, Shumway was considered the father of heart transplantation, and he'd almost been the first to perform one. On November 20, 1967, he announced that he was ready for a transplant, what would have been the first ever. He had a patient and was waiting for a donor.

The wait proved too long. He lost the race to Barnard by

thirty-three days. (Shumway's first transplant, the world's fourth, fared no better than the others, the patient surviving for just two weeks.)

Many years later, it would become clear exactly how Barnard had won. Shumway had been limited by international ethical conventions on certifying death. At the time, brain death was not sufficient; the heart had to have stopped on its own. That meant surgeons sometimes watched helplessly as potential donors slowly wasted away, damaging their tissues beyond recovery. Barnard was bound by the same strictures, but was under less scrutiny from a despised government desperate for the feel of international legitimacy. As was disclosed forty years later by Barnard's brother, Marcus, in Donald McRae's 2006 book about that first transplant, *Every Second Counts,* Barnard had gotten that first donor heart to stop by stopping it. He'd furtively injected it with paralyzing potassium until the donor became officially deceased.

In operating room 6, Lefrak had also injected potassium into Eva's exhausted heart, for an entirely different reason. When the heart was still, the extraction was easier. Once it was free of her body it became a specimen for the lab, for any secrets it might offer up to help take the "idiopathic" out of cardiomyopathy.

At a signal from Lefrak, the Igloo was brought in from operating room 12. The triple-bagged heart was unpackaged and laid out on a tray.

Unbidden, Mary Dellinger passed Lefrak a suture. She knew exactly what came next—much of what remained was sophisticated needlework. Dellinger had been helping Lefrak with this for two years, at the doctor's side since the beginning, a constant presence during most of the rehearsals. She was one of those invaluable surgical nurses whose hand was there with the next needed instrument even before the surgeon thought to reach for it.

In 1986, the only way to practice transplanting hearts was to transplant hearts, which meant, for Lefrak, a tip from a pathologist or morgue attendant, followed by an awkward conversation with next of kin, followed by hours at the morgue, working with a new cadaver. There had been more than a dozen such dry runs. The most memorable had been on February 27, 1986, the day before Christiaan Barnard's testimony in Richmond. Gamely, Barnard had agreed to join Lefrak in the morgue. There he sat at the head of the gurney and kibitzed as Lefrak rehearsed with a corpse.

From that day, Dellinger kept several photos—Barnard, gracious with his time, posing with the doctors and nurses. She also kept two indelible memories—one wistful, one amusing. Wistful: the inescapable pathos of Barnard's hands, still expressive, still usable for most things, but clearly stiff and gnarled, no longer supple enough for the thing that saved lives. Amusing: All the nurses bore witness to this one. Barnard was an irrepressible roué, an earnest, unapologetic, indiscriminately libidinous, joyfully incorrigible hands-on flirt.

IN THE OPERATING ROOM, some of the sewing was as simple as splicing severed vessels, hose to hose, end to end. The whole transplant was a meticulous, repetitive process. Sew, check for leaks. Sew, check for leaks. This took hours. The sun rose. The sewing and checking continued.

When all connections had been sealed and the perfusionist

began to slowly warm the blood, Lefrak released the cross-clamp on the aorta and the new heart began to tremble. A good sign. It was not beating, but it was fibrillating.

What happened next defied everything most people presume about the human heart. Lefrak lowered Eva's head, cupped her new heart with his left hand and tilted the bottom of it up so it became the highest point in her body. Then he accepted from Mary Dellinger a long 18-gauge hypodermic needle and stabbed it into the heart's apex, clean through the muscle to the cavity of the left ventricle. From the plastic collet of the needle came a bloody froth. When that stopped, Lefrak withdrew the needle, then pushed it in again, a few millimeters away. More bubbles.

If a heart is sliced by the thrust of a knife, that is usually fatal. If it is pierced by a bullet, it is nearly always fatal. But the heart is, in the end, a muscle, and as anyone knows who has ever gotten a vaccination in the arm—or anyone familiar with the overdose scene in *Pulp Fiction*—muscles can withstand and survive a needle. They close back up and heal instantly. Lefrak repeated this unnerving stab of the needle more than a dozen times. The goal was to empty the heart of all air bubbles before reconnecting it to its prime source of blood, via the venae cavae. Air bubbles cause embolisms, and embolisms cause brain damage.

Satisfied all the air was gone—no more froth—Lefrak allowed the heart to fill with blood.

Typically, at this point, nothing happens. No beat. That doesn't occur until the blood is fully warmed, from 79 degrees to 98.6, and that process is gradual. Even then, often, nothing happens; with the majority of heart transplants, electric shock must be used to start the organ. The electrode paddles were readied.

They weren't needed. After the heart was fully warmed and Lefrak massaged it by hand for a minute or two, Mark Willey's heart started beating. His heart? Her heart? For the moment, pronouns became ambiguous.

It was an imperfect beat—the right atrium was stuttering—but that soon resolved.

In an understandable deviation from procedure, Aaron Hill abandoned his heart-lung machine, walked up behind Lefrak and looked over the doctor's shoulder, to take in the moment. The beat was strong, a young man's heart in a young woman's body, in powerful, controlled spasm. Clench and release, clench and release. The sutures all held.

It's perhaps odd, but twenty-eight years later there is no consensus on what happened next. Lefrak, who disdains shows of emotion in his operating room, remembers no celebration at all. Anesthesiologist Mokie Shakoor recalls the slowly building *thup-thup-thup* of applause through a circle of latex gloves. Speir thinks he may have reached around the table to shake Lefrak's hand. The clearest memory belongs to Mary Dellinger.

Dellinger remembers an almost matter-of-fact atmosphere, not a letdown or an anticlimax, but an exhilarating satisfied collective nod. Of course it had worked. They had practiced so obsessively with the dead, there was no way it was not going to work for the living.

After major procedures, surgeons dictate operative notes, for the record. These tend to be laconic affairs, heavy on technical language, empty of drama. This one was no different, and it also reflected Lefrak's distaste for showmanship. It was three pages long, single spaced on a manual typewriter. Under "Operation" it says "orthotopic cardiac transplantation," just as it might have said "tonsillectomy." After three long paragraphs describing the patient's history, her diagnosis, the medications that had been tried and failed, the prep of her body, and the mechanics of cardiopulmonary bypass, Lefrak summarized the entire four-hour transplant in one sentence: "The donor heart was sutured in place using the standardized technique." Like a successful fisherman giving credit to his line, he then notes the sutures were made with "3-0 Prolene." Finally: "The patient was taken to the surgical intensive care unit in satisfactory condition."

TWENTY-EIGHT YEARS LATER, at seventy-one, Lefrak had just eased into retirement.

He and his wife, Trudy, have five adult daughters. The Lefraks live in one of the grandest homes in stately McLean, Virginia. It's a mansion on a hill, a feat of modern architecture and design in which much of the furniture and infrastructure looks as though it was carved out of the same enormous tree.

Unlike Christiaan Barnard, Ed Lefrak had an unforced retirement. His hands are fine. He uses them to resew his granddaughters' loved-ragged stuffed toys, and sometimes hauls out the surgical spectacles with those little telescopes to untangle his wife's necklaces. Once a month, he and Trudy—a registered nurse—volunteer their time at a free medical clinic in Arlington, Virginia, treating the uninsured for problems as plebeian as hemorrhoids.

Lefrak is one of those rare and lucky individuals whose personal fortune allows the sort of generosity of spirit we all like to think we'd show if we just had the resources. Most of us are never tested on this. For those who are, the rewards can be complicated.

In 1998, Lefrak was part of a medical team that volunteered to care for Nicaraguan peasants after Hurricane Mitch nearly annihilated the country, killing thousands, displacing hundreds of thousands, destroying hospitals, distributing willy-nilly through the floodwaters hundreds of active land mines left over from the Contra insurgency of the 1980s. Many lives and limbs were lost.

In Corinto, a poor coastal city ravaged by flooding, Lefrak found himself moved by the plight of a sickly fourteen-year-old girl, one hardship in all the rubble that was not wrought by Mitch. The mitral valve in Maria Eliset Centeno Hernandez's heart had been damaged from a bout with rheumatic fever at age nine. Her lungs were bubbly with blood, her breathing shallow and liquid. Lefrak knew what lay in store for her—a lingering death in her twenties, if she even made it that far, considering her straits. Orphaned at an early age, Maria lived with her doting grandmother and disabled brother in a leaky tin-roofed shack without electricity or running water. Dinner was sometimes bread and coffee.

Working with an international charity organization, Lefrak brought Maria to Virginia, put her up for a few weeks in his palatial home, and then, in a grueling daylong surgery, sliced open her heart and gave it a new valve. All of it was a gift—from Lefrak, his colleagues, and his hospital.

Before the operation, Maria could barely move. A week afterward, she was Rollerblading around the Lefraks' home and bonding with ten-year-old Mikaela, the youngest Lefrak daughter. Her suitcases fat with new clothes and toys, Maria returned with boundless joy and reckless energy to the reality that awaited her in the dispiriting grit of Corinto, Nicaragua—population 15,000.

Was it too much, too fast, with hope too easily extinguished? Eighteen months later, Maria was pregnant. Six years later, she was dead. Lefrak doesn't know what took her—but he does know she lived unwisely and did not take care of her health. On his desk, he keeps a picture of Maria, and of her two children, a boy and a girl. The boy's middle name is Eduardo, named for the doctor who had saved the mother's life.

When Lefrak allows himself to, he still sees Maria at fourteen, dimply, joyful, with a cereal-bowl haircut, looking like a little girl but for her strangely complex grown-up eyes.

FAIRFAX HOSPITAL—NOW CALLED Inova Fairfax—has become one of the leading heart transplant centers in the country. Its chief surgeon is Alan Speir.

Heart transplantation is now close to commonplace, with more than two thousand performed in the United States alone. It extends life, but is not without problems, still. For reasons that are not yet clear, transplant recipients tend to develop coronary artery disease more rapidly than most people. Transplant survival rates, while vastly better than before, are still not extraordinary. Only half survive for ten years or more. Fifteen years is considered excellent. Twenty is remarkable. Twenty-five is nearly unheard of. Also, for unknown reasons, survival rates for black patients are significantly lower than for white patients.

What, then, explains Eva Baisey, here in her living room, thirty-two years after her surgery, one of the longest-living transplant patients on the planet, joking about how she sometimes forgets to take her meds?

"I don't always take cyclosporine twice a day like I'm supposed to," she says in a conspiratorial whisper. "I'll remember after three or four days when I feel a little flutter or it skips a beat."

Eva considers what this must sound like. A big smile.

"Don't tell Dr. Lefrak. He'll *kill* me."

She and Dr. Lefrak remain friends. He calls her every December twenty-eighth, every anniversary of the surgery that saved her life. He has done it thirty-one times.

Eva Baisey is a formidable presence, with long, striking purplish braids. She is in a perpetual happy battle with her weight, something she talks about a lot. What she doesn't talk about much are the events of Christmas week 1986.

When she woke after surgery, Eva asked her ICU nurse to see the Sunday newspaper. The nurse laughed. Sunday was history; Eva had slept clear through it. So the nurse handed Eva the Monday *Washington Post*. She was on page 1.

Soon Eva would get the bad news: She could not be a nurse. Her compromised immune system made it too dangerous for her to be around the sick. She was crushed by this; ever since childhood, all she'd ever wanted to do, she said, was to "help old people and babies." So for a time she studied computer science and worked with those machines, though, as she puts it now without irony, "my heart wasn't in it."

After five years, Eva's immune system seemed fine and her doctors relented. She was cleared to be a nurse, and that's what she is. She works at a MedStar clinic. She helps old people and babies. She lives in a nice garden apartment in District Heights, Maryland, not far from her son and her daughter, a security guard who braids Eva's hair, and her mom, Barbara, who still has her back.

Eva says that in the black community, there is still some mistrust about donating organs, a suspicion that for African Americans the transplant business is a one-way street in the wrong direction. She tries to dispel that notion wherever and whenever she can.

Doctors working with transplant patients have noticed that many of them tend to be incurious about the lives of the people whose hearts beat in their chest, or the circumstances of their deaths. It's not ingratitude—it's a form of self-defense. There is a burden in merely surviving this surgery and remaining optimistic, and it does not help to incorporate someone else's tragedy into the narrative of your life. Living for one is hard enough.

Eva's like that. It has helped her to think of her new heart as a thing, more like a prosthetic device than a part from another human being. She knew about the murder, of course—it, too, was in the newspapers—but she never asked about the details, didn't really want details, and did not hear them until this very day.

Taking this all in is Eva's son, Antonio, who was not yet two at the time of the operation. Antonio is a slight, elegant, soft-spoken young man who is politically liberal but once worked as a waiter in a Republican country club. He held his tongue at work and hides a smile about that. Antonio has stayed quiet, too, for most of the last two hours, listening to the story of his mother's deteriorating illness, her near death, and of the murder that saved her life.

"This is the first time I've heard a lot of this," he says, shaking his head.

Doctors tend not to speculate why one transplant works so well and others do not. Surely it helped that Mark Willey's heart was fresh, that it had spent only minutes outside his body when it went into Eva's. But hundreds of down-the-hall transplants haven't been nearly as successful as this one. Other donors have been in better physical shape than Mark, other recipients in better physical shape than Eva. Nothing convincingly explains the strange chemistry, the alchemy, that has kept the heart of a sullen, violent, tormented criminal beating for so long in a gentle mother's chest. Her coronary arteries—*his* coronary arteries—are amazingly clear.

Eva has never before been asked whether it bothered her that she's got the heart of a murderer. She is asked it now. She opens her mouth, then closes it again. She looks at Antonio, gets no help there, then back at the person who posed that impertinent question.

Finally: "Okay, it could have been a car accident. Someone dying for no reason at all. Something meaningless."

This is better, she said. "Someone loved someone so hard they couldn't bear to live without them. Yes, it's selfish. I don't want anyone to love me to death. But it all comes out of a need to be wanted, to passionately connect with another person. That is not meaningless. That comes out of something good. And something good came out of that."

Eva is right. She didn't get a murderer's heart, exactly. She got a broken heart. It fixed her, and she fixed it.

3:00 A.M., Bristol, Rhode Island

The exact time it happened is a guess, but an educated one, based on available data and applicable mythology. We're placing it at three A.M., the stillest part of the night and the start of the medieval witching hour, when demons were said to dance with the Devil.

By 5:30 A.M., indisputably, the deed had been done. That was when a faculty member looked up into the early morning skyscape over Roger Williams College, a 140-acre, 2,000-student liberal arts institution in this picturesque New England seaport town, and gasped. Given the events of the previous month, his first thought was no doubt some variant of "Oh, shit."

What happened here on December 28, 1986, had its beginnings in the spring of that year. That was when Kevin Jordan, a professor of historic preservation, was given an old weather vane by a friend at the local water company, where it had been kept in storage for years. It was a primitive vane manufactured in the late 1800s, wrought of copper, partially gilded, and partially oxidized to a Statue of Liberty green. It was almost three feet high and weighed about twenty pounds.

It depicted an early Native American archer with a three-feather headdress, holding a bow in one hand and an oversized arrow in the other. On his back was an empty quiver. The archer, who swiveled on a pole, was looking to his left, always into the wind. He sat atop a fixed ring depicting north, south, east, and west.

The vane was not formidable in size, but it was well crafted and detailed. Etched into the stabilizer "tail" were symbols of nature: nuts and berries and such.

Jordan had had the thing lightly restored, including the patching up of a few bullet holes. Weather vanes are a tempting target for yahoos with rifles; when you hit them at just the right angle, they spin.

The man who gave Jordan the vane said it was a likeness of a warlike seventeenth-century Wampanoag Indian sachem named Metacomet. The professor knew that made it rare and valuable and excitingly local. The Wampanoags roamed the Bristol area three centuries before. What to do with it?

That question seemed easily answered. Jordan and his students had recently restored a huge old barn on campus and converted it into a performing arts center. On the top of the barn was a cupola, and on top of the cupola was nothing. Once it had been capped by a weather vane, but the vane had been stolen many years before, in the 1970s, during a rash of thefts of these quaint New England barn-toppers. Antique vanes had a high resale value, and there was a spirited black market for them. The thieves were brazen and inventive. Some scaled the steeply pitched barn roofs using grappling hooks. Some went further. Old weather vanes often were only lightly attached to their bases or had just been slid down onto a fitted pole. This made them vulnerable to helicopter thieves, who would just dangle a rope with a hook and yank. In the 1970s you could rent a copter for $200 an hour, and there were plenty of jaded ex-Vietnam pilots looking for a quick payday. Many weather vanes were stolen that way.

Jordan was aware of all this, and he was no one's fool. So he and his students hauled Metacomet up to the top of the barn and secured it with a collet below roof level. Just to be extra safe, they employed sturdy screws of three different designs, with three different types of heads, requiring three different types of screwdrivers. A helicopter assault would likely be fruitless. A grappling-hook assault would certainly be complicated.

The barn was the highest point on campus, and the weather vane was the highest point on the barn; ergo, Metacomet looked down on the whole school and all that was in it. And that's where this story ends, peaceably, with everyone proud and content and safe under the protective, watchful eye of a fierce warrior.

Not.

That is not where this story ends, because this was Roger Williams College, which emphatically put the *liberal* in *liberal arts*. It was a bastion of progressive pedagogy and cultural sensitivity and robust epistemological, semiotic, heuristic debate over matters large and small, and even very small.

This was the 1980s, and the students themselves—though bright and of inclusive and progressive bent—were not much into protest or identity politics. Most of them didn't give a rat's ass about the new weather vane. Few gave any thought at all to the question of whether it was appropriate to have an ancient Native American symbol fly over their mostly euro-white campus. Many of the students didn't even know what the image was, all the way up there at the top of the barn. One student squinted into the sun and decided it was a rooster. The kids, mostly, just didn't care.

But the faculty had come of age in the 1960s. They were one-time righteous activists, now bemused and benumbed by the political apathy that surrounded them. They were spoiling for a fight. The new weather vane became the focus of a strong if effete debate among the academics.

The school had been founded in the name of the colonial-era theologian who admired Native Americans, studied their language till he could speak it, and supported their demands for fair treatment. Might not this weather vane be seen, legitimately, as homage to that early, magnificent cross-cultural handshake? Or was it something else entirely? Was it what we today call *cultural appropriation,* a final indignity against a tribe twice decimated by their encounter with white Europeans—first in an outbreak of leptospirosis against which they were helpless, and second in their bloody two-year war against the English colonists, in a desperate effort to oust them from New England?

As it happens, that ill-fated anti-colonial campaign was led by Metacomet. He didn't survive it. Shot in the heart, he fell face-first to his death in the mud of a swamp right here, near Bristol.

Metacomet was unloved by the colonists. Hearing news of his death, Cotton Mather was said to have proclaimed from the pulpit that "God has sent us the head of a Leviathan, for a feast."

Metacomet's head was not eaten. That would have been the act of savages, not Englishmen. Instead, his head was placed on a pike high outside a British fort—physically resembling a weather vane, actually—and it remained there, rotting, for twenty years until it was just a skull. His body was quartered and hung from tree limbs. His severed right hand was awarded to the soldier who shot him—an Indian turncoat, as it happens. Metacomet's wife and nine-year-old son were sold into slavery.

Couldn't you argue that hoisting this weather vane high over the school was an overdue apology to Metacomet and his tribe? Or could it be that it was more of a final thumb in the eye, a wiggle of the butt, right in their faces?

It was a lot to chew on, and the faculty of Roger Williams College gnawed it to the bone. As bones of contention go, this one was pretty slender: a three-foot object that you couldn't clearly make out from the ground forty-five feet away.

Meetings were held. Lines were drawn. Tempers flared. American studies instructor Richard Potter, of Native American descent, announced that he would not attend a performance at the barn until the weather vane was gone. This annoyed many of his colleagues in a place where participatory collegiality was valued. "There really has been a great amount of hostility," Potter grumped at the time. This got into the newspapers.

Eventually the anti-vaners persuaded the faculty senate to ask the president of the college to have Metacomet taken down. The pro-vaners were indignant; they said the anti-vaners had rammed the measure through without proper time for contemplation and debate. They demanded that a decision be reconsidered at the next senate meeting in February. The president of the college, William H. Rizzini, mulled the situation, stalling for time. "I'm going to hold off on making a decision until both sides have a chance to air their views," he said. "We'll see what comes out of it and then I'll get into the fray."

By now the media had begun to show up. TV stations. AP and UPI. Small newspapers, medium-sized newspapers, and eventually *The New York Times.* For all of them, this was fun.

Donald Whitworth, a psychology instructor who is one-quarter Cherokee, told the *Times* the vane "reduces us to the level of the whale, the chicken, or the horse," which are other antique weather vane staples. That was true, but so were Greek gods, manly charioteers, Viking warriors, and beautiful women seated in half-moons, their hair flying in the wind.

William Grandgeorge, coordinator of the drama department, responded to Whitworth: "This isn't a rendition of an Indian holding an arrow in his teeth. It's a dignified rendition of what I assume was a very dignified man."

The matter was at a tense standstill, awaiting official action. The media went home.

And then more drama. A Roger Williams student delivered a bombshell. He had been looking through tattered old weather vane catalogues and discovered, in the catalogue of the J. Harris Co., late of Boston, Massachusetts, this precise weather vane. It was not an image of Metacomet at all. It was of Massasoit, Metacomet's father, and a very, very different sort of man. Arguably, a great man.

The media returned. The new stories appeared on December 14, 1986.

It turns out that Massasoit was a significant player in American history. He attended the very first Thanksgiving in 1621, the most famous meal in American history, dining with the Pilgrims of Plymouth Colony. His contribution to the meager table is said to have turned it into a feast: five newly slain deer.

Could this be why he was depicted not aiming an arrow, but keeping it peaceably at his side?

Massasoit and his deputy, Squanto, are often credited with saving the early colonists' lives, contributing food and teaching them survival skills to gut it out through the bitter winter. A friend of William Bradford, Myles Standish, and other colonial leaders, Massasoit also became something of a double agent, warning the colonists of impending attacks by other tribes. Suddenly there was a new narrative to embrace: Massasoit as a hero of the early American people. You could argue that a weather vane depicting Massasoit was no different from a weather vane depicting George Washington, couldn't you?

Not so fast, Kemosabe.

Some anti-vaners argued that this changed nothing and may even have made things worse: Whoever that guy with the arrow is, to Americans he's just the generic stereotype of the savage Indian. And with this new knowledge—that the actual Indian depicted was a peaceable man—that lie is even greater.

"We shouldn't be educating them to see people stereotypically," Richard Potter told the *Times*. "Symbols deal on emotional levels. You can't control what a symbol does. I could put up a Hopi symbol for earth or land, but it would offend many people. It happens to be a swastika."

Battle lines remained drawn.

It should be noted that the argument may have seemed painfully academic, but it was not without merit on both sides. Had it been conducted without rancor, in conference rooms among respectful peers, perhaps with interested students in attendance, it might have contributed to a broader cultural understanding on campus. But that's not how it went down. The stink was very public and caustic. And because of that, it attracted the media, who turned it into the most famous weather vane in the world. And because of that, something else became widely known. Almost every story about the vane mentioned that it was rare and precious. Jordan had told reporters he knew of only two or three others exactly like it. Its value was estimated at between $75,000 and $150,000. Also part of the narrative, of course, were the extensive measures that had been taken to make it safe from theft.

Which brings us back to the unfortunate events of the early morning hours of December 28, 1986.

Police surmised that there had been at least two and probably three thieves. They were very likely newspaper readers. They stole onto the campus in a car or truck some time between two A.M.—the last time the weather vane had been seen—and just before dawn, when its disappearance was first noticed. They were aided by the darkness of that slivery moon. They had come well prepared, probably with a blunt instrument and some muffling device to mask the sound of glass breaking in a ground-floor window. They'd brought a complete set of screwdrivers with different heads. The whole operation had probably taken less than half an hour.

Single-handedly, in a brief span of time, the thieves had solved the college's internal sociopolitical problem, but they'd charged at least $75,000 for their services.

The weather vane has never been recovered or replaced. Above the cupola is nothing.

3:02 A.M., Falls City, Nebraska

If the fixture that overheated had been on the Christmas tree, there might have been enough early pop and crackle to wake the man sleeping just a few feet away. But the fire started in a makeshift lamp swaddled in macrame that was hanging from the underside of a stairwell. So it likely smoldered in dry rope, then burned into old wood, slow and noiseless, poisoning the air before the fire raged. The house was still. The house stayed still too long.

The call went out at 3:02, phoned in from the home of the family across the street, relayed by a dispatcher simultaneously to both the police and the fire department. The pumper truck had to be roused, manned, and maneuvered, which is why patrolman Marty Eickhoff was first on the scene, in his cruiser.

In most places, the house at 1224 Morton Street would be called a bungalow, but that term's too pretentious for small-town Nebraskans. In Falls City, population 4,990, the cheerless home on a street corner near the southern side of town was called a one-and-a-half, which describes it adequately, a cheap clapboard box with a rickety porch and a second half-story on top, with a slope-roofed attic bedroom. Rent was under a hundred a month.

As he approached in his car, Eickhoff saw the little house throwing way too much light into the darkness. Then flames tonguing out of the front, worryingly near the gas meter. A car stood at a weird angle in the street, as though the driver had come in fast, saw the fire, braked hard, and fishtailed. Finally Eickhoff saw a young woman in the front yard, screaming. The car was hers. There were people trying to console her.

Eickhoff heard "babies," and "inside," and bolted to where he was directed, the bedroom on the right side of the house.

A second patrol car skidded up. This was Duane Armbruster. In time, Armbruster would become a lifer on the city's small police force—its main crime investigator and eventually its chief—so he would see his share of bad, but this would stick as the bleakest night ever.

The bedroom window was smashed in. Investigators would later learn the screaming woman was the babies' mother, and she had pulled up to the house after a night out with friends. Desperation overcame caution. She had done that to the window with her fists.

Hot air from inside hit Eickhoff as though from a bellows. Because he moonlighted as a firefighter, he knew the peril he faced: Superheated air can take out your lungs in one breath. The fire truck was en route, with its protective gear and breathing packs, but there was no time to wait for it. Eickhoff took a gulp of cool night air, held it, and pushed his face into the furnace.

The room was filled from the ceiling down with black smoke.

Midway, where it thinned some, the policeman could make out two small shapes on a bed a few feet away. The children were just beyond his reach, so he grabbed the headboard and tried to shimmy the whole bed toward him. It went maybe a foot, then stopped, as though something were blocking it.

Back out, grab a breath, back in. Armbruster was beside him now, and two neighbors. The men managed to seize the sheet and reel it in toward them until the shapes were close enough to grab and pull through the window. An ambulance was on the way, but it would not be needed, at least not for the children.

The men gently laid the two-year-old boy and one-year-old girl on the ground. A small mercy: They were not burned. But they were baked.

By now the firemen had arrived, and from the neighbors they learned there was probably someone else in the house. Protected by gear, cooled in the mist from the fire hose, they went in and found a male adult on the floor.

Firefighters carried Todd Thrane out of the building. He was limp and unconscious, but there was a faint pulse, so they tried CPR. He made it into the ambulance alive but did not survive the ride to the hospital. The coroner would report that all victims had died of smoke inhalation.

On this slowest weekend for news, three dead in a house fire in the middle of nowhere was enough to make it onto the national wires. The UPI story identified the dead man, who was only nineteen, as the babysitter.

Wire service articles tend to be written in what journalists call an inverted pyramid. That means that you cram the most important facts at the top and let the story taper down from there. This permits busy newspaper editors, with limited space, to cut from the bottom without worrying that they're losing salient details.

Most papers—among them, *The New York Times*—carried just a paragraph. Three dead, two infants and their teenaged babysitter. Where the story ran a paragraph or two longer, readers learned the additional puzzling fact that the babysitter had lived in the house.

As it turns out, Todd Thrane was babysitting, but he wasn't the babysitter. No one got the whole story, which was poignant and textured and deep. And of course no one could have known of the Gothic shadows it would cast.

TODD THRANE WAS as complicated as it gets and as simple as they come. He liked things loud—fireworks, pro wrestling, motorcycles, deer hunting, heavy machinery, heavy metal. First he liked girls, and then women. He liked cars and he liked drinking, and he didn't mind mixing the two.

He was a cipher, a deeply good-natured boy who, at fifteen, had become a recidivist truant and ambitious carouser, so wild and contrarian that his mother sent him from her home in Lincoln to live with her brother on a farm in Falls City, to straighten him out. He was so laconic nobody could really tell you what he was thinking about anything important, yet so sensitive and vulnerable he never got over his parents' untidy divorce, which started with an infidelity so blatant it couldn't be hidden or minimized or talked around.

That's where most of it started, with the divorce. Just about everyone who knew Todd Thrane agrees on that, if not on much else. In the extended Thrane family, some hard feelings remain and some regrets linger, much of it over what happened to its youngest son.

Bill Thrane had a master's degree in special education, but he worked in the grocery business. His wife, Judith, was a licensed hairdresser, but worked as a bookkeeper. The three Thrane boys grew up understanding that life sometimes entails compromise; also, that there were rules, and you lived by them, and if you didn't, there were consequences. When he was little, Todd once lit a remarkably competent bonfire under the backyard deck and almost burned it down. "I don't think he sat down for a week after that," his brother Allen recalls. "Didn't do it again."

As a child, Todd had cherubic altar-boy looks, with a chubby face, a diffident smile, and a lush mushroom cap of corn-silk hair. He was a scamp, but he could surprise you with his tenderness. One summer he worked on a farm pulling weeds from the bean fields; it was clear he wanted money of his own but unclear why, and he wouldn't say. Suspicions mounted. It turned out he was saving for a fancy birthday present for his mom, a wicker chair he'd known she wanted.

There's no "good" age for a child to weather a divorce, nor is there consensus among experts about which age is the worst. But you won't get many arguments that eleven stinks. It is when you are solidifying a sense of self; a stable, structured, loving home life provides a template for how to adjust to adulthood. Divorcing parents of preadolescents are particularly urged to strive for normalcy: Tamp down the drama. Avoid accusations of betrayal. Eliminate the tawdry.

Todd was eleven on the day his mother took him and his middle brother, Tim, to visit their father in the hospital, where Bill Thrane was being treated for a minor problem. When the boys walked into the room, a young woman was on the bed, too.

As Tim remembers it, not much talking ensued. No introductions were offered. The woman just got up and left, and afterward, the conversation between their mom and dad seemed dreadfully strained. "We'll discuss it when I get home," Bill said to Judy under his breath.

But he never came home. He was just . . . gone.

There wasn't much conversation in the Thrane home about what had happened, and things stayed that way—an oppressive secret too awful to articulate—until one day when Tim and his older brother, Allen, were out for a drive and happened to see their father's car outside a house they didn't recognize. Allen remembers the moment frozen, as though it were an old-fashioned snapshot, the kind from those primitive harsh flash cameras that shattered the bulb in the process of taking the photo: Dad, sheepish in the front yard, that lady at the front door, backlit in a floral pastel dress. That's when the boys in the family knew for sure that their father was not coming back, and why. The older brothers made peace with this over time, but Todd never really did.

One day not long afterward, Judy Thrane came home from work to find that her husband had let himself in during the day and hauled away their bedroom furniture. That night Todd watched his mother go to sleep on the floor. The next day he found and confronted his father with all the tight-lipped, chin-quivering, beetle-browed righteous indignation an eleven-year-old could muster. It was apparently formidable. Bill Thrane wound up po-nying up for a new bed.

Todd didn't talk much about the divorce, or the incident at the hospital, or the news of the lady in the floral dress, or any feelings he had about any of this. There was fury, but it was inarticulate. One day, after quarreling with Allen over some trifle, he calmly walked outside and kicked a big dent in the fender of his big brother's car.

It was all part of a nihilistic shift of attitude. Todd began act-ing as if rules no longer had any meaning.

Curfews were imposed and ignored. School attendance be-came, in Todd's judgment, optional. His bedroom was in the basement, and it had a window that could pivot open, so it be-came his doggie door to freedom. He found ways to get beer. Judy remembers warning her son that he was flirting with juve-nile delinquency and seemed destined for Boys Town. She meant it as a warning; he seemed to take it as a compliment.

The strange thing about Todd's misbehavior was that he sel-dom tried to hide it. There was a system: He announced his in-tentions, his mom freaked out and forbade it, and then he did it. It was after he informed her that he was not going to be attending school anymore that Todd found himself living a hundred miles away, on Uncle Benny's farm in Falls City.

Falls City was founded in 1857 at the southeastern corner of what was then the territory of Nebraska. It wasn't much to look at, and by 1986 it was even less. The dinky four-foot-high wa-terfalls for which the city was grandiosely named had long gone dry. The population was dwindling, and the economy—once built around railroads and oil—was in decline. Falls City still had its farmers, and its farmers still had a certain stubborn pugnacity, a trait dating to the Civil War era, when the townspeople conspired to keep a dangerous secret. A barn in Falls City was the first Underground Railroad stop in Nebraska for fugitive slaves from Kansas. According to lore, radical abolitionist John Brown, though wanted on capital charges, was said to have strode through Falls City without fear.

Benny Sickle grew up on his father's farm a few miles out of town, and he was still there but running the place in 1982 when his likable but incorrigible nephew arrived one day from Lincoln. It was a Sunday. Benny took one look at Todd, of whom he was about to take legal custody and full disciplinary responsibility, and phoned a friend. The friend was a barber. The Lord's Day notwithstanding, Todd got his moppy, mullety mess shorn close, right that day. New sheriff, new rules.

Benny's daughter LeAnn was just about Todd's age. She remembers her friends' fascination with this young city slicker, particularly the girls. To the teenagers of Falls City, Lincoln was Babylon, USA, and LeAnn's cousin was a tantalizing mystery. He wasn't cherubic anymore. His face had thinned. Farmwork was hardening his body. His mouth was taut, like Clint Eastwood's. His emerald eyes squinted out at you with a promise of mischief. He was glib, almost too glib for his own good. He didn't care for school and he never read a book he didn't absolutely have to, but he picked things up and could talk about most any subject, or at least artfully bullshit around it. He once told his mom that he'd probably stop drinking when he hit twenty-one, because then it would be legal, and what's the fun in that?

Show a group of women a photo of Todd Thrane from his late teens, and you get a consistent reaction, customized by age. Each compares him to a sandy-haired, bad-boy leading man with whom she is or had once been smitten. James Dean, for some. For some, Leonardo DiCaprio or Heath Ledger. Jude Law. The youngest summon Ryan Gosling. Todd's good looks were cinematic, and there was a half-hitch in his walk, a kind of swagger.

For a time, he took well to the greater structure at his uncle's home. He was a reliable farmhand who worked prodigiously when he worked. But the city, such as it was, beckoned. There was some nightlife there, and once again, curfews became optional. Familiar cycles ensued: escape, punishment, atonement, escape. Too often Todd came home drunk.

He somehow made it through high school, which ended Uncle Benny's responsibilities, none too soon for the Falls City Thranes. Briefly back at home in Lincoln, Todd got a job in a meat market, a job he lost when he picked up a DUI. Then he returned to Falls City, where he got a job in a grocery store, a job he lost when he picked up a DWI. Two drunkenness arrests in three months. It was May 1986, and things were out of control.

Something complicated was bedeviling Todd, and he was using booze as an anesthetic. He showed up at his court appearance amiably but obviously smashed. Unamused, the judge instructed him to sober up and afforded him ample time to accomplish that—thirty days in the county jail. It was the low point in the short, troubled life of Todd Thrane.

His older cousin Donna O'Grady visited him in jail. She talked to him in his cell. He looked small. It was the first time she had ever seen him scared. "Don't let this be your life," she implored him.

It's anyone's guess what Todd's life might have been, had he survived the fire, or had there been no fire at all. The most optimistic guesses come from those who were familiar with the events of Todd's final summer and fall, beginning on the day he first walked into that flimsy one-and-a-half on 1224 Morton Street. Becky Gill lived there.

Todd had gone there with his friend Ron Gill, who was getting a divorce from Becky but still hung around some, hoping for a reconciliation. Ron had somewhere else to be, so for a time he left Todd with Becky, which turned out to be a tactical error, romantically. They became an official couple soon after, and not long after that, Todd moved in.

Becky was twenty. She was smallish and appealing in a hot-blooded sort of way—think Stockard Channing in *Grease*. She drank and smoked. She kept rowdy company. She took crap from no one. She was refreshingly cynical. You could have called her wild and hard and loose, or you could have called her scrappy and sassy and free-spirited, depending on how much you liked her.

Todd liked her, but what he seemed to like most of all were her moppets—Savannah, the one-year-old, and older brother, Tony, who was two. When he was around the children, Todd softened. Everyone saw it.

There are photos of Todd on the Sickle farm that year, with Becky's two children, his arms protectively around them. In one snapshot he's on a three-wheeler dirt bike, with a pig-tailed Savannah in his lap. She is jubilantly pointing toward the sky, as if just discovering clouds. Todd looks not at her but at the camera. He's smiling confidently, with what looks very much like pride.

It was as though the children had broken through to some

vulnerable part of Todd that had been stashed away, around age eleven, for safekeeping.

Not all of Todd's relatives were crazy about Becky—in their view, she was part of the party crowd from which they were trying to wean Todd. But they couldn't deny or dislike the change that was coming over him. He was drinking less, and also less purposefully; sometimes it seemed he'd made that change for the children, with whom he was aligned in friendly conspiracy. There was the time Becky sent Todd out with money to buy her cigarettes. He returned instead with candy canes for Tony and Savannah, and got chewed out, but took it with a grin.

A week before his death Todd went to visit his parents in Lincoln for the Christmas holidays. He spent the first day with his father, with whom he was reconnecting, followed by a boisterous Christmas Eve with his mother and brothers, where three young men became boys again. They arm-wrestled. Allen let Todd drive his motorcycle around town, which was risky and arguably irresponsible, but also a welcome sign of trust: Not only did Todd have no motorcycle license but his driver's license had been suspended for a year over the drinking mess.

As it happens, Todd wasn't supposed to be back home on Sunday the twenty-eighth. His plan had been to stay in Lincoln through New Year's. But he changed his mind and asked his mom to drive him back early, on Friday. When she told him that her car was in the shop, he said he'd hitchhike. So she borrowed a friend's car.

Accounts differ about the events of those final few days, and they are likely influenced by what feels comfortable in the memory. Judy says Todd was anxious to get home because he'd had a tiff with Becky and they'd made up over the phone, so he just wanted to be with her. Becky says there was no tiff, that everything was great between them at the end. Tim says that when Todd couldn't reach Becky by phone and learned the children were with grandparents, he began to worry about where Becky was and with whom. Allen remembers that Todd was just "homesick." Allen is the diplomat in the family.

There is also the question of just what Todd brought back with him that day. There were definitely Christmas presents for him, Becky, and the kids. Becky remembers one gift in particular that came into the house that day, but Judy says no, that Todd had had it long before the fatal weekend. Judy was good at needlework, and she had made the decorative part of it herself. It was a hanging lamp festooned with homemade macrame.

Fire investigators never figured out exactly what went wrong with that lamp. It's possible the socket was faulty, or maybe the bulb. It's also possible that the bulb being used was of too high wattage to be safely nestled near combustible sisal. Understandably, the family doesn't like to dwell on these details, because what does it matter?

Here's what matters. About fifteen minutes before three A.M., Todd Thrane awoke to an all-too-real nightmare. He was likely already dizzy from smoke. The front door lay eight feet to his left; the children's bedroom eight feet to his right. He moved right.

In the Thrane family, this moment is recounted with reverence. Allen remembers being told that Todd's body was found on the floor, tantalizingly close to the front door, with a baby under each arm. It is not true, but it is not far from the truth. The truth needs no embellishment. Todd Thrane died a hero.

His sooty handprints were on the edge of Savannah's crib; Becky saw them when she numbly inspected the scene in the ruined house the day after the fire. The house would be bulldozed soon after.

Todd had evidently gone for the little girl first, lifted her from the crib, then lurched with her over to Tony's bed. Todd had to have been operating on adrenaline and pure stubborn will, because he was approaching unconsciousness. The air was thick with toxins: carbon monoxide, carbon dioxide, and hydrogen cyanide, all of which would have had his head pounding. His eyes would have been red and watering, his vision a blur. He would have been alternatively gasping for air, then seized with a paroxysm of coughing. His lungs were burning, literally.

Smoke inhalation can take you down in a second. When Todd dropped, he managed to roll Savannah onto the bed with her brother. We know that because he was right there with them. It had been Todd's body, right below the babies, that had prevented patrolman Marty Eickhoff from pulling the bed to the window.

Wouldn't anyone have risked his life to save two infants left in his care? Maybe. Probably. But can anyone really know that about himself, unless he's faced such a stark choice in a moment of blind terror?

So that's what can be said, at the very least, of the likable, exasperating, incorrigible Todd Thrane. With his last breaths, he turned toward the flames and the children he'd come to love, and his life ended on that note of grace.

But Todd Thrane's story doesn't wrap up that easily, and it doesn't end with his death. The end hasn't been written yet. It could go any number of ways.

Only a few people knew it, but on the day she lost her young lover and her two children, Becky Gill was pregnant with Todd's baby.

IT IS 2013. Todd's baby is twenty-six. At the moment he's backing a dump truck down a driveway. He's got three tons of gravel to deliver.

Mark Gill has hazel eyes that squint out at you with a promise of mischief. His mouth is taut, like Eastwood's. He's got his father's chiseled musculature, which he carries on his father's smallish frame. Women look at him and think *bad-boy leading man.* There's a half-hitch in his walk, a hint of a swagger. He's glib, sometimes too glib for his own good. He grew up a chronic truant with a taste for booze and pills. He seems to know a little about every subject, or at least can artfully bullshit around it. He likes things loud. He likes motorcycles and owns one—a Suzuki GSX-R1000—his "crotch rocket," he calls it. It can approach 200 miles an hour, which he says he'd never, ever do because it's illegal and you could get in real trouble, and then he smiles big and looks away.

Mark lives in Colorado Springs, Colorado, where he is operations manager for a garden supply company. He lives in a camper on the company's eighteen-acre property, which is fine with his bosses, especially since it lets him work an eighty-hour week if he wants to, which he often does. His mom, Becky, lives close by with his stepfather, and they're all friends. Until this particular weekend, when a writer came to town with questions for Becky, Mark had never heard the full story about what happened to his father. He got it from her at a Waffle House, sitting silently, the third person at the table, taking it in, intense but emotionless and stone-faced, which is his customary expression. He is preternaturally self-possessed, which seems masterful, but also a little off-putting. It's as though he is part Zen master and part sociopath. He doesn't challenge that description. He says it sounds about right. It's the place you get to, he says, when you grow up like he did.

AFTER THE FIRE, before the funeral, there was a viewing just for the family. Outside the room, Bill Thrane approached Becky, and what he snarled at her remains indelible: "Are you going to beg my forgiveness for killing my son?"

Then he told her she didn't belong there, and that he wouldn't permit her in to see the body. Wordlessly, elegantly, Judy took Becky's trembling hand, and the two women walked in together.

It's hard to fault anyone for his or her behavior during those dreadful days; surely it was not the first time a grieving person found a scapegoat. Other Thranes wondered why Becky was out that night and with whom. She says it was a girlfriend, a woman who is now dead, and there is no evidence to doubt her or any reason to want to. And why would anyone really care?

Bill Thrane cared. Through his grief and likely his guilt—he wept through the funeral, the first time either of his remaining sons ever saw their father in tears—he saw Becky as a Jezebel whom he would put nothing past. One day after Mark was born, Bill arrived at Becky's house and asked to see the baby. After a long scrutiny at cribside, Becky remembers, Bill turned to his new wife. "You can go get the presents from the car," he said. "This is my grandson."

In those final days of his life, Todd had known Becky was pregnant. He was ecstatic, telling his family that he and Becky were planning on marrying in the summer. Allen remembers his kid brother talking about baby names. He was partial to Oscar, everyone remembers.

At the funeral home, Allen Thrane recalls Becky couldn't tear her eyes off him. He understood why. The two had not met before that day, and he and Todd looked very much alike.

Allen is fifty-six now; he'd worked most of his life in the printing business and now owns a restaurant in Branson, Missouri. You look at him, and there's a good chance you're looking at what Todd might look like today. He's still got his hair, still a sandy blond, a little fleshy in the face, a little prosperous in the middle, still a handsome man.

He is talking about his nephew, Mark Gill. "I have a lot of guilt in my heart about him."

Guilt?

"I think my brother would be upset with me."

There's something Allen's trying to get out, and it isn't coming easily.

"After the fire, and even after that, my wife and I talked about legally adopting Mark. We really wanted to do it."

They thought they could make a convincing case that it would be for everyone's good—both for the baby and for Becky, who had a lot to recover from without the stress of single motherhood. And it's not as though the baby would be out of her life.

But Allen never had the heart or nerve to broach it. "How do you ask a woman who just lost two children to give up her third?"

Though the Thranes were part of the first few years of Mark's life, Becky eventually moved to Colorado, and they lost contact. Allen wishes things had gone differently.

He is really struggling with this. He starts to explain, stops, starts again. He doesn't want to say anything bad about anyone. He doesn't want to be judgmental or sound elitist. But facts are facts.

"I have three children. One is a lawyer. One is a doctor. One is an accountant. My children grew up with opportunities. Mark grew up very poor. The house was dirty. He didn't eat as well as we did. If Mark had been our son . . ."

His voice catches.

". . . he wouldn't have felt he had to rob banks."

MARK GILL HAS DUMPED out the gravel in the driveway and is heading back to his work. It's a Sunday. On his right upper arm is a big tattoo. It's monochrome, a skull drawn in thin blue lines. It's an okay tat job, considering.

"Unfortunately, it is the by-product of impatience," Mark says with a tight smile. He means he should have waited for that particular procedure until he got out of prison. "I was young and I didn't understand the ramifications." He means walking around for the rest of your life with a semi-lame tattoo.

The first thing you notice about Mark Gill is how he speaks. He's a high school dropout with a GED, but he's got a lush vocabulary that he deploys preemptively, the way Frederick Douglass did, as though to controvert any assumptions you may have about his intelligence or sophistication. He learned to speak well in prison, from books. It was part of a plan that he hatched in the early months of his seven-plus years in custody.

"Don't let this be your life," Donna O'Grady had begged her cousin Todd in his jail cell. Mark Gill didn't have a Donna. He was alone, but he gave himself that talk.

"I went to prison with the mentality that this was not going to become the defining point of my life," he says. "I was not going to live a life of jackassery. Inside, I spent a great deal of time in inner reflection. I read an immense number of books. I studied philosophy, religion, architecture, civics, politics. I read Nietzsche. I read Marcus Aurelius. I read Sun Tzu's *Art of War*. Surprisingly enough, I read Webster's dictionary twelve times. I read books about living off the grid. I read books about gardening. Anything I could get my hands on."

Todd Thrane's unfinished life seemed circumscribed almost from the start, stunted by bad luck and then compounded by bad choices. He was a young man who seemed intelligent and charming enough to be more than he was, to aim higher than he did. It is tempting to think of the son as the father's second chance. And when you do that, you find yourself in some interesting territory.

We are inside Mark's camper, which is parked at the back of Don's Garden Shop, a sprawling venue that sits under a breathtaking expanse of the northern Rocky Mountains. It's dominated by Pikes Peak; the view from that summit is said to have inspired Katharine Lee Bates to write "America the Beautiful." Had Bates looked out today and seen Don's Garden Shop, the song might have had one more stanza, an oddball one.

Don's sells custom-made soils, mulch, fertilizer, firewood, paving materials, deck lumber, landscaping stones, and prefab garden sheds, but what stands out are the gargantuan lawn ornaments. The place is a menagerie of gigantic concrete and iron figurines—bears, stallions, turtles, wolves, frogs, and people. Mark's camper sits between a statue of St. Francis of Assisi and the shed that houses his shiny black Suzuki that can hit 200 but never does—wink wink, nudge nudge. The juxtaposition seems fitting.

The camper is a 26-footer, and it is so austere inside that it nearly landed Mark back in jail, because his parole officer took a look around and didn't believe anyone was actually living there, as Mark had sworn he was. "I lived in a cell not much bigger than that," Mark says dryly, pointing to the bed. "This is fine."

His vices these days, other than the bike, are coffee and Marlboros. He's a teetotaler; it's a condition of his parole, and he's tested frequently. He got out after serving half of a fourteen-year sentence he negotiated in return for a guilty plea. It was a pretty good deal for him, because he had indeed robbed banks—seven attempts, four successful—and they had him dead to rights.

HE WAS EIGHTEEN. He'd just dropped out of high school. He was living with the eighteen-year-old mother of his year-old daughter. He had a job as an auto mechanic. Like his father, he was good with cars. And like his father, he grew up missing a father.

By the time he was eight, Becky had remarried and moved from Falls City to Colorado. Mark got along with his stepfather, but his stepfather was a busy man. He worked in construction and was often away on big jobs for weeks or even months at a time.

At eighteen, "I was sort of looking for a father figure," Mark says. He took what he could get, which was the company of his landlord, Thomas Bastian. Bastian, who was twenty-seven, had a criminal record for domestic abuse and assault. Man and young man became drinking and carousing buddies, and then conspirators in one of the more pathetic crime sprees Colorado Springs has ever seen.

Mark and Tom were heavily into crystal meth, Ecstasy, and ketamine. They wanted more, but hadn't the bucks for it.

"We were just riding down the street one day," Mark says, "and we said, 'Well, let's rob a bank.'" They laughed about it for a bit—until they stopped laughing.

Bastian's wife had worked in a bank, and she'd told her husband something intriguing: In a robbery, tellers are instructed to hand over money and offer no resistance, even if there is no weapon presented, even if no overt threat is made. Being a bank robber sounded like being a panhandler in a neighborhood of bleeding hearts. You ask, they give.

Tom and Mark hit their first bank on October 4, 2005. It was the World Savings Bank on South Nevada Avenue.

Mark waited in the car while Bastian went in. The older man came out grinning with a thousand-plus in cash, and they drove away and that was it. No one ran out of the bank waving a gun or even shaking a fist. There was no police pursuit.

Here's a koan that must be particularly fascinating when one is hopped up on meth and Special K: If you pull off a bank heist and no one seems to care, was there a crime at all?

They'd agreed Mark would pull off the next one while Tom drove getaway. Mark approached a teller at Key Bank, passed her a note informing her that she was being robbed and requesting the contents of the till. Request approved. Mark sauntered out to the car, heart pounding, heat nowhere in sight, a few more thousand in hand.

Days of chemically infused partying followed. Then things got a little nuts.

The newly minted bank robbers decided they weren't getting enough money. Only so much could be filched from the till at a single teller's station. They felt they needed to get into the little safes at the tellers' feet, the ones full of cash to replenish the tills. And the only way to do that and to make sure there was no funny business with hidden alarms was to leap the counter, *Dog Day Afternoon* style. This required two men in the bank as well as a getaway driver, so Mark roped in a third guy named Richard, who happened to be his mom's next-door neighbor. There was not a lot of quality control going on, on any level.

What they lacked in sophistication they made up for in melodrama.

"We became cinematic," Mark says. "When we walked in, we put on masks. Shouted for everyone to freeze. We took over the bank."

They were armed only with BB guns, Mark says. No life was ever in danger. But they also had loud voices and that sense of implacable evil conferred by masks. Mark's was an army-issue gas mask. He looked like an alien with a gun.

These robberies were planned, but only haphazardly. The team thought ahead about some things but not about others. They knew to leave behind any stack of bills, however big and whatever the denomination, if it could not be riffled deep through to the center. That's because those exploding dye packets are generally hidden in the middle of hollowed-out stacks. Also, they did enough research to know they should order people to freeze in place: Mark had heard that if you order a captive to move, you are technically taking a hostage, and it might trigger an additional charge of kidnapping.

But they never stopped to think that their lucky run of police indifference would probably end once they started acting like the Baby Face Nelson gang. They never considered disabling surveillance cameras. They never considered muddying their license tags. They never weighed what might have been a prudent strategy: expanding their ambit of operations to other cities, under different police jurisdictions. So in the space of six weeks they became one hellacious local crime spree for Colorado Springs, one that demanded task-force attention.

Their final heist was a return to Key Bank, the scene of Mark's first successful, gentlemanly, panhandler-type robbery. This one involved threats and gas masks and brandished weapons, and it went badly.

Richard had forgotten to riffle his stacks of bills. The robbers discovered this as they were driving away in Tom's Honda when the bag exploded with an ominous *whuump* and the car filled with red smoke and tear gas. Dye bombs are triggered by an inverse-proximity fuse: At a certain distance from the bank, they detonate.

Gasping for air, eyes tearing, Mark threw the stinking, smoking sack out of the car, with its big stack of phony fifties—along with real money, too, now made unspendable by telltale red splatter.

Things got worse. Evidently someone had written down the numbers on their license plate. They were apprehended not long

afterward. Because he had no criminal record, Mark was released on $10,000 bond, posted by his mother and stepfather.

The low point of Todd Thrane's life had happened at nineteen, as he sulked in jail on two drunk driving charges. The low
point of his son's life may be what happened to him after his arrest. He skipped out on bond and fled to Florida.

How could he do that to his mother?

"At that point," he says expressionlessly, with that curious de-
tachment, "I was consciously cutting all ties to anyone I'd ever
known and loved." It was a simple, practical decision, he says,
that seemed regrettable but necessary. Just do it. Don't look back.

We can only speculate whether Todd Thrane was going to
turn his life around, but we know that at a critical moment he
made a critical decision, that it was the right thing to do, and that
it ended his life. Mark Gill had a critical moment, too, of a different sort but of no less moment. It was also the right thing to
do, and in his case it very likely saved his life.

It came in Destin, Florida, two weeks after he disappeared
from Colorado. He was in the front seat of the truck he had
stolen opportunistically, because someone had left his keys in
the ignition. A police officer had stopped him and was approaching on foot. Mark knew the cop would run his name against a
national database of fugitives, and that he would be going away
for a long time. What Mark also knew, and the police officer did
not, was that he had a loaded 9-millimeter handgun within
reach.

"I considered shooting him in the head. I thought about it."

Mark Gill meets your eyes. It's still impressive and still disturbing, that emotional disconnect. He reminds you of Camus's

Meursault, the impenetrable protagonist of *The Stranger*, who acts but does not feel.

Mark has been talking for six hours over two days, and he's expressed regrets but no remorse. He's copped to having been stupid, but not to having been bad or immoral—not for stealing things, or for running out on his responsibilities, or for terrifying people. Not for having a child at sixteen and not really being around for her. He says he doesn't feel guilty about anything he's done, because it's all in the past, and it has nothing to do with what he is now and where he is going. Like Meursault, he deals with his history as if it were a series of things that simply happened, as though to a completely different person. Which, in a sense, is true.

"I thought about shooting the police officer in the head," he says blandly, "but then I did not."

IN HIS BOOKING PHOTO, Walton County Inmate No. 06003797, DOB 7/18/87, is wearing an orange prison-issue jumpsuit and an expression that tries for bravado but looks a lot more like fear. He's wide-eyed, up against a cinder-block wall. He seems like someone who has just been slapped awake. He's got a ratty little perimeter beard on a face too young to support a mustache. He is a person who has just decided not to murder a cop. He is about to head into what he will later call the luckiest seven and a half years of his life.

The charges on which he'd been arrested included grand theft auto and possession of concealed weapons; together, they'd get him a year in Florida. The bank robbery would add six more in Colorado, which he would spend in the Bent County Correctional Facility, a privately run prison with, as it happens, an extensive program that lets you order books from city libraries.

After he got out in the winter of 2012 he started cold-calling for jobs. When he showed up at Don's Garden Shop, he spoke with Paula Humphrey, Don's wife and co-owner. He said he was a parolee living in a halfway house, that he had robbed banks, that he was determined to radically change the course of his life, that he had learned a little about gardening in prison, and that he desperately needed a job. To Paula, he seemed extremely intense but also extremely focused, which impressed her. She told him they don't hire in the winter, but to come back on March 1 or after. On March 1, exactly, he was back. That impressed her, too.

What happened next impressed her even more. One of the crappiest jobs at Don's Garden Shop is splitting tree trunks and branches into firewood, using a primitive gas-driven single-piston splitter device. The work is repetitive, boring, and dangerous, which is not a good combination. Typically, newbies dawdle, trying to parcel out the work at a tolerable pace. Don and Paula set Mark down with pieces of tree and the machine, and came back an hour later to find a small forest of cordwood. It was like the work of a man possessed.

He was hired on at minimum wage to do entry-level work. He watched, learned, and two years later is being groomed to take over the management of the place. He has become indispensable.

"He makes $850 a week, more than anyone else here," Paula

says. She mulls this, and laughs. "Actually, it's close to what we make."

Paula, sixty-two, considers herself a good judge of character. Beyond just liking Mark Gill, she respects and trusts him. He handles money. There has never been a problem.

Paula acknowledges that Mark is not easy to get to know, that there is a remoteness about him, but she doesn't see it as lack of empathy. She sees it as caution, as though there is a place he won't let people get to, a vulnerable part of himself that's tucked away for safekeeping.

"I think," she says, "he's afraid of being hurt."

IT'S ANYONE'S GUESS what Mark Gill's life would be like had his father not died in the fire, or had Allen Thrane worked up the nerve to make his case for adoption. One thing leads to another, which leads to another. Some connections are made, some are missed, and all of it shapes a life.

Bill Thrane, who started it all by walking out on his family, had a sense of all that near the end of his life. In 2005, he telephoned his grandson out of the blue. They had not seen each other since Mark was a baby. He identified himself as Grandpa Thrane. He was sick, he said, and he wanted to reconnect. It was part of an extended farewell tour Bill Thrane was conducting, trying to mend old wounds. Bill and Mark talked cordially for a bit, and agreed to talk again and maybe schedule a visit. But nothing ever came of it, because in just a few weeks, Mark would get the idea to rob a bank. By the time he got out of prison, his grandfather was dead, buried in Lincoln next to Todd.

————

THE STRANGER, the man who seems to be part Zen master and part sociopath, is digging into his steak. He eats Continental style—knife in the right hand, fork in the left, tines down, all smooth and transitionless. He taught himself that in prison, too. The reinvention of Mark Gill has been meticulously engineered.

If Paula Humphrey is right and Mark is vulnerable, it's well disguised. He thinks highly of himself and isn't bashful about saying it.

He says, "My work ethic is ridiculous."

He says, "My mind is a sponge."

He says, "I am extremely personable."

He is. But there is the feel of a salesman to Mark Gill, the feel of a man perpetually trying to close a deal. He looks you straight in the eye all the time, and uses your name in conversation more than he needs to. He answers questions with disarming bluntness, yet you get the impression this is not so much a devotion to truth as a sense that bluntness impresses others.

You want to ask if this might all be part of that strategic reinvention. Is it possible this new life with its new focus is not so much a moral conversion as the next thing he's trying because the last thing didn't work out? Actually you do ask it, and he grins and does the bluntness thing.

"Someone once asked Edison how he felt about trying to make a lightbulb and failing a thousand times. Edison said it wasn't failure, exactly. He said, 'I learned something. I learned a thousand ways that don't work.'"

After prison, Mark got a second tattoo. This one was inked by a pro. It's bold Thai lettering running across his chest, a Buddhist motto he found in a book. Translated, it says, "Oneself is one's own mainstay." He interprets this to mean that in the end a person can rely only on himself. He sees it as a guiding principle, a hard reality summoning personal toughness and rigor.

He's right about what it means, but it wasn't meant to stand alone. It's actually said to be from the writings of the Buddha himself, the beginning of a thought that is completed a few lines later: "Evil is done by oneself; by oneself is one defiled. Evil is left undone by oneself; by oneself is one cleansed."

It's not entirely clear if Mark has gotten there yet in his reinvention, or if he plans to. Maybe.

You ask him what the chances are that he will ever be in prison again.

"Slim," he says, forking his steak into his mouth in that smooth, smooth move.

Slim to none?

"Slim," he says. "Just slim."

EPILOGUE:

It is late 2018. Mark doesn't respond to emails. Mark doesn't answer his phone. Paula Humphrey answers hers, at Don's Garden Shop.

No, she says, Mark doesn't work here anymore. He left over a year ago. He'd had some health problems, she said, and then his work began to deteriorate as he started to befriend some of her clients who happened to be in the pot-growing business.

Marijuana is now legal in Colorado. This opened new, legit

opportunities for entrepreneurs. Mark, Paula says, hungered to be part of that. It became his main focus, and when Mark focuses on something, it is with blinding intensity.

Mark still lives in the area, but Paula hasn't heard from him in a while. You should see what he's up to, she says, with some concern in her voice.

Mark finally answers his phone.

"It's pretty much what Paula says. I just ventured away and decided to do my own thing."

He seems to want the conversation to end there. But he is courtly, open and accommodating, still. It's his thing.

"Are you in the pot business?"

"Only to an extent, in a roundabout way. As a convicted felon, I can't do it directly. I build greenhouses. I consult on custom soils, show 'em how to start up their plots."

"Pot plots?"

"Mostly."

"Have you stayed out of trouble with the law?"

"I wish I could say yes. I wish I could tell you that. But I am in litigation now. I have a criminal matter pending. Nothing's been filed yet. We are hoping to avoid that. Under advice of counsel, I can't say more."

"Is it a violent crime?"

"No."

Might you wind up back in jail?

There's just a slight pause. A beat and a half. A momentary hiccup in his extraordinary composure.

"I might. Such is life."

5:45 A.M., Bartlett, Tennessee

In a cozy Colonial in a cozy cul-de-sac in this somnolent suburb of Memphis, all was dark but for the faint glow on the living room floor and its fainter flicker on the ceiling. The source of the light was the screen of a Nintendo game, where Mario the plumber was nimbly navigating his obstacle course, hopping and dancing through the Mushroom Kingdom on a quest to rescue Princess Toadstool from Mario's archnemesis, Bowser, the evil turtle monster.

Asleep on the floor were the home's three golden retrievers and their girl, Ryan Sledge, who was nine. At the controls of the game was Ryan's friend, Heather Hamilton, who was eleven. This was a sleepover for Heather, but her sleep ended early.

Heather lived a few houses down with her brother and her mom, who was a devout Mormon and who did not permit her children to play Nintendo. She felt it ungodly, partly because she thought it distasteful that the kids *wanted* it so badly, having tussled for it on the one occasion a borrowed game was allowed into the house. There was disagreeable violence on the screen as well—jellyfish and birds and all sorts of fauna got popped into oblivion. But mostly, as Heather would theorize many years later, her mom didn't like it because—though primitive by today's standards—it was visually more realistic than other contemporary video games, like Atari. Nintendo seemed too *lifelike,* which bothered her mother. Life should not be made trivial or silly.

So for Heather Hamilton, a Goody-Two-Shoes in all other ways, a straight-A student who liked to clean the house to surprise her mother, the Mushroom Kingdom was thrilling, forbidden territory.

She and Ryan had been playing Super Mario Bros. well into the night until they conked out, right there on the floor. Heather hadn't found the princess, but she had reached world eight, the final tier. She'd gotten hungrily close, so close that the desire to beat the game simmered through her mind and woke her just after five A.M.

In the wee hours of the morning, on the floor still, in the dark, Heather played four hours straight. A singularly obedient child, this was her first tentative act of sedition. She was being insubordinate, and in defiance of her religion, at least as interpreted by her mother. It was all feeling so good. Then suddenly it got immeasurably better. Triumphal music rang out, Mario cleared a final obstacle, and there he was beside the princess, who was free at last. The game congratulated Heather and told her there were no more worlds to conquer. Skilled Nintendo players got here occasionally, but Heather was a furtive novice, playing on borrowed time, and this was something.

There had been no one to witness her feat. She was like a golfer who gets a hole in one while playing alone.

What happened next might seem peculiar unless you understood this particular little girl. Heather was unusually intense, more solemn and serious than most eleven-year-olds. As an adult, she would read about the impostor syndrome, which afflicts successful people who secretly doubt their worth and are always looking to prove to themselves that they deserve their success— and the adult Heather would think: *That was me, an impostor in training, at eleven.*

And so in this quiet house, bursting with self-validation made all the richer by defying rules she considered unjust, Heather got up from the floor and commandeered a scrap of paper from Ryan's backpack. On it, she wrote:

December 28, 1986
Today I saved the princess!

And then in her schoolgirl script, she signed her name.

Heather walked home and put the paper in a shoebox in her closet, where she kept balls of scavenged aluminum foil and other priceless oddball preteen treasures. She had chosen the words for this homemade certificate shrewdly; they were sufficiently ambiguous that they would not betray her misdeed even if her mom found it. The scrap of paper would remain in that box for years. Even later in her teens she would get it out sometimes and study it.

IT'S TEMPTING FOR A BIOGRAPHER to draw too much significance from a single moment in someone's life—to find defining meaning in something that may only be trivial.

Still, consider what happened to the little girl who chose insubordination, and won, on December 28, 1986:

She dutifully went to Brigham Young University, where she took up drugs, discovered sex, and in the end, decided that the religion to which she had been born was stifling and hypocritical, and jettisoned it. This resulted in a meeting with her mother in a Chili's restaurant, where, over salsa and tears, Heather was informed that, one, her mom knew she was living in sin with a boyfriend and strongly disapproved; and two, that until she accepted the Mormon Jesus, their relationship was severed. And it was. The two women grew distant.

Heather got a job in Los Angeles with a start-up tech firm, doing work she disliked, surrounded by some people for whom she had contempt. What she really wanted to do was write—she liked making observations about life, the more jaundiced the better—so she started a blog in February 2001. It was an extremely impolite blog. Seditious, even. For reasons too boring to explain, she called it dooce.com.

Yes, you may have heard of it. We'll get to that in a minute.

When September 11 came, Heather Hamilton seethed for two days and then took to her computer. She began typing and did not stop for some time.

She wrote about Mormonism and how she believed it strangled free thought. Then she suggested that if a prophet in the Mormon church had ordered his minions to hijack planes and fly them into buildings, they would have done it just as readily and just as enthusiastically, and just as convinced of the rightness of it, as the Al Qaeda murderers had. During that summer her blog was getting about sixty visitors a day. She figured what she wrote would go out into the ether like smoke and quickly dissipate into nothing.

It didn't. Her brother found it—he later claimed that divine inspiration had led him to a computer and to Google, and to type in his sister's name and gasp. Heather having abandoned Mormonism was bad enough, but to have blasphemed so publicly and poisonously was a betrayal of, well, God. What little family comity was left was ruptured completely.

Defiantly Heather kept up the blog and the vitriol.

Back then, in the early days, Heather sometimes trafficked in anonymous character assassination, making withering, caustic observations about her coworkers. She never called out anyone or the company by name, and told only trusted friends at work about it. So she felt safe in writing this about her boss:

> When she talks with her hands she looks like she's molesting the air around her, sticking her fingers in holes and around forbidden curves. Often the air around her is the air around me, and my air doesn't appreciate it. . . . Her right index finger is fondling my monitor. Her left hand is pinching an invisible nipple in the air behind my head.

She wrote:

> I hate that the Tech Producer doesn't know how to use e-mail. He's the goddamn TECH Producer, for crying out loud. I hate that one of the 10 vice-presidents in this 30-person company wasn't born with an "indoor" voice but with a shrill, monotone,

speaking-over-a-passing-F-16 outdoor voice. And he loves to hear himself speak, even if just to himself.

She was profane, astringent, and wildly politically incorrect. One day her blog was a list of ten items titled *Reasons the Asian Database Administrator is so Fucking Annoying.* (Item 8: *Because, as far as you can tell, he hasn't brushed his teeth since he was hired eight months ago.*)

And so forth. Brutal stuff, some of it.

Naively, Heather Hamilton felt insulated from discovery. Back then, no one really understood the Internet, with its power to exponentiate the spread of information and its bottomless potential for cruelty, conferred by anonymity.

Someone ratted her out. She suspects a disgruntled former boyfriend, but doesn't know for sure.

One day in February 2002, she was at work when she heard boisterous laughter from a nearby office. Then it spread, office to office. The informant had used a generic Hotmail address to send her blog to each of the many vice-presidents of the company.

At first the reaction seemed contained. People found it funny. But when she arrived at work a few days later, there were people surrounding her desk. Cardboard boxes for her stuff. The gig, as they say, was up. She was being fired for insubordination. It was February 26. She went home and blogged about it.

I lost my job today. My direct boss and the human resources representative pulled me into one of three relatively tiny conference rooms and informed me that The Company no longer had any use for me. Essentially, they explained, they didn't like what I had expressed on my website. I got fired because of dooce.com.

She closed down dooce.com. She cried for days. She eloped with her boyfriend and became Heather Armstrong. She thought her online life was destroyed. That is because she did not yet understand the Internet.

Heather Armstrong had just become an Internet curiosity: So far as anyone could tell, she was the first person to be fired for blogging. The Web lit up. The blogosphere exploded. Her dismissal became a lightning rod for free-speech advocates. She reopened dooce.com. Traffic to her site doubled, then tripled, then quadrupled, then entered a tier of multiplication for which no familiar mathematical terms exist.

She would even enter the common lexicon—the expression *to be dooced* came to mean—well, exactly what happened to her. On December 10, 2009, the word was an answer on *Jeopardy!* ("Rhymes with 'juiced,' it means to lose one's job because of one's blog. Coined by blogger Heather Armstrong.")

Over the next few years, Armstrong turned her blog inward, writing almost exclusively about her life. She'd had a baby, she suffered postpartum depression. She blogged it all honestly, hiding no anguish, not sparing herself. Much of what she wrote was focused on trivial things—her new Maytag washer broke; her dogs were hyperactive—but through it all, she kept her acid voice and didn't forswear the profanity. Dooce.com proved a bracingly arch alternative to the pablum-esque family-oriented blogs. Not much was sacred. ("That's the miracle of babies," she wrote, "their ability to lay bare the tender, beating hearts of raging assholes.")

She gained more than a million followers on Twitter.

She's telegenic—a tall, striking blonde with a prominent chin, with which she often leads fearlessly. She got on *Oprah*. In 2011, when *The New York Times Magazine* profiled her, it called her the "Queen of the Mommy Bloggers." By this time, her website was getting 20,000 unique visitors a day or more, and because of the explosion of online advertising, her income soared. She hired employees. Her husband quit his job to manage the site. The *Times* and *The Wall Street Journal* estimated she was pulling in $30,000 to $50,000 a month, a range she today says was inflated, but not by much. (She didn't correct them at the time. The Web rewards perceived success with more success.)

Armstrong lives in Salt Lake City now. Divorced three years, she is a single parent to two girls, Marlo Iris, ten, and Leta Elise, fifteen.

Leta has been a particularly interesting child. As soon as Armstrong started writing about her as a toddler—gimlet-eyed appraisals, as usual—readers began tactfully offering advice. Leta, who shunned physical contact and seemed unusually withdrawn, was probably autistic, people suggested.

She was tested. She wasn't. She was just a little . . . difficult. Over the years, her relationship with her mother was at times strained—Heather was a perfectionist, authoritarian type, and Leta was a perfectionist, question-authority type, and these characteristics collided in the predictable way, particularly in the preteen years, with predictably histrionic encounters.

It was during that period, in late 2013, that Leta got a Nintendo 2DS for Christmas. (On Christmas morning, she'd found it stashed in the oven after following a maddening trail of clues.)

The handheld device had come loaded from the factory with a starter game or two.

On the Friday after Christmas, Leta, then nine, was hunched over her new toy, squinting through her cutely big eyeglasses, dying. Losing lives like crazy. Getting frustrated. Her mother walked by and instantly recognized the music she was hearing. It was Super Mario Bros. It had more sophisticated graphic interfaces, but it was the same damn game. Same minefield to navigate. Same goal.

This happened to be Friday, December 28, 2013, twenty-seven years to the day after eleven-year-old Heather Hamilton first rescued the princess.

Heather sat down next to her daughter and held out her hand. Laughingly, Leta coughed up the console. This was going to be ugly. She had no doubt Mom would be a dingus at video games.

Leta sat back smugly. Then her eyes widened.

"It was amazing," Armstrong says today. "It came back immediately. It's like hearing a song you haven't heard for years, but you can still finish the lines. I still had the muscle memory."

Mario raced through the obstacle course, nimbly hopping and dancing through the Mushroom Kingdom, blithely assassinating birds and fish, picking up bonuses, gaining extra lives. Level 3, 4, 5 . . .

"MOM, YOU'RE SO GOOD AT THIS."

Mom had never seemed good at anything kid-like. Mom was good at being a mom by telling her daughters what to do.

For the next few hours, mother and daughter, antagonists no more, sat side by side and played a video game together, really together, for the first time. They never got to the princess that day—Leta eventually got bored and started deliberately running Mario off ledges to his death. But the dozens of years between them, and the power mismatch, disappeared, just like that.

"Leta and I are best friends now," Armstrong says.

And Armstrong and *her* mother?

A pause. "Great. Actually, things could not be better between us."

How did that happen?

It happened, she said, when each woman—the rabidly devout Mormon and the rabidly devout atheist—inched toward a middle ground. Armstrong's mother reconsidered how painful it would be not to know her grandchildren. And that happened to coincide with a problem she could solve: Armstrong and her then husband were both out of work and needed a basement to crash in. It turns out there was one waiting for them in Utah. Hearts were softening in both directions.

Heather's mother had risen from saleslady to become a top executive in Avon Products. "We both realized," Armstrong says today, "that in some ways I am her. Ambition, intuition, commitment. She made me that way."

Armstrong shut down dooce.com in 2015 for a while, for two reasons. She felt she was becoming uncomfortably beholden to her advertisers, but more important, she felt Leta—this was a mommy blog, and kids are fodder to be relentlessly chronicled—was becoming resentful about her loss of privacy. When the blog stopped, that took a lot of pressure off.

As of late 2017, dooce.com was off and running again, but with some of the angry edge taken off. Heather Armstrong wasn't softening, exactly, but she was growing up. She wrote a memoir—*The Valedictorian of Being Dead*—about going through a life-threatening controversial treatment for depression. She moved in with a boyfriend who had two live-at-home kids of his own, so, to her amusement and bemusement, the outlaw, piss-and-vinegar, single-warrior single parent got transformed into a doughty *Brady Bunch* mom, gamely trying to make the whole wacky blended-family thing work, dadgum it.

Things seem to be working out just fine.

And that defiant scrap of paper from December 28, 1986?

"My mother threw the whole box out one day, cleaning up. It's in a landfill somewhere." The big issue, buried at last.

6:35 A.M., San Diego, California

The exit sign said MERCY ROAD, but on this morning, both words were a lie. There was no road, and there would be no mercy.

Newlyweds Cynthia Knott and Bill Weick got off the freeway at the exit, pulled their Volkswagen Beetle up to the ROAD CLOSED sign, and stopped. They didn't know what lay beyond it.

Beyond it, the off-ramp curved down onto old Highway 395, which the freeway had replaced. Now it was just an underused bike trail leading to a deserted highway overpass overlooking a steep canyon with a dry creek bed. The area was so desolate and forbidding that it was a go-to spot for the furtive: undocumented migrants sharing meals, hookers giving blow jobs, junkies getting off, and sometimes, police officers stealing a forbidden snooze or a smoke or a few minutes of solitude to write their reports. On this nearly moonless morning, the place was empty and dark and pillowed in fog.

Cynthia and Bill had been crisscrossing the freeway for any clue to the whereabouts of Cynthia's twenty-year-old kid sister, Cara. This was their second stop at Mercy Road that night; the first time they had obeyed the sign. They were obedient by nature, but they were at the end of their rope. Should they go in?

Cara Knott had phoned her parents at 8:30, saying she was leaving her boyfriend's house and driving to theirs, a forty-minute shot down Interstate 15 from Escondido to El Cajon. Nearly two hours later, with no Cara at home and no further word from her—she was always punctual and always kept her family alerted to delays—the large Knott family had mobilized a search party. Multiple cars began retracing Cara's route, exploring off-ramps. Cara's mother, Joyce Knott, and Cheryl, the third sister, stayed home, coordinating phone calls, trying hospitals and police stations, trying Cara's friends. Trying anyone they could think of.

It had gone on for hours. The Knotts had traversed every inch of highway. The whole night had passed, and dawn was just breaking. And now, in desperation, Bill Weick eased his car around the sign. Alert for axle-breaking ruts, he drove almost a quarter of a mile past piles of trash into the eerie dark and silence, and then they saw it: Cara's white Volkswagen Beetle, parked at an odd angle in a dead end, inexplicably far from the highway.

For a split second, elation. Then fear. Then hope—a sliver of it, anyway. After a night of nothing, here was *something*.

Cynthia ran to the car. The engine was off, the keys in the ignition. No Cara. (*If she got out to walk, why would she leave her keys?*) The driver's side window was half open. (*She would never crack the window in a place like this, not for anyone.*) On the passenger seat, a receipt for gas from a station some ten miles away. (*Did someone see her in the station and follow her?*) In the back seat, Cara's pocketbook, with money and credit cards. (*Not good at all.*) No Cara. Husband and wife bellowed her name into the fog. No Cara.

Cynthia and Bill got back in their car and pulled away to find a pay phone. Finally, at least, the police would *have* to listen.

WE ARRIVE AT CERTAIN assumptions about the things in life we need not fear and those that we must. It's a necessary accommodation to negotiate this world without falling prisoner to all its attendant terrors. For Southern Californians, the events of that miserable night in 1986 and the discoveries that followed would rupture that fundamental compact about the people and institutions we can intuitively trust. And it would set an anguished father on a lifelong crusade on behalf of crime victims—designed perhaps as much to save his sanity as to right a wrong.

The father was Sam Knott, a tall, florid-faced, raspy-voiced man who counseled people on their investments. It was he who had taken the phone call from Cara at 8:30 that Saturday night as his family sat around the Christmas tree, did a jigsaw puzzle, and watched a VHS tape of Disney's *Sleeping Beauty*. (This family enjoyed cornball.) And it was Sam who sat bolt upright when Cara was more than an hour and a half late and announced that he knew something was wrong. Sam was intuitive. In court, he would describe that moment in mystical terms: "It was a call to my soul."

At one point on the nightlong search, Sam Knott stopped two police officers to tell them of his missing daughter. The officers informed him that a person had to be missing twenty-four hours before an APB could be issued. It was an inviolable policy, they said. Later in the night, briefly back home and making phone calls, Sam was told much the same thing but in a more callous way. One dispatcher urged him not to worry because "girls will be girls." A California Highway Patrol dispatcher told him she could retire if she had a dollar for every briefly missing young person who turns up fine—if it is a woman, presumably blushing and debauched. Then the dispatcher blandly suggested that Sam "check the jails."

Sam did not check the jails. Cara, the youngest Knott daughter, was almost a caricature of a nice girl—congenial, sweet-natured, law-abiding almost to a fault. At the zoo, privately deputizing herself, she would stop strangers from feeding the animals. In no-smoking areas, she'd ask smokers to desist. If she saw a guy littering, she'd pick the trash up, hand it back to him, and politely point out the closest trash can. How many people have the personality to pull this off without being dismissed as a scold? Cara did.

A top student at San Diego State, she was an ardent environmentalist and an athlete who ran the high hurdles and won. She was also a chocolate-eyed beauty with blond Farrah Fawcett hair and an authentic full-face smile—a head-turner who seemed naively oblivious to her own allure. Once, on a trip to Europe, a man who found himself unexpectedly in her presence accidentally walked into a swimming pool. Cara had no idea what had just happened or why.

Cara Knott's high school photo—the one that would be given out to the press by a grieving family on December 28, 1986—was so lovely and heartbreakingly wholesome that it would push her story onto front pages even in some newspapers outside of California.

Bill Weick and Cynthia Knott finally reached a pay phone, and the San Diego police finally had an inarguable reason to mobilize.

JIM SPEARS WAS THE FIRST patrol officer to drive to the scene, speeding down I-15 to Mercy Road. After being briefed by Cynthia and Bill, Spears approached Cara's car. He put on gloves, reached inside, and half turned the key. The gas gauge crept all the way to full. It was an automatic transmission, in park. Still outside, Spears hit the ignition. The engine started up and idled just fine for a few seconds until he shut it off.

Spears did not tell the family why he'd done that, in case they hadn't figured it out, because the results were not encouraging. Cara's 1968 VW was old, but the engine and battery were evidently fine. It was not car trouble that brought her here. An unalarming explanation for her absence was getting more unlikely, but Spears felt it was still possible, right until the moment he looked down at the driver's side door and saw a small drop of what appeared to be blood.

He didn't tell the family about this, either. He just asked them to stay away from the car. Thirty years later, Spears would remember how the sight of blood put him into "instant crime-scene mode." A second officer, Mary Cornicelli, had arrived, and right on her tail, Sam Knott. Sam just followed her squad car in, wanting to ask for help, never expecting to find Cynthia there or Cara's VW.

Jim Spears radioed his acting sergeant, Bill Maheu. Spears

knew he had to be careful in what he said, both because the family was within earshot and because local journalists monitored police radio transmissions and understood cop talk—the last thing Spears needed were reporters crawling around the scene. What he wanted to tell Maheu was that he had "possible 187," which meant a homicide. But all he actually said was that he was requesting backup. Maheu took in the urgency of his patrolman's voice and understood. He decided to drive to the scene himself.

After calling the police, Cynthia had gotten back on the pay phone, alerting the family. So by the time Maheu pulled into the Mercy Road exit, another car had arrived, and then a third. Cara's sister Cheryl drove in from the south with her grandfather. Then, from the north, Cara's boyfriend, Wayne Bautista. It had likely been years since that many people were together at one time, for one purpose, at Mercy Road.

Like all the cops in the area, Maheu knew the reputation of this phantom exit. He knew its remoteness led to the occasional transactional liaison, but he dismissed this idea almost immediately when he saw these people. His experience told him that when there is something sordid or irresponsible or mentally unstable in the background of a missing person, if this was a likely runaway, you can usually read it in the faces of friends and family. One or two of them would be less distraught than the others. They would *know*. But out on Mercy Road, Maheu was looking at a large, engaged, attractive family uniformly scared out of its wits.

The sergeant drove back to the station so he'd have a secure line to call for homicide detectives and a K-9 officer. Then he returned to the scene. This time he decided to approach it from the north. He got off at the next exit, Poway Road, parked, and walked back toward Mercy Road along the old highway bridge. That gave him a good view of the whole canyon. He glanced left and right, saw nothing out of the ordinary, and then looked down toward the creek bed, sixty-five feet below, which is when he drew a sharp breath.

Maheu was young for a sergeant—only twenty-seven—but he was long on experience, some of it harrowing. Thirty years later, he would remember finding Cara Knott's body as one of just a handful of on-the-job memories that he could not erase. It's not the violence that sticks with him, exactly—for police officers, violence can become both banal and routine. Maheu tends to remember moments that take him inside himself.

Just two years before, he had been at the scene of the San Ysidro McDonald's massacre, one of the worst mass killings in American history. A mentally ill man with assault weapons had opened fire in a crowded McDonald's, methodically murdering twenty-one people as they cowered, aiming deliberately to pick off children as their mothers tried to shield them. One of the dead was eight months old. By the time Maheu arrived with a SWAT team, the killer had already been taken down. The evidence of James Huberty's savagery was all over, but the thing that stays with Maheu most vividly was meeting the eyes of a survivor, a teenager in a McDonald's uniform, as she was stumbling out of the restaurant. She was not physically injured, but her face told him that she would never be the same person she was when she arrived at work that day. What he remembers feeling was profound futility. There are things no cop can fix.

On Mercy Road, Maheu took Spears aside and quietly told him that he'd seen a woman's body under the bridge. The two men headed down to the creek bed by foot, accompanied by a police dog and his handler, who had just arrived. As they walked, the men put on surgical gloves. They disappeared from the view of the Knotts.

Cara was on her back, wearing white half boots, purple sweat pants, and a white sweatshirt, lying in a bed of pebbles and scrub brush and trash. Her left arm was across her chest. She could have been asleep, except for the blood that dappled her shirt. Spears felt for her carotid artery, but he knew it was futile even before he found no pulse. Her neck was as cold as the chill in the air, and stiff with rigor mortis.

This was the indelible moment for Maheu. A graceful young woman with impeccably manicured nails, fully engaged in life, beloved by a big family that was about to have the worst day of their lives become immeasurably worse . . . dumped like a sack of garbage.

Had the two men inspected further, they would have seen the cause of death, but that wasn't their job. At this point, Maheu and Spears had two responsibilities. The first was hard: They'd need to preserve a sprawling crime scene down here in the canyon and up on the bridge until the homicide detectives arrived. Their second job was harder.

"I'll do it," said Spears. He'd grown up in Brooklyn and feels it toughened him. He had a way of compartmentalizing things, of doing his job without *feeling* his job, and he thought he could handle this.

So it was Spears who walked ahead, alone, to Sam Knott. Before he could say anything, Sam met his eyes and said, "You found my daughter." Sam was a shrewd and observant man, a good poker player. From the moment he'd seen Maheu and Spears slipping on gloves, Sam knew.

It turns out Spears wasn't entirely right about compartmentalizing. He had trouble finding his voice, then trouble keeping it level and steady. His eyes welled. Finally: "Your daughter. She's dead."

The shock of such a disclosure often leaves family members uncomprehending, unwilling to accept it emotionally, and for some small time they'll speak of the dead in the present tense. But Sam Knott had been given some minutes to prepare for this. He said to Spears: "If you had only known her. My daughter was an angel."

Then he walked to his family and told them, and they sagged into one another's embraces.

LATER IN THE DAY, the coroner would find broken bones and ruptured organs and conclude Cara Knott had been thrown from the highway bridge, a six-story fall that accounted for much of the blood and most of the injuries; one police officer told the Los Angeles Times "she was like a frozen Milky Way that's been slammed against a table." But it wasn't the fall that had killed Cara. Over the orbit of her right eye she had a deep, shattering bruise. That also had not been fatal, but it had at least initially incapacitated her, which was what allowed her murderer to slip some sort of noose around her neck and strangle her to death. The ligature had necklaced her with welts and bruises, three separate strands of them, meaning at some point she'd likely writhed and struggled for her life. Or possibly the murderer had twice readjusted this grip, for better bite. In either event, the coroner concluded, death had come from asphyxiation.

IT'S ODD WHAT PROFESSIONALS take away from a scene of violent death. They tend to focus on small things. Homicide detective Bill Nulton, called to Mercy Road on his day off, had seen hundreds of bodies. The thing he remembers is that the fall had exposed Cara's midriff, a little hint of belly, which made her seem even more violated and vulnerable. He had to keep the crime scene intact, so he couldn't pull the shirt down. Nulton also saw that Cara wasn't wearing a bra, and it troubled him that he was going to have to ask the family about that. If going braless had not been Cara's custom, possibly there had been some sort of sex crime? And if so—where was the bra?

But the family confirmed she sometimes went without a bra, and the coroner determined she hadn't been sexually assaulted, a fact that became part of the puzzle.

And it was a puzzle. For some reason, a good-natured, intelligent, demure, cautious young woman had threaded her car around a barrier and driven a quarter of a mile into a scary place, where she was bludgeoned, then strangled to death for no apparent reason. This wasn't robbery. This wasn't a carjacking. There was no rape. None of it made any sense.

If you have a suspicion about how Cara Knott came to arrive

at that place and why she was murdered, it is likely because you are reading this in the twenty-first century, not in 1986. You are comparatively jaded. In 1986, certain things were unthinkable.

In the first couple of days after the murder, not a single investigator saw where this was heading. The cops had one working theory, which proved to be right: That Cara would have driven to that remote spot only with or at the direction of someone she thought she could trust. So the initial suspicion fell on Wayne Bautista, Cara's boyfriend. But that proved to be wrong.

On the third day, there was a break in the case, and within a couple of weeks the identity of the prime suspect leaked out among members of the San Diego police. Bill Maheu remembers hearing about it from his fellow officer, Mary Cornicelli. And he remembers thinking: *Of course.*

WHEN POLICE FIND themselves with little to go on, they often seek help from the public, which means cooperating with the media, particularly TV stations. Put it all out there—maybe someone saw something. There may never have been a case in which this strategy worked better.

Police assisted the local ABC affiliate to put together a quick CrimeStoppers segment, using actors to show Cara stopping at a Chevron gas station off the interstate, near Bear Valley. The local NBC affiliate asked the California Highway Patrol to send an officer for a ride-around feature on vehicular safety—advising motorists on what to do, and what not to do, if they are alone at the wheel and encounter trouble. CHiPs offered up Craig Peyer, as they did so often for liaisons with the public. The patrolman presented well, if a bit unsmilingly. With his close-cropped hair and lugubrious manner, he bore a superficial resemblance to Sergeant Joe Friday. Just the facts, ma'am.

Peyer, thirty-six, was straitlaced, by the book, businesslike—the guy who wrote up the most summonses, who kept his cruiser spotless, his shirt crisp, his pants creased, his shoes gleaming. As he rode with young TV reporter Rory Devine on Monday night, he stayed on message, as he usually did, his solemn voice urging caution.

The video is still out there: Peyer, at the wheel at night, talks while keeping his eyes riveted on the road. He advises people who have car trouble to stay in their vehicles, even overnight if need be, even if a stranger stops and offers help. What he says next is so terse and blunt, it's clearly intended to stay with you:

"Don't get into anyone else's car, because you're at their mercy. Being a female you could get raped. Robbed, if you are a male. Um, all the way to where you could be killed."

Thirty years later, Rory Devine, the TV reporter, would remember two unusual things about this otherwise routine assignment. She wanted to film some of the interview at Mercy Road, but Peyer nixed that. Never said why.

The second thing she remembers is Peyer stopping his car to help out a guy who ran out of gas. That put a question in her mind, one that hadn't occurred to her before:

"I did say to him, 'What if it's a *cop* who stops you?' and he said, 'Well, that's kind of a different story.'"

And . . .

"And I just let it go."

———

ON DAY THREE, phone calls started coming in. Some callers had seen CrimeStoppers. Some had seen Rory Devine's ride-along with Peyer. All had heard or read about Mercy Road as the scene of the crime. And a large number of the calls were from or on behalf of women—women who'd had strange, disturbing encounters with an officer Craig Peyer, on Mercy Road.

The women were all young with long hair and trim figures, and all had been alone at the wheel. Most were blondes. Several drove VW Beetles. They told roughly the identical story: Using his lights and blaring PA system, Peyer would pull them over on Interstate 15 for some trivial infraction that many cops might ignore—a busted taillight, misaligned headlights, failing to signal a lane change. ("Red Honda, please pull over on the right.") The right was invariably Mercy Road. Then in many cases he'd direct them around the barrier, after which things would get . . . unnerving.

Sometimes he'd get in their cars or invite them into his. He'd engage them in small talk, sometimes for an excruciatingly long time. Sometimes it was about their driving or the daunting price of Southern California real estate. Sometimes he'd lecture them on how dangerous it is to be a woman traveling alone. Sometimes he'd compliment their appearance. ("You have beautiful eyes.") Sometimes he'd inquire whether they had boyfriends. He creeped out a twenty-two-year-old department store security guard by asking if she'd ever watched females in the dressing rooms, changing clothes.

Altogether, about two dozen women had contacted the San Diego police to complain about a thoroughly skeevy encounter with patrolman Craig Peyer. Though none had been physically assaulted, and though they tended to agree the officer had been outwardly polite, many had been rattled by what they thought bordered on predatory behavior. He *had* to know he was making them uncomfortable. Several drove off with their hands trembling. Several said that he'd been so flirtatious they expected him to call them and ask them out.

It was during these first two weeks that word leaked out to the rank-and-file San Diego police that detectives were looking at a cop as the possible killer. Which is when acting sergeant Bill Maheu had his disturbing revelation.

It *was* someone Cara thought she could trust.

CRAIG PEYER WAS a thirteen-year CHiPs veteran with an unblemished record. Family man, nice suburban home, three kids in a blended marriage. Under questioning, he denied ever having stopped or seen Cara Knott that night. He produced his logbook, which showed that he'd given out a ticket at another part of the county at 9:20, roughly the time Cara was killed.

In the initial stages, police treated the investigation of Craig Peyer as a lead on which to show due diligence and then move on. Sure, this particular Sergeant Friday might turn out to be a creep who got his jollies by hitting on hot young blondes in situations with a power imbalance, but nothing about his past suggested criminality, certainly not a capacity for murder.

Still, they were obliged to check him out. What they found sickened them.

Late on the night of the murder, Peyer had walked into the stationhouse with bloody welts and abrasions on his face and right arm, and a story of how he had gotten them. He even filed a report: At the police station gas pumps, he said, he had stumbled on spilled gasoline and hit his head on a chain link fence. Investigators went to the gas pumps and took measurements. To have hit the chain link with his face, they concluded, he would have to have taken a running start and launched himself at it, like a high jumper.

Tire marks at the scene of the murder suggested the presence of a second vehicle, one that left in a hurry, burning rubber. It was a big, squat car: The distance between the tire tracks was fifty-three inches. Police cruisers are big, squat cars. The distance between Peyer's tires was fifty-three inches.

Those things were suspicious but circumstantial, as were the blood tests. The droplet of blood Jim Spears had seen on Cara Knott's car door was too small to yield any information, but investigators had found a larger drop on Cara Knott's white boot. Cara's blood was type O. The drop on the boot was type A, as was Peyer's. This was before reliable DNA testing, but taken together with the few genetic markers found in the blood, experts determined the drop was rare enough that it could belong to only 1 in 161 people in the San Diego area. This abbreviated field included Craig Peyer, but also some 12,000 other people.

Detectives found no microscopic traces of Peyer in Cara's car, or of Cara in Peyer's car, or of blood inside either car. But they did learn that Peyer had meticulously cleaned out and hosed down his cruiser more than once in the days after the murder.

In Peyer's trunk, detectives found a four-foot length of rope that was not standard-issue police equipment. It was narrow and braided, and its topology neatly matched the welts on Cara Knott's neck. But a forensic search of the rope showed no microscopic shreds of skin or blood on it. Had he scrubbed it clean? Had the rope been longer before the murder, with the lethal part now discarded? Or was this all just a red herring?

Investigators went back to Peyer's logbook to check out his principal alibi. He had written thirteen tickets that night, which was a ton for most patrolmen, but pretty standard for Peyer, known among his peers as a "hot pencil." The logbook was meticulous, typical of Peyer. It was a three-ring binder into which he had entered the date and time of every traffic stop he'd made.

It showed that he gave a speeding ticket to a woman at 7:45 and another to a man shortly after eight P.M. Then there was an uncharacteristically long gap before the next ticket was issued. It was for a broken taillight. That's the one that showed 9:20, around the time of the murder. But there was something odd about this entry. The time looked altered.

Detectives found the recipient, a high school student named Jean-Pierre Gulli. The teenager told them the stop had been at ten P.M. The officer, he said, seemed to be in a big hurry, and had initially put the time as 10:30 on his ticket. But then, Gulli said, the officer scratched that out and made it 9:20. Investigators found the ticket itself. It had been altered, too.

Finally came the most intriguing clue of all. It was the size of an eyelash.

On Cara Knott's clothing, detectives had found a single tiny gold-colored fiber. It matched nothing Cara was wearing. It was so unusual looking—ostentatious gold, as though not from a garment but from some sort of ornamental display—that it stuck in the mind of the forensic fiber expert, John Simms. So when Simms was given the uniform that Peyer had worn on the night of the murder, he saw something he might have otherwise overlooked. The uniform was bland khaki, but it had a CHiPs insignia on a shoulder, and the insignia had gold braiding.

Simms extracted a fiber and put both samples under a polarized light microscope; they were at least highly similar. Both were pigmented rayon, and when the pigments were further studied under a spectrophotometer, they were chemically identical. It was a perfect match of what turned out to be a rare type of thread. Peyer kept his uniforms in spotless condition, so his lasted longer than most other officers'. Its patch was more than five years old. Almost all CHiPs patrolmen had newer uniforms, with patches that had been made using a different dyeing process, showing a different spectrophotometric profile.

This nailed it for them. Craig Peyer had betrayed his badge, and it then betrayed him.

On January 15, 1987, he was charged with first-degree murder.

NEWS OF THE KILLING had disturbed San Diego, but news of Peyer's arrest traumatized it. That basic social contract—you obey police and in return they protect you—had been shredded. Ordinary highway stops became tense encounters. Young women began refusing to pull over in areas that were not brightly illuminated. At least one arrest was made for this disobedience, but a court over-turned it. Quickly the state passed a law allowing motorists stopped by police to pull ahead as far as they wanted, into a place they felt safe. Law enforcement organizations were outraged; gov-ernment seemed to be saying the public was justified in fearing police.

Bringing the case against Peyer was Joseph Van Orshoven, a well-regarded prosecutor with a well-known drinking problem. He was in his late fifties, craggy-faced, silver-haired, sober of mien. This 1987 trial, his last big one, was a disaster.

Juries like things neatly sealed. The absence of a smoking gun—say, an eyewitness to the crime or a fingerprint match—is always a challenge for a district attorney.

Although a parade of young blond female witnesses extrava-gantly established Peyer's disturbing behavior, not one woman said he was impolite or touched her inappropriately. The blood and fiber evidence was highly suggestive, but not conclusive.

No one could clearly place Peyer at the scene of the crime at the time of the crime. The defense took advantage of some of Van Orshoven's sloppiness to turn small discrepancies in evi-dence into what seemed like significant holes in the case. Some prosecution witnesses had not been properly prepared: Canny cross-examination of the coroner made it seem as though the time of death could not even be approximated, undercutting the sig-nificance of Peyer's logbook adjustments. After seven days, the jury declared itself deadlocked, split seven to five for conviction. Craig Peyer went free, pending a new trial. It came the following year. This time things would be different.

A new prosecutor was chosen—Paul Pfingst, a recent arrival

in San Diego. At thirty-five, he had been an assistant district attorney from New York, a hotshot who had already won more than twenty murder convictions. Pale, fair-haired, and sharp-featured, he looked like a cross between Art Garfunkel and William Hurt.

Pfingst was determined to learn from Van Orshoven's mistakes, among them having marginalized the Knott family. No one was more emotionally involved in this case than the Knotts, particularly its patriarch, and Pfingst realized they could be a resource. In the days after the mistrial, Sam Knott, on his own, had assembled in his home seven of the jurors and debriefed them about what had gone wrong. Pfingst listened to Knott and learned. He also saw some things Van Orshoven had missed, particularly regarding Peyer's movements on the night of the murder.

Just as Nazis' meticulous record-keeping created evidentiary problems for them when they faced tribunals of justice, Peyer's hot pencil had given prosecutors a gift. By stopping so many cars that night and recording where and when he had done so, Peyer had allowed Pfingst to create a convincing timeline of the patrol route he had taken. And because Cara had gotten gas not long before her murder and the receipt was time-stamped, Pfingst could match times and places and probable rates of speed to place the officer and the victim at roughly the identical place on Interstate 15 at roughly the identical moment. As Cara was getting back onto the highway, heading south after gassing up at Bear Valley, Peyer was following his circular route, making a U-turn on the interstate, getting back on, going south . . . at Bear Valley. Pfingst blew up the timeline into a huge, convincing exhibit.

According to testimony, just days before her murder Cara Knott had taken a course in self-defense. The instructor advised women not to be docile. If things become threatening, Cara had been told, "explode" toward the eyes and throat. Use your nails. Claw and gouge. Craig Peyer's injuries, the prosecution contended, precisely reflected that lesson perhaps too well learned.

After giving his testimony, Bill Maheu remembers walking out of the courtroom, seeing a bench filled with attractive, long-haired blondes, and smiling to himself. The parade of lovelies was about to begin again. But among them he noticed one young man. The man also had long blond hair. He'd been stopped by Peyer at Mercy Road, too. And of all the blondes, only the man testified he had not been detained for a long time. When Peyer walked up to the window from behind, the man said, the patrolman looked at him and quickly sent him on his way.

And finally, there was a surprise witness. Not long before trial, Pfingst heard from a young woman named Traci Koenig who claimed she'd been on I-15 the night of the murder. She said she'd seen a white VW bug with a woman inside get pulled over by a highway patrolman at the Mercy Road exit, between eight and nine o'clock.

Pfingst was skeptical. Where was Traci Koenig for the first trial? Why was she showing up now? He figured she might be a publicity seeker or a nut, but both possibilities evaporated when he met her. She hadn't been alone that night—she'd been with her fiancé, who confirmed the sighting. She had also told her parents about it both before and after news of the murder broke, and they confirmed it to Pfingst, too.

Why had she not come forward before? Because, Traci said, she had a secret she did not want to have to disclose in testimony— an arrest for retail theft—and because, based on news reports, prosecutors seemed to have had a good case without her. Now she felt guilty.

The defense went nuts at this eleventh-hour bombshell. But Traci and her boyfriend were allowed to testify. At last there was an eyewitness, if not to the crime itself then to its ominous beginnings. It was devastating to Peyer's case.

It was not the trial's most unforgettable moment, though. That came when Pfingst put Sam Knott on the stand, to testify about the morning of December 28, when Cara's body was discovered. As Sam described his lone car ride home from Mercy Road at midday, when he was agonizing over just how to tell his wife, Joyce, that their youngest daughter was dead, he wept, which was to be expected. What was unexpected was the way this father's sorrow drenched the courtroom and crept into nearly everyone's heart.

Paul Pfingst, sixty-five, is now a partner in a San Diego law firm. "I have tried many murder cases and supervised hundreds more," he says. "I have seen victims and victims' families get up and testify, and I've seen people touched by them. But I never saw anything like this, before or since. Everyone in the courtroom was crying. Jurors were crying. The *defense* lawyers were crying. I have never been known for sentimentality—legions of people wonder if I have any sentiment at all—and *I* was crying. On the bench, the judge, Richard Huffman, tried to rotate his chair away from the jurors, so they couldn't see. But he was crying."

Through his attorneys, Craig Peyer maintained his innocence, though he never testified. On June 22, 1988, he was convicted of first-degree murder. He got twenty-five years to life.

———

THE CASE WAS over for everyone but a small cadre of appeals attorneys, and Sam Knott. For Sam Knott, things had barely begun.

Since the night of the murder, Sam had become intimately familiar with a law enforcement system he felt was fatally corrupted, not by intentional misconduct but by institutional indifference and disorganization. He was particularly galled to learn that before the murder, at least two women had complained to CHiPs superiors about Peyer's behavior during traffic stops; not only were the complaints dismissed, but Peyer was complimented for being so friendly and thorough.

Sam Knott felt that his family had been betrayed by the system and that he was going to be the one to fix it. It would be a deeply personal crusade, and it would keep the memory of Cara alive. To those close to Sam, it sometimes seemed that in his mind, it kept Cara herself alive.

Sam understood he had the benefit of public sympathy, and he was determined not to squander it. In public appearances, he kept his rage in check, but his indignation was front and center always. His voice was measured, his comportment stoic. He never, ever uttered Peyer's name, not to family and friends, not in interviews with the media, not in lobbying meetings, not in testimony. His daughter's killer simply became "the monster." This Manichaean view helped him frame the issue: There are monsters out there; all the rest of us must mobilize against them.

Sam Knott had developed a game plan. He typed it up as something of a manifesto, dozens of pages, single spaced, divided into chapters. Some still survive.

Here's chapter 11, which is about making improvements in CHiPs. Chapter 11 has twenty-one subsections. Each item is both pragmatic and personal, with Sam's outrage evident in every occasional stressed, capitalized, and boldfaced syllable.

Subsection 3: The recognition on the part of the CHP that it is an Intolerable Situation to Not Know the Location of All Officers in the Field by the field supervisory sergeant or duty watch commander.

Subsection 7: The development of an Educational Program for all dispatchers and CHP personnel . . . that specifically addresses Attitude Question or Mindset that a Call-in by a Citizen Is Somehow a Meaningless Call-in by a Traffic Violator or a Lawbreaker. This bureaucratic attitude on the part of the CHP was a fundamental element that contributed to Cara's murder. The failure by the CHP supervisory staff to take seriously or hear the alarm calls from concerned citizens about a dangerous traffic stop made in a dark and desolate area.

Sam Knott's first specific target was the Mercy Road exit itself. Within weeks he had hectored local authorities into sealing it off. Next he attacked the twenty-four-hour missing-persons rule—some local police jurisdictions even insisted on forty-eight hours—and won that at the statehouse in Sacramento. A new law, enacted in response to his testimony, elevated the status of missing-persons reports, meaning police agencies had to activate search protocols immediately if there were reasonable grounds to suspect foul play.

Outraged that police labs were not availing themselves of the most modern science, Knott pestered authorities until the federal government awarded the first national grant for research in DNA forensics to the sexual assault unit at a medical center in Seattle. It would be the start of a revolution in public funding for DNA testing.

On behalf of his family, Sam Knott also filed a $7.5 million wrongful death claim against the state and CHiPs. The family would eventually—many years later—settle for $2.7 million.

The Knotts became concerned by Sam's obsession. His health was beginning to fail, and the stress of his crusade didn't help. He was diverting more and more time to it, so the family's finances were suffering. But Sam was unstoppable. He began to lobby for cameras and GPS devices on police cars—the technology for both was there, but largely unused in law enforcement—to keep tabs on where officers are and what they are doing. Public servants were beginning to cringe when Sam Knott showed up at their office doors; few welcomed his dreadnought approach, though most were in genuine awe of it.

After an eight-year crusade, by 1996, Sam had persuaded the state to help set up a memorial garden under the old highway bridge, near the spot where Cara's body had thudded to the ground. It was dedicated to victims of violent crimes. The old bridge—formerly the Los Penasquitos Creek Bridge—was renamed the Cara Knott Memorial Bridge. The road leading down to the oak grove became Cara Way. The initial plantings were oak saplings Sam Knott had grown in his backyard, from acorns.

The San Diego Crime Victims Oak Garden is a serene place, with hiking paths, planned and impromptu artwork, and a big central gazebo. The preferred method of remembrance is an engraved garden stone. Cara's is a simple white one that reads: *Cara Knott, In Loving Memory 1966–1986.*

Nearby is a stone for Charles "Chuck" Crow (*Forever in our hearts*), a young father shot to death in his Jeep in 2006 during an encounter with a rancher onto whose property he had driven. When the rancher was acquitted of manslaughter, Crow's mother left the courtroom, begging sheriff's deputies to shoot her, too. Exactly what had happened during the fatal confrontation is in dispute, but what is clear is that the shooter was more than ably represented in court. His lawyer was Paul Pfingst. The criminal justice system is not without bittersweet ironies.

And it still must deal with the incomprehensible: One stone is for Leah Tadeo, who was seventeen when she was shotgunned to death by a man who thought she had slighted him by crossing out his nickname, which had been soaped onto a mirror during a party. He's in prison for life.

The grove bears testament to the timelessness of grief. Engraved on a stone for Nikki Benedict is a 1960s peace symbol and these words: *Still skipping stones and feeling groovy.* Nikki was killed in 1967, at age fourteen, stabbed in the heart while walking home from a friend's house not far from Mercy Road. The killer has never been found.

As often as he could, Sam Knott would return to the memorial grove, which is where he was on the afternoon of November 30, 2000, tidying up Cara's small ring of stones and clearing some brush. When he was done, he got in his car and drove back up toward the interstate.

What happened next is part surmise: It was dinnertime. To head home, Sam should have turned left when he reached I-15, but instead, inexplicably, he turned right. It may be that he felt the coronary coming. He drove a short distance, until he was just over Cara's memorial, a hundred feet above it. Responsible as always, he pulled over to the side of the road and died. He was sixty-three.

"Half of him died there," says Paul Pfingst. "The other half had died on December 28, 1986."

Of the circumstances of Sam's death, Pfingst says: "It was the wrong time, but the perfect place. I like to think it was divine intervention. When it was Sam's time to go, I like to think he was directed to that spot to take his last breath."

There's now a stone for Sam Knott in the crime victims memorial. He was, after all, a crime victim, too.

CRAIG PEYER has never confessed. Though his guilt is obvious, some mystery remains. How did a harmlessly creepy police officer become a cold-blooded murderer? What, exactly, happened that night between the cop and his victim?

Paul Pfingst believes he knows. He spent weeks re-creating that traffic stop in his mind, cross-checking it against available evidence, testing it against what he knew of the personalities of the killer and victim, so he could lay it out to a jury in a persuasive narrative.

As Pfingst talks about it thirty years later, it is as though no time has passed. "It is an escalating pattern of misbehavior. The pattern involves stopping attractive women on the highway and exercising control over them. Their responses were to try to please him, to avoid getting a ticket. It made Peyer feel manly. It was a sick appetite, and it became an addiction."

In the days before he killed Cara, Peyer was getting bolder and more outrageous, stopping more women, bringing them further into the desolation of the Mercy Road dead end, holding them longer, sometimes for more than an hour. It was a compulsion that was getting out of hand. On December 26, the day before Cara was killed, he pulled over three separate women at Mercy Road for lengthy, skin-crawling interrogations in a place so far off the highway that it was beyond the range of a scream. Then Cara.

Paul Pfingst:

We know Cara had an inoperative light over her license plate. That's probably the pretext under which he stops her. He directs her into this unsafe place. She realizes there is something very wrong about this place, how isolated it is, and she is alarmed. Her car is facing back toward the highway. His car is facing her, and I think it is blocking her escape. When he approaches her, she gets out of her car. They are both out of their cars. She's a track star; if she has to, she is thinking she can outrun him back up to the highway, where she will be comparatively safe. It all happens outside the cars, which is why there's no evidence inside either one.

She is the kind of person who will speak up for herself, and she has her father's strong sense of right and wrong. She is no doormat. She is the kind of person who will say, "I'm going to report this. I am going to tell my family, I'm going to tell my father."

He doesn't know what to do except what cops do, which is take control, issue directives. It doesn't go well with her. When he attempts to reassure her, it has the opposite effect. When things go off script, he is not someone able to summon reassuring personal vibes. I think at this point there is physical touching. Maybe he pulls her arm. She becomes indignant. She says, "You can't do this." She struggles to pull away, and he restrains her with greater force. Now her self-defense training kicks in. She goes for his face. He reacts instinctively, reflexively. He is already holding his flashlight. He hits her over the head with it. She's down.

Now he recognizes this is all falling apart. He had treated her not like a young woman but like some DUI guy who was violently resisting arrest. He realizes there is no way this can be explainable. Any investigation will certainly uncover his prior behavior, certainly result in termination of his career and maybe his marriage. His whole identity, his ego, is tied up in being a CHiPs officer. Now he's got to kill her.

How do you kill a gal and leave as few traces as possible? He can pummel her and get blood all over himself—that doesn't make any sense. He can't shoot her because ballistics would get him. He can't just throw her off the bridge. It's a soft river bottom, with leaves and debris and muck. She might survive the fall. Remember this is all happening in real time; there is no time to reflect. He must act. He can strangle her, but if you do it with your bare hands, you might leave evidence, skin under the fingernails. Plus, it's too personal. You have to push down, looking at her looking up at you doing it. He's making this up as he's going along. He's full of adrenaline.

Then he remembers, and goes to his trunk. This is where a misunderstanding becomes first-degree murder. It is so cold and cruel and premeditated. Maybe she is coming to. He lays her prone, on her belly, wraps the rope around her neck and strangles her from the back. Maybe he's got a knee between her shoulder blades. His hands are in close to the neck. It takes less time than you think. Less than four minutes. It's done.

Now he has a big problem. Ideally, he brings the body to somewhere where it would deteriorate, where animals would get to it before people find it. But what do you do with her car? You can't move it because you'd have to get in it. But as soon as her car is discovered, everything will unravel. You can't transport her anywhere, because her blood will get in your car. You do the best you can.

You put her on *the top* of your car. You can hose that off, and you will. You drive a few hundred feet to the overpass and throw her over. But you do have to carry her to the roof of the car and then to the bridge. You try to be careful—try to avoid blood on her, but there are fibers that transfer, and one of them is gold. . . .

Then you burn rubber getting out of there. You have to get back on the road before it becomes more obvious you are missing. You've got to write tickets to cover your ass.

THE ONE PERSON who can confirm or correct that narrative, won't. Craig Peyer's consistent and continuing story is that he never met Cara Knott. It has been his story for thirty years.

And yet.

One fact neither jury ever heard was that in the days after the killing and before Peyer's arrest, he volunteered to take a lie detector exam administered by the police. Independently reviewing the results, four separate polygraph operators concluded he was lying when he answered no to two relevant questions. They were: "Are you responsible for the death of Cara Knott?" and "Regarding the death of Cara Knott, did you strangle her and throw her body off that bridge?"

And then there is this:

Not long after winning the Peyer case, Paul Pfingst became San Diego's district attorney, and he instituted a new policy, the first of its kind in the country: In cases where it might expose a miscarriage of justice, his office would use public funds to conduct DNA tests on old evidence in convictions obtained before 1993, before DNA testing was used. All he would require was a request from the convict. Pfingst's office identified more than seven hundred such cases, one of which was Craig Peyer's.

DNA testing has been a godsend for the unjustly convicted. Nationally, it has exonerated dozens of people and set them free, some from death row.

In 2003, Pfingst's co-counsel in the Peyer trial, Joan Stein, contacted Peyer's lawyers. If Peyer requests it, she said, the county will retest the blood in the case, including the spot of blood on Cara Knott's boot, which had been central to his conviction. If under more rigorous testing it turned out not to be Peyer's, he might get a new trial.

Days went by. Then the answer came: No, thanks.

A few months later, at his parole hearing, Peyer's attorneys announced in advance that he would take no questions. Stein, however, was allowed to have one of hers entered into the record, and it was read aloud at the hearing. It was: "If you are innocent, as you maintain, why did you decline to have a DNA test that could prove it?"

Peyer remained silent, staring straight ahead.

No, he didn't get parole. He didn't in 2008, either. Or 2012. He's up next in 2027.

6:40 A.M., Flagstaff, Arizona

Cynthia Manuel sat in her living room, a mug of coffee beside her. This was her time of day, the minutes she stole for herself most mornings. Raspberry and Barley pressed in, catlike, petitioning for affection.

Cynthia was writing in a blue-lined hardcover notebook, the kind you buy at the office supply store for $1.95. The binding was turquoise, as was her choice of felt-tip; she loved the gemstone color, which is said to inspire serenity and good fortune. That was the first of two ironies. The second was the brand name on the front of the book: Simple Record. Inside, in girlish, looping longhand, without blot or erasure or cross-out, as was her custom, Cynthia Manuel was dissecting in excruciating, unsimple detail the bewildering collapse of her new marriage.

Don-Paul, her husband of six months, lay sleeping in the bedroom down the hall after yet another restless, thrashing night. For weeks they'd both known they were doomed as a couple, but on this day, in her notebook, Cynthia began to grapple with why. Uncharacteristically she'd missed a few days since the last entry. She'd been thinking. The house was quiet. Small sounds carried.

"In his sleep he sighs," she wrote. "Resigned, condemned, tormented sighs . . ."

Manuel, thirty-nine, was the owner of a bookstore, a once-divorced mother of an eleven-year-old girl, a beekeeper, an earnest, committed eat-what-you-raise farmer, and above all, a diarist. She'd been writing in a journal almost every day since she was sixteen.

As is true of most diaries, hers was intended for an audience of one. Privately chronicling one's life as it unfolds is, for some, a compulsion. For others, it is psychotherapy. For literary figures, it can be a liberating rough first draft unencumbered by the professional's need for restraint—dirty ore awaiting refinement. Virginia Woolf did that. So does David Sedaris.

The least forthright diaries tend to be those written to be shared. Many belong to people in the gyre of history or those convinced they will be, people who want to marshal facts strategically to control the narrative in forgiving ways, for the benefit of historians. Ronald Reagan kept a diary.

As it happened, on this same day that Cynthia Manuel was grimly facing the truth, the president of the United States was gingerly avoiding it.

At a hotel in Los Angeles where he was on Christmas vacation, Reagan would dryly write that he had met with his son and daughter and their families and discussed with them the newly unraveling Iran-Contra affair. It didn't have that name yet, nor the eventual, largely universal verdict of it as a scandal. Reagan simply called it Iran.

It was huge and audacious and stupid. A team of ideologues in his administration had run amok, secretly funneling to supposedly anticommunist Nicaraguan rebels the profits from covert

American arms sales to the rogue anti-American theocracy of Iran. Operating out of the White House, the ham-fisted scheme was almost comically sinister, with cooked books, shredded files, bagmen, and even a launderer: Israel was the front, the ostensible arms merchant, covering up the true source of the weaponry. In return, at least in theory, Iran would agree to exert its influence to secure the release of American hostages held in Lebanon. It was unambiguously illegal and arguably deeply immoral: We were arming an unscrupulous enemy in a volatile neighborhood of the globe, then funneling the proceeds to a group that was, among multiple unsavory things, selling cocaine to Americans. When the facts of the Iran-Contra affair spilled out, they exposed the unnerving disengagement of the president's hitherto vaunted "hands-off" management style. It was one of several reasons why some historians would come to wonder whether the dementia that would infantilize Reagan in his last years had actually begun to take hold during his presidency.

That remains speculation. What is clear is that this head of state initially failed to grasp the gravity of the scandal and remained incurious about it for far too long. By late December, enough of this had leaked out that a congressional investigation had begun and a special prosecutor had been named.

Reagan was that dry, dutiful, cover-your-ass, man-of-destiny diarist. He was seldom introspective, even less so on matters that might impel self-doubt or imperil his formidable ideological resolve. This, in its entirety, was what Ronald Reagan wrote in his diary on December 28, 1986, about his meeting with his kids and others: "Subject again Iran and why I don't display anger etc. fire someone. I think Im doing it right."

Cynthia Manuel's diary entry on the day ran on for three dense, loose-leaf-sized pages. There was nothing dry or dutiful about it. She wrote:

His friends exclaim how wonderful it must be to live with someone who has such a golden sense of life's humor. Well, I was fooled, too.

She and Don-Paul Benjamin had met less than a year before, in early January, when he walked into her small bookstore in Fort Collins, Colorado, to try to persuade her to display some copies of his self-published book. Benjamin was a college administrator, but also drew books of cartoons—whimsical, single-panel jokes, not quite *The Far Side,* but not without humor. Manuel was charmed—less, perhaps, by the book than by a man confident enough to hand you his work and invite you to leaf through it as he watched, yet vulnerable enough that you could feel his worry. She agreed to take a few copies. At closing time, Benjamin invited her to a bar, where he drew little penguins on napkins and cheerful little suns with faces. In six months, they'd be married.

It wasn't exactly love at first sight for either; they were insufficiently idealistic for that, too old and callused by past romantic failures. What happened to Cynthia Manuel and Don-Paul Benjamin that day in January might best be described as "settling at first sight." Each saw a need the other filled.

Benjamin was a lifelong bachelor, wary of women after some painful rejections, including two rebuffed marriage proposals. At forty-one, he was living in his parents' garage, knowing that had to change, soon. He told himself that he liked the idea of a financially independent wife, and one with a child: an instant family, at middle age. Plus, this woman was cute—doe-eyed, petite, with long dark hair, a recidivist hippie who seemed effortlessly retro; she wore wide-brimmed hats and rocked the look.

For Cynthia, here was a father for her daughter, Morgan, a difficult child in sullen rebellion. Manuel's first marriage was also impulsive, taking hold in a bohemian commune, and had ended almost before it began. Morgan had seen her father only once, at age three. There were tensions between mother and daughter— "oppositional defiance," as Morgan would describe it many years later. At eleven, she was a handful. Cynthia felt her daughter was in need of the sort of imposing authority figure she could no longer be. And Don-Paul would be easy to wake up next to, a sinewy man, cowboy lanky, seemingly at ease in his own skin.

And he drew smiling little suns.

From the diary, December 28, 1986:

One could go far with that humor. It could transport you over life's rough spots. We would be laughing through our tragedies. . . .

Right after their engagement, Benjamin got a new job, and they had to move from Colorado to Arizona. Things had to be done too quickly. To Cynthia, looking back, what happened next seems portentous.

There wasn't time to find a new owner for the animals Cynthia was raising on her acre and a half—there were chickens, a doe, some baby goats—so despite misgivings, she had them slaughtered and gave the meat to friends. Farmers live with death, of course, and accommodate it unemotionally, but only as part of a deliberate, natural process with a measured end. This was a bloodbath, a frenzy of unnecessary killing followed by an added indignity: Much of the gift meat, Manuel would discover, went uneaten. So it had just been butchery, in a disturbing sense of the word, and she felt complicit—"shell-shocked," as she would later put it.

Next came the phone call. It was from a saleswoman at a mall in Flagstaff.

Cynthia had sent her new husband and her daughter ahead to Arizona in late summer, to find a house and enroll Morgan in school, while Cynthia stayed behind to close down the farm and the store. On this night, Don-Paul had decided to take Morgan to buy a swimsuit. This was an idea so unwise on its face that it could only have occurred to a lifelong bachelor—someone oblivious to the likelihood that an emotionally volatile eleven-year-old girl in a self-conscious adolescent standoff with her body might not want to perform this particular shopping task in front of a man she barely knew, and might not take well to being hurried, or come to think of it, even being *looked* at.

Morgan dawdled. Don-Paul fumed. Morgan wanted to try on a few more. Don-Paul exploded. Morgan wept. Things got so publicly loud and potentially creepy that a saleswoman intervened, at which point Don-Paul loudly instructed her to mind her own business, which was not a good impulse under the circumstances. The saleswoman threatened to call the police unless she was satisfied she was not witnessing something abusive. Hence the long-distance phone call. Cynthia calmed things down, but the rupture between stepfather and stepdaughter would never really be repaired.

It was the first strong clue that Cynthia had not married the man she thought she was marrying. There would be more and they would arrive swiftly. He'd said he liked animals, but once they were living together, he'd banished her big, goofy tailless dog, Panda, to live outside, and complained sourly about the sound of cat collars jingling in the night. He'd seemed easygoing; now he was peevish. He'd never seemed to worry about money before, and she had never asked about his finances; now he was secretive about his checking account, and told her that all she meant to him was "bills, bills, bills." He'd been sweep-you-off-your-feet romantic; now he contrived to go to sleep early, to avoid intimacy. He'd seemed open, but in Flagstaff he closed himself off, with unexplained disappearances. He was furtive to the point that Cynthia suspected infidelity. He had a rage that seemed to be building, particularly against Morgan, whose intractability was only stiffened by conflict. Once he balled a fist at her and said, "There's gonna be some hitting going on."

Once, on a family trip to Target to buy back-to-school supplies, Don-Paul threw into the shopping cart, wordlessly, without explanation, in there among the backpacks and the binders and the colored pencils, an axe.

An axe. Years later, Cynthia would look back at 1986, the worst year of her life, and call it, only half jokingly, the year of the axe murder that never happened.

On Christmas, when the base of the tree was swimming in presents, there was not one from Don-Paul, for anyone.

From Cynthia's diary on December 28:

Don-Paul's humor does not go beneath the surface. It is a defense he learned in childhood. It helps people to like him. It smooths things over socially. It prevents people from getting too close.

Marriage, Cynthia realized, had forced an intimacy on him, one he was emotionally unequipped for. Under the stress of that, and of a new job that was going badly, and a willfully resentful child, something ugly emerged.

TODAY, DON-PAUL BENJAMIN is Donald Paul Benjamin. At sixty-nine, he's semiretired, working as an itinerant teacher, traveling to grade schools to give art lessons to kids. He does quirky, easy-to-replicate, skillfully simple drawings of the cactus-and-coyote type. He's still cowboy lanky, with a gray goatee and twinkly eyes. It's easy to see how well he engages with children. And it's easy to see how, if this particular man suddenly showed an explosive temper, you'd feel ambushed.

Twenty-eight years later, Benjamin heard for the first time the words from Cynthia's diary entry from December 28, 1986. You might expect defensiveness or an attempt to mold the narrative. There was neither.

"She was right," he said. "There's some of the Robin Williams syndrome in me. Sadness, darkness, whatever, under the humor. It was the thing I didn't show her, until we were in Flagstaff and it bubbled over."

Reliving this seemed to unburden him.

"Once, at the dinner table, when Morgan acted up over something, something little, I got up and stormed out of the house. Slamming doors, the whole thing. I spent the night with a friend. Morgan was the adolescent, but how was *that* for an adolescent reaction from me? I remember my words exactly because I regret them, and I still think of them fairly often because I am ashamed. I said to Cynthia, 'Keep that little bitch away from me!'"

If his rage surprised Cynthia, Cynthia held some surprises for Don-Paul, too. She hadn't told him just how difficult her daughter could be, though she'd surely known it. But there was something subtler that remained hidden. Just days after the new family first got together, Don-Paul's father died suddenly. There was unfinished business between the two men—lingering oppositional defiance of its own—and Don-Paul was poleaxed with grief and guilt. When he fell apart, he found little sympathy from his new family.

"Cynthia didn't get that. She was like, 'He was old, he was sick, what are you getting so upset about?'"

It seemed cold to him—not unfeeling so much as fatalistic, the reaction of someone who lived with an expectation of pain. Once, when he took his new bride out to meet some of his friends, one of them took him aside and confided: "I didn't think you'd wind up with someone so negative." It opened his eyes: There was in Cynthia a certain melancholy, a baseline despondency he hadn't seen in Colorado. Many years later, Cynthia would explain it this way: She has always lived, she says, with "crocodiles."

As it happens, it was all in her diary, on that singular entry of December 28, 1986. Don-Paul, she wrote, "was to be a balance to my deep sadness."

How was I to know that he did not see exactly who I was either? My negative outlook on the world has surprised him. I hid that in my animals, my garden, my activity. If you are busy you don't have time to think about it. If you shut yourself off from the rest of the world on a little farm you can ignore the great cruelties of the world. You can create your own separate peace . . . When my choices are gone, as they are in Flagstaff, I have no alternative but to see it in an inescapable, every day sort of way. When there is no way to look the other way, so to speak, it all becomes so oppressive.

She'd nailed it all, in barely four hundred words. For the best of reasons, Cynthia Manuel and Don-Paul Benjamin had tried to make things work, but they never really stopped "dating" until it was too late. Their courtship turned out to be a mutual well-intentioned lie. Deliberately or inadvertently, each left something hidden. In the end, instead of finding a complement in each other, instead of being stronger together than alone, they had gotten an unnerving echo of the darker part of themselves.

Neither tried marriage again. To this day, when Benjamin has to fill out a form asking his marital status—single? married? divorced? widowed?—he sometimes hesitates over it. His marriage was so long ago and so brief and so terribly mistaken, it's as though it never was.

After the disaster, Cynthia and her daughter moved back to Colorado, and she reopened her bookstore, the Eclectic Reader. Once, just a few years ago, Don-Paul walked into that store, just like that. He was in town and decided to do it, on impulse. And just for a moment, to each it seemed familiar and a little exciting. And then the feeling went away.

AND WHAT OF MORGAN, the inadvertent flashpoint of this dreadfully failed marriage?

"That was my last year of childhood, really. The last time I played with dolls," she said. "The next year, there was makeup and there were boys."

She is Morgan Williams now, living in Portland. She's just about the age her mother was on December 28, 1986. She's been married for six years, with two little girls with big beautiful blond curls, which come from daddy. Like her mother, Morgan is dark-haired and pretty.

Unlike her mother, who tried to busy herself into avoiding other people's troubles, Morgan ran toward them. She's a labor and delivery room nurse who specializes in high-risk pregnancies. She sees a lot of newborns die, and some of their mothers, too.

Life is essentially a fatal disease of indeterminate duration. You can either cry at the unfairness of this or laugh at its absurdity. Morgan grew up in the presence of Option 1 and chose Option 2 for herself. Her sense of humor is dry and self-deprecatory. Asked to describe herself physically, she says, "I am not small, like my mom. Sadly, I missed the hobbit gene. My mom says I'm big-boned. The BMI scale says I'm obese. I say, curvy with some extra padding."

In college, Morgan had a boyfriend whom she liked, but she dumped him when she realized he was cheating on her. Later came a more serious relationship, one that might well have ended in an impulsive marriage, had Morgan been more like her mother.

"At the start I was thinking, *You need to make this work*," she says. "But then I realized I was putting up with a lot of things I shouldn't have been putting up with. It was all pot and video games for him, and hanging out with his friends, and he was bad-mouthing me. I was trying to turn him into a fiancé, maybe by having a kid, and then suddenly I said no."

"It was a close call," she says, laughing.

The man Morgan eventually married, Lee Williams, is a different sort of person entirely. Different from that boyfriend and different from Morgan. Morgan is still temperamental. Lee is not, so when she needs calming, he calms her. Lee can't handle money, but Morgan can and does. Their marriage started out with residual financial problems from his profligate past, and that could have gotten messy and testy, but Morgan simply declared that they were now a single entity, with one bank account and no secrets. As part of one fiduciary entity, she helped them whittle down the debt until it disappeared.

"I know where my husband is. I know what he spends. It's working. I believe in my marriage," Morgan says.

So did this good marriage have anything to do with the bad marriage she'd seen unravel so messily in Flagstaff?

Initially Morgan says no.

"I don't remember that year with sadness. I had good friends in school. I mean, I was aware of the tensions in the house and the lack of trust between Mom and Don-Paul. That was the worst part, and it was bad. But I had an escape."

There was a vacant lot across the street, she explains, the

ruins of where a house had once stood. It had a steep set of cement stairs that probably once led up to the front door, but now led to rubble. There were bushes in which a child could hide. The whole thing was ghostly, like a demolished movie set, which was good for fantasizing, particularly if you were eleven and in need of a refuge.

From that old lot you could look back and see the unhappy house. It had a big skinny wrought-iron letter S on the chimney stack, in an odd attenuated wicked-looking font.

"When I was outside across the street," Morgan said, "I played house. I continually narrated a story in my head, and I would get lost in it. It was almost like I was writing a story. I was really into *Little House on the Prairie*, and that's what it was like. I was fascinated by pioneer life."

So when she was by herself in her pretend home, writing her own little story, she became the mother in a close family, overcoming hardships by pulling together?

Morgan is laughing now. "We had six children, and we had love and we were happy."

So maybe that year in Flagstaff did affect her, just a little bit.

8:15 A.M., Cedar Rapids, Iowa

Linda was up first, and up to something. Ed could see that through sleep-squinty eyes as his wife went for her suitcase and rummaged deep. He was just sitting up in bed when she'd retrieved his present and handed it over with a smile.

It was Ed Krug's thirtieth birthday. He and Linda were bunking with Ed's kid sister in a holiday visit that would soon turn into a neighborhood reconnaissance mission. Ed and Linda were Cedar Rapids kids—they'd met here in high school—but they'd moved east when Ed went to law school at Boston College, and they stayed after he landed his first job with a Boston firm. On this trip, they were rediscovering the quiet charm of Cedar Rapids and started talking about moving back west.

It wasn't that Ed's Boston law practice was suffering—far from it. To his colleagues and adversaries, he was already evolving into Killer Krug, the nom de guerre for his balls-to-the-wall style of litigation.

Killer was not a nickname he would have imagined for himself when he was eleven, idolizing Bobby Kennedy for his devotion to the poor and socially marginalized. Over the years, he kept a photo of Bobby, campaigning from a flatbed truck in 1968 in a sweat-damp white shirt and tie, reaching out to an enthusiastic crowd in the rural South, braced by his friend and bodyguard Rosey Grier, who just months later would wrestle the gun from the assassin as Bobby lay mortally wounded on a hotel kitchen floor.

But young Ed Krug's idealistic ardor had gotten some prag-matic competition when he nailed a prized summer internship with a Cleveland firm. It paid $2,400 a month in 1981 dollars, and Ed came to believe there was no sin in doing well.

At thirty, he specialized in personal injury cases, but he didn't represent the personally injured. He was on the other side, hired to defend businesses and utilities accused of negligence or other civil wrongs. You could call that a sellout, and some people do, but there are two sides to most cases, and just as some corpora-tions are rapacious and careless and reckless, some people who sue them are opportunists and frauds. Ed had no qualms about being on the big-money side of this divide, the side where law-yers billed by the quarter hour and didn't have to gamble on con-tingency fees. And if this sometimes made him the adversary of grievously injured people—well, that was the nature of the work. His favorite opening phrase in cross-examination was "Isn't it true that . . . ?" which turns every question, however innocuous, into an accusation. Young Killer Krug was taking well to personal injury defense.

He never thought much about *why* he put in such long hours, or the ferocity with which he filled those hours, other than that's what lawyers do, if they're ambitious. And that was true, but there was another answer, too. It would only come many years later, and it would not come easily.

Ed's birthday present from Linda was the size of a brick and weighed almost as much. Under the gift wrap was a Sony Discman D-50, miniaturized to the limits of 1985 technology, still priced for its novelty. Just as the first pocket calculators sold for $240 in 1971 and performed only middle-school arithmetic, the first portable CD player was huge, heavy, and ludicrously impractical. It worked fine on a desktop, but was "portable" mostly as luggage. For one thing, it had no battery: To be carried in the street, it had to be connected to a bulky battery pack and slung over a shoulder, and it still tended to skip when jostled. Linda had paid extravagantly—$350—but Ed loved it, mostly for the grand, sweet illogic of its timing.

Linda could have given him the big old box a few days early, before they left Boston, and saved herself the hassle of schlepping it on the plane. But that wasn't an option, because Linda knew Ed better than anyone else. Like many other children of a distressed home—Ed's father was a flop-down doorstep drunk and a serial philanderer, his mother a docile go-along—Ed grew up with a hunger for order and harmony and affection. Small gestures meant a lot. He also was saddled with one of those unlucky Christmas-week birthdays, the classic childhood gyp. So Linda made sure, as always, that Ed was going to get a Christmas present *and* a birthday present, and they would be distinct events, and that was that. The Discman got schlepped.

By conventional measures, Ed and Linda Krug were the happiest of couples, devoted to each other in a way that a romantic would find adorable and a cynic might find cloying. She called him Bo. He called her . . . Bo. It was short for *bobo*, which is Spanish slang for a simpleton, and which, in an amiable way, fit.

Theirs was the sappy togetherness of a couple who met as teenagers, explored sex for the first time with each other, and who never found any reason to look elsewhere. Ed was likably sharp-featured and wore a mustache during the last years you could do that and not look like a sleazebag. Bo still thought Bo had a sweet, round face and a fabulous behind. They were a cute, attractive, sexy couple. Bo and Bo had been together for exactly half of their lives.

Many years later, Linda would remember this thirtieth birthday gift only vaguely. To Ed the memory of it would be indelible, in the way other similar moments became indelible: yet another time that Linda had shown a private knowledge of him that went beyond thoughtfulness and affection into something suggesting predestination—a marriage of souls, as he saw it, the sort of spiritual gift one tampers with at one's own peril. Ed harvested those moments with gratitude—he needed them. He was keeping score because he felt he had to.

The outwardly perfect married life of Ed Krug had a secret interior soliloquy. Inside, he was Hamlet, pacing the dank corridors of Elsinore, dithering over what to do about a problem of life-altering dimensions, one he'd told no one about, ever.

To Linda, the lure of Cedar Rapids involved family (she missed hers) and finance—Boston in 1986 was among the most expensive cities to live in. Ed gave lip service to those things, too, but he had a bigger motive. To him, Boston was Babylon, a source of temptation that imperiled everything. Cedar Rapids was small and safe, a comfort-food city, literally. There's a Quaker Oats factory downtown, and many days the streets smelled of cinnamon or Cap'n Crunch's Crunch Berries. Ed could not make the things that were happening in his head go away, but he could limit the likelihood that he would succumb to them and ruin everything. The seductive blandness of Cap'n Crunchland could help.

On the way in from Boston, their plane had been forced to land in Davenport. Through the eighty-mile bus ride to Cedar Rapids in the middle of the night, Ed Krug was mesmerized by the darkness that mantled the Iowa countryside. It was quiet and peaceful and safe. *Perfect,* Ed said to himself. *This could work.*

THE THOUGHT, in some primitive preadolescent form, first arose in Ed Krug's brain one summer weekend afternoon in Parlin, New Jersey, as the ice cream truck tootled its arrival down the street. For the price of a cone, a cute nine-year-old girl with olive skin and Brillo hair was being importuned to drop her drawers for the enlightenment of a small group of neighborhood boys, among them Eddie Krug, age eight.

It was hot and she was hungry. Currency changed hands. Shorts, then undies, slid down to the knees. Arms akimbo, mouth set defiantly, the young lady held the pose for what was adjudged a contractually adequate length of time. Then pants were pulled up, heart rates slowed, ice cream got licked, and life, slightly sweetened, continued for the boys in the street of Parlin, New Jersey, in 1964.

Exactly what the other boys thought of this moment we can only presume. We know what Ed Krug thought, because it would stay in his mind, in one form or another, for most of the rest of his life.

Clean lines.

In those few seconds, Ed had looked not with desire but with envy. He had seen an anatomical perfection—simple, elegant, symmetrical architecture—that he'd found wanting in himself. In time he would come to think of the flesh between his legs as "my penis and scrotum blob." He hated it.

As the years passed, Ed Krug's secret longings would mature and crystallize. First he wanted to wear girls' lingerie, an urge he initially satisfied in his teens when he stole into his sister's bedroom, put on panties, and pranced in front of mirrors.

He was attracted to girls, but also to boys, in a secret seditious way. Once, when he saw his own brother naked, he experienced a thrill that confused him. In time, the two impulses merged into a simple sexual narrative in his mind, and it would not go away: Ed in women's clothing, in the presence of a lustful, admiring man.

Linda did not know any of this. She did not know that her husband leafed through a Victoria's Secret catalogue with an entirely different sort of prurience than most men did. She did not know that he went on furtive buying sprees and hid caches of women's underwear, then threw them out, determined to shake his "habit," then bought more. She did not know that her seemingly robust sex life was half jury-rigged; in his mind, Ed often had a movie playing, and it involved him, dressed as a woman, submitting to a handsome goateed man. "Do with me as you please," Ed would whisper. The cheesy melodrama was, of course, all in his head.

Linda wasn't going to find out about any of this any time soon. Ed was riven by indecision, tormented by what he desperately hoped was a controllable quirk. He kept track of the times he was "lingerie sober" and when he backslid. In Boston, he'd found himself reading the same-sex personals in the back of *The Phoenix*, the city's gritty alternative weekly, then nervously throwing them away. The Combat Zone—Boston's gay, sleazy demimonde—

beckoned. He once sneaked into a movie house there, noticed men leaving in pairs for a back room. It thrilled and terrified him. He was afraid of AIDS, afraid of giving it to Linda. He was afraid of losing her and the full, rich life they shared. About a year after their thirtieth birthday scouting mission, they would indeed move back to Cedar Rapids.

To call Ed's cross-dressing a compulsion is accurate but misleading. It would be like calling ingesting nutrients a compulsion. Wearing women's clothes seemed right to him, an acknowledgment of what he was supposed to be and what he was supposed to do.

Many lawyers will tell you that their legal training helps in other areas of their lives. It gives them a template for how to marshal thoughts efficiently, how to deal with others in productive ways. But courtroom trials—theaters with their own separate realities—also teach you to compartmentalize. Plus, the practice of civil law is in part about the deft deployment of accommodation and compromise. These things were of no help at all to the Hamlet in Ed.

In 1986, he was still yo-yoing back and forth in his mind over what he really was, what he really wanted, and what he was willing to sacrifice to get it. Some things would bring him clarity, but it was an adrenaline-scary sort of clarity. It would happen when he was cross-dressing. It would happen during the crystallizing climax of solitary sex, moments spent dressed as a woman, in his mind, in the company of that goateed man, who would at last do with him—her?—what he pleased.

Then there were the other moments, the ones that were not visceral but intellectual. Those provided a sort of comforting white noise, the promise of what he considered a "normal" life, with a wife and children, achieved by arriving at a simple accommodation with oneself: How much self-deception and self-denial can you endure? He was, after all, married to a woman he loved, for all the right reasons except one. That was pretty close to perfection, wasn't it?

December 28, 1986, presented one of those white-noise times. A return to Cedar Rapids was in their future, and it would help him forget his urges. Ed the lawyer told Ed the husband that Linda the wife was too wonderful an asset to squander.

It would take Ed Krug another decade and a half, years filled with therapy and thoughts of suicide, to fully realize what he was and to wholly embrace it. At his center he was not, as he had initially assumed, a man who wanted sex with men. He was a woman who wanted sex with men. And maybe with women, too. It was a complicated landscape.

But for the moment, there was Linda and her gift, which, as it happens, came with its own soundtrack. Linda had picked out an inaugural CD. It was the album *December* by George Winston, the easy-listening 1970s classical pianist, respected by some, derided by others as the composer of Muzak for hippies.

December was a surrender to serenity, an album of pure contentment, without a dissonant note. At the center of it was Pachelbel's Canon, that soothing, lilting seventeenth-century piece for strings. The name may not be familiar, but you'd know it if you heard it. It's the reassuring selection that modern churches sometimes play at weddings when the ceremony is running late and you need to tamp down the anxiety.

It was white noise. It was comfort food. It did the job. On the last weekend of 1986, Ed Krug was pretty sure he could hang on to what he had.

DECEMBER 2014.

Yes, she's pretty.

Ellie Krug is better looking than Ed. Ed's weak chin is now Ellie's dainty one. His ferrety beak became a perky nose, thanks to a plastic surgeon. His hair had been short, dark, and corporate-lawyer nondescript; hers is long and silky blond, and she likes to toss it. He always grappled with stubble and lost; her complexion, befriended by makeup, is clear. Her hands and wrists are large for a woman, but when offset by generous bracelets, look just fine.

Ellen Krug, Esq., is one of very few lawyers in history to have argued before juries as both a man and a woman. In her very first jury trial, still unsteady on heels, still with male genitalia under her skirt, she asked the judge if she could tell the prospective jury that she was transgender. The judge deferred to the opposing counsel.

"He's going to think like a man," Ellie figured. "He's going to think the jury will see a freak show." Ellie, as a woman, felt the opposite: that a jury would see it as a sign of painful honesty in the face of difficult circumstances, and extend that sentiment to her client.

"We have no objection," opposing counsel said, with the faintest hint of a smirk.

Ellie won the trial.

Long divorced from Linda, Ellie's not seeing anyone right now. She misses Linda, she says, every day.

"I don't have a soul mate anymore, and I very much want to be in love," she says, and then answers your next question before it is asked. "Yes, I have lost a great deal. I used to confuse loss with regret. I don't do that anymore. I do not regret what I did. If I hadn't, I don't think I'd be alive now. I had to become me, and I had no real choice in that."

Her voice is still masculine. On the phone, you're talking to a man. But in person, the voice is part of a larger picture that is unambiguously female.

A year after the thirtieth birthday present, when Ed and Linda did move back to Cedar Rapids, Ed found the quiet he sought, but no peace. Three years later, in 1990, his father blew his brains out in the bathtub. When going through Tom Krug's papers, Ed came across ample evidence of his father's lifelong infidelities, with a tantalizing rider attached: Bizarrely, he'd kept coded diaries of his conquests, and some of them were men.

Not long after his father's death, Ed and Linda—infertile as a couple—adopted two baby girls from South Korea. The Krugs' life was so outwardly normal that when *The Gazette* started a Sunday feature series on happy nuclear families in Cedar Rapids, Ed submitted an application, and the Krugs of Knollwood Drive were chosen for a segment.

It ran on Sunday, May 4, 1997. The story began on page 1 and then filled three more pages inside. It was about a workaholic dad—the Krug Law Firm was doing well—who manufactured time for his family. There was a lavish photo spread of a happy family after dinner: Ed and Linda in jeans, Ed in wire-rims, a flannel shirt, and his perpetual Nixonian five-o'clock shadow, dancing with the girls, reading to the girls on the bed, Saturday morning at Donutland for a daddy-and-daughters breakfast.

Ed had made this article happen. It was a stratagem, and even then he recognized it for what it was, a self-imposed obstacle to make it harder for him to do what he eventually did. It's the suicide bomber technique: You make a heroic video to force your own hand, using the specter of shame as a threat to preempt cold feet.

You can actually see it as you read that old newspaper story now. Ed seems to be talking himself into—or out of—something:

"This is one lucky family," he tells the *Gazette* reporter. "Lucky that Linda and I have a great relationship. Lucky that I make a good living. Lucky that we have the girls."

Translation: What sort of damn fool would *dare* monkey with this mojo?

Here's how strange it got. Ed and Linda became family counselors at their Roman Catholic church, teaching newlyweds and troubled couples how to stay in a long, loving relationship. They'd typically start out asking their students to say what was the best thing about their marriage, and the teachers would answer the question first. Linda would say, "I am married to my best friend." Ed would say: "We have a history, and it's deep. I can turn to Linda anytime and say, 'Do you remember . . . ' and she does."

Both statements were true. But Linda was in real time, looking ahead. Ed was in the past, clawing at the scenery, trying to hang on.

It all might have stayed that way if not for September 11, 2001.

Two of the hijacked planes had originated in Boston on routes familiar to the much-traveled lawyer. Ed could blink and see himself there in his customary window seat, watching buildings loom up way too close, realizing he was about to die without ever becoming the person he felt he really was. That was the day he decided he was living as a liar and a coward, the day Ed resolved to become Ellen. It did not go smoothly.

What he would put his family through—particularly Linda—was excruciating. His confessions came out gradually, over years, in partial reveals—hedged, qualified, lawyerlike, as little as Ed could disclose at each step as he still fought to salvage, somehow, his marriage. He liked lingerie, but was not gay. He liked lingerie but was maybe gay. He felt like a woman, but it was an urge he could and would fight. He was a woman and he couldn't fight it. He would leave. He would stay. He would leave. He once left for good, then came back, on the same night. He finally moved out on April 30, 2004.

Everyone was hurt, but the greatest injury was to the couple's older daughter. On the day Ed and Linda announced they would separate, and explained more or less why, the still shell-shocked Linda buried her resentment and bravely put up a united front. But their fourteen-year-old bolted for her bedroom and lay on her bed in a fetal position, weeping. It was simply too much.

But this time the separation held. For Linda, there would be romance and remarriage. For Ed, psychological counseling. Hormone treatments. Breast implants. A butt job, a face tweak, the reduction of her Adam's apple. The last, most tangible remnants of Ed Krug disappeared on September 14, 2010, on an operating table in Scottsdale, Arizona.

THERE'S ONE MORE twist to the story. Can you see it coming? Ed couldn't.

With the end of Ed, someone else went away. Killer Krug. Yes, somehow, the balls to the wall are gone, too.

You can do a chicken-egg analysis of this and never get a completely satisfactory answer, but the fact is that Ellen Krug is a different kind of lawyer, a kinder kind; or as one former courtroom adversary unsmilingly informed her one day over lunch: "You were a real asshole as a man."

Was Ed always secretly Ellie, with Killer Krug being a facade— a desperate subconscious stratagem to seem "manly"? Or did something in the physical and chemical feminizing of Ed— estrogen in, testosterone out, curves replacing edges—change the lawyer's basic disposition? Or was it a matter of frustration aggression: Was Ed Krug so bottled up with the anger of living a lie that he took it out savagely in his professional life?

Ellie Krug listens to these three possibilities, laughs, and says, "Yes."

The fact is, she lost the taste for blood. It had begun in 2008 when she was still presenting to the world as a man and got the most gruesome case of her life, a man crippled and terribly disfigured in a transportation accident. He lost both legs, part of his colon, and most of his buttocks.

Ellie—still Ed, to the world—got to the grisly scene an hour or two after it happened; blood and tissue was everywhere.

The situation was messy in other ways, too. The Krug Law Firm's client was not the victim. The client, as usual, was the defendant corporation. And what became clear from accident reconstruction was that whatever negligence the defendant may have shown, the victim was also significantly complicit. If that did not outright absolve the defendant, it surely softened the plaintiff's case.

It would be the job of the company's lawyer to negotiate a modest settlement by convincing the victim that he'd lose at trial because the accident was all his fault, and the law firm was prepared to fight tooth and nail to prove it. It's a sort of extortion, but perfectly legit. Lawyers do it all the time. Killer Krug never had a problem with it.

The victim showed up for a pretrial mediation session in a wheelchair, a half-sized man, focused fury in his eyes. How great was his resolve? He'd had the date of his accident tattooed large on a forearm.

Ed Krug, Esq., woman masquerading as man, tried to muster the customary thunder, but it didn't come. She said the words, but they lacked conviction. The plaintiff was not intimidated; he tersely declined to consider a settlement, so the case would proceed to trial.

In the view of the corporate client, its lawyer's performance had been so lacking—so inexcusably contaminated by a hint of a tinge of a shred of compassion—that they took him off the case.

"I was relieved," Ellie Krug says now.

HER FIRST WIN AS A WOMAN was followed by what seemed like professional disaster; her firm's biggest client dropped her. She believes she knows why. She believes it because she never got a good explanation. In the end, the reason didn't matter: The Krug Law Firm could no longer support itself and had to close.

Soon something worse happened. Ellie's oldest daughter, last seen here at fourteen in a fetal position on her bed, just could not handle the weirdness. She cut Ellie out of her life. Ellie's strategy was to fall back, give space, and hope for a change of heart or a miracle or both.

Both came in December 2014. In the middle of a personal crisis, daughter needed a father. In an eye-opening moment, she realized that she still had one, one who just happened to smell nice and come in an unconventional shape. At twenty-four, daughter moved to Minneapolis and began living with Ellie.

"It was," Ellen says, "the greatest Christmas present in my life." And birthday?

"And birthday." Just this once, Christmas and birthday together was just fine.

Since her final surgery, Ellie has had three short romances, one with a man and two with women. She treasures one particular moment from the boudoir, when a woman smiled and said, "I love your doctor."

Ellie's lonely. She's not surprised that it's been hard.

"Look, I'm a transsexual, and this is Minneapolis, not Boston. Also, I'm fifty-eight. If I were thirty-two, I'd belong to a generation that's unafraid of being variant."

She's still looking. She gives lectures on the complicated experience of being transsexual. She has written a book, *Getting to Ellen*, published in 2013 by a small Minneapolis imprint. Its sales have been only in the hundreds, but the online reviews are grand, many from transsexuals at various stages of transition who see their story in hers.

Ellen is working again, although not making nearly as much as Ed Krug did. She is executive director of Call for Justice, a Minneapolis nonprofit she started.

Society provides free legal assistance for people accused of crimes—the Supreme Court compelled that—but those same people can be plumb out of luck when their legal troubles are of a different nature. It's a national problem called the justice gap, and that's what Call for Justice seeks to close. It cuts through red tape to find quality legal help for low- and moderate-income people in acute need of legal assistance of a noncriminal nature, such as those facing eviction or foreclosure.

Three years after the organization came into existence, the American Bar Association gave Call for Justice its Louis M. Brown Award, which goes yearly to the firm or organization in the United Sates that most creatively expands the public's access to legal services. Call for Justice has made a huge difference to small lives. It's about as far as you can get from Killer Krug, but a lot closer to Bobby Kennedy.

10:50 A.M., Dallas, Texas

The alarm came in as a code 3: house fire, 1303 Exeter Street. That address was in the most threadbare corner of Oak Cliff, a Dallas neighborhood of bygone notoriety, containing both the boardinghouse in which Lee Oswald lived and the movie theater in which he tried to hide. Code 3 meant get there yesterday, and the benighted address added a little extra urgency: Dallas firefighters, particularly those of color, sometimes moved a little faster to the poorest areas, where nobody had much and houses tended to be uninsured.

On this day, Richard Lane was the Nozzle. That is what the men at Engine Station 23 called the guy manning the hose. As the engine took the corner from Kushla onto Exeter, Lane couldn't see much smoke, which he knew might be illusory. Just as people sometimes die in cars that barely seem damaged, feeble-looking fires are sometimes the most deadly.

The house was a dingy white clapboard box—one story, pitched roof, attic crawl space, four small rooms. What little smoke Lane saw came from the front. There was a hydrant twenty feet away, but he realized it wouldn't be needed—there'd be enough water in the pumper of the truck. Anyway, containing the flames instantly became a secondary concern. Kids inside, said the paramedics, who'd driven up moments before.

There's a calculation firefighters sometimes face when time is essential and lives are at stake. Do you take an extra few seconds to wrestle on headgear with an oxygen feed, or do you just bull your way in, finding your good air in the mist near the nozzle of the hose? It's a primitive trick, but it usually works if you have the nerve to try.

On December 28, 1986, Richard Lane had an overabundance of nerve. He was thirty-five and felt at the top of his game. Just three weeks before, the Pop Warner Jr. Pee Wee division football team he coached, a squad of eight-, nine-, and ten-year-olds, won the state championship. In those days his self-confidence was also boosted by booze and black mollies, which is what people in the South call what people in the North call black beauties, which are amphetamines. The fact is, Richard Lane's life was careering toward a precipice, one he didn't foresee. He felt invincible.

No headgear. As it happens, the brash decision might have saved a life.

The driver kicked in the front door and Lane plunged in ahead of him, sucking air from the hose. On his hands and knees—to see, you have to get below the densest smoke—he knew he was in a bedroom. There was a structure that had once been a bed, but the wooden frame had burned clean through and the mattress was on the floor, aflame. The next few moments were hard to handle.

Lane thought he heard something, so he shushed his partner till he heard it again. It was part moan, part whimper, and Lane crawled toward it. On the floor was a baby half pinned under the mattress. Even in the instant he allowed himself to look, Lane could see the injuries were ghastly. The fire had eaten at the baby's limbs. It had scourged the baby's face. The little thing seemed more dead than alive.

With his Kevlar gloves, Lane picked up the smoldering child—a boy, though Lane couldn't have told you that at the time—and handed him out to paramedics through a window they had smashed in. They raced off to Parkland Memorial, the same hospital where, twenty-three years before, both JFK and his assassin had been pronounced dead. The fire had been of the deceptively lethal kind. It was contained in minutes. The house, at least, would be spared.

The cowboy culture of the 1980s urban firehouse rewarded the tight-lipped and punished the sensitive, which meant firefighters did not readily traffic in feelings. You didn't share. You didn't vent. Shit happens; you forget it and move on to the next shit. So by the Monday after the Sunday of the fire, Lane had managed to put this particular horror behind him. But one of his closest friends, a British-born nurse named Christine Owens, worked in the burn unit at Parkland Memorial. On that Monday, Lane happened to be talking to her, and she mentioned her most recent admission, a heartbreaker. It was a baby boy from Oak Cliff named Michael Anthony Green Jr., not yet sixteen months old, burned over three-quarters of his body, deeply disfigured, dreadfully disabled.

Lane waited for the inevitable. It didn't come. It took him a moment to process this.

"Are you telling me that he *lived?*"

––––––––

THE HOUSE STILL STANDS. The clapboard is rotting from age and damp. Some of the window treatments are soiled sheets. It's still tenanted by people living thin.

Across town, in a municipal government complex, the sign above Richard Lane's desk reads CASE MANAGER. He still works for the city of Dallas, but he's not a cowboy anymore. Life hasn't exactly humbled him, but it's delivered a sense of proportion and priorities. He's in charge of community outreach to the homeless, a job he's good at but that he knows he's lucky to have, considering.

Lane is an imposing man with a beguiling combination of humility and hubris. He mythologizes his life, both the good and the ugly, nimbly summoning milestone dates from memory. "Joined the Fire Department on February 28, 1977. Was terminated for cause in June 8, 1988. Returned to city employment on February 23, 2001."

Those last two dates represent his fall and his redemption. At the time of the fire at 1303 Exeter, Lane says, he was in entropy, spiraling toward a bad end, and things would intensify in the ensuing year and a half: "Lying, cheating, stealing, dealing. Booze, pills. Wet or dry, I got high."

Like the man himself, Lane's smile is big and off-center, owing to a missing front tooth. He could have had that fixed long ago but chose not to, he says, because it is so jarring. He got the gap during his hell-raising years, when he was not paying attention to his health, and now, every morning, his bathroom mirror reminds him of a place to which he has no intention of returning.

He'll return to the day of the fire, if reluctantly. There are things about it he has not talked about, not in detail, not even to his wife, not in thirty years.

The paramedics had said there were "kids" inside, and in this case the plural had been accurate. In that smoky furnace of a room, there had been two babies. When Lane first saw the burning bed, he said, it became clear that the mattress had detached first on one side, then the other, which meant that it had likely pitched the children onto the floor, then fell on top of them. Before he heard the whimper of the baby boy, he had found the baby girl. She was fully under the mattress, and she was beyond help.

How did he know that?

"It was obvious."

How?

Lane has a thick hide and a penchant for melodrama, but this is not easy. "When I touched her," he finally says, "she exploded."

She . . .

"Exploded. Edema effect. Swollen. Gases."

Lane looks away. "Only seen that one othe. time. Two too many."

Her name was Flocheri Chambers, nicknamed Candi. She was Michael Green's older sister, not yet three years old. Michael had evidently survived because of an accident of kinetics. He had rolled partly free of that lethal mattress.

Not long after the fire, Lane's life became what could be euphemistically termed "eventful." When his then-wife complained to him about his intemperate ways, he instructed her to kiss his ass, which turned out to be a tactical error because she had him busted on drug possession. He avoided jail through deferred adjudication, which meant he only had to stay out of trouble for a while, which turned out to be more difficult than you'd think. Violating his probation, he fled the country, becoming a fugitive in England, where he almost managed to start a new, unentangled life.

"Unfortunately," he says, "wherever I go, I take me."

And . . . ?

"Whupped a guy's ass." Eye roll. "Over a woman." When he was taken into custody, the fugitive warrant was discovered, which got him a trip back to the United States. ("Went to prison August 23, 1989 . . .") He served six months.

Today Lane is married to his best friend, which sounds like an empty cliché, except in his case it is literally true. His wife is Christine Owens Lane, the British-born burn-unit nurse who first told him that Michael Green had lived. ("I met her on December 10, 1980 . . .")

It was a platonic relationship from the get-go, but a solid one—so much so that when Lane got out of jail, Christine was the only person who was there for him. Their economic needs dovetailed, so they became hands-off roommates for years until the day that Lane informed Christine he felt ready to start a real adult life and buy a house, so he was moving out. That was the moment Christine burst into tears, the same moment that Richard Lane had his belated "duh" insight—yes, that particular province of the thickheaded male.

"That is when it hit me," he says, smiling.

When *what* hit you?

"That she wanted to be married."

And?

"That, you know. She loved me."

And?

Smile, teeth, gap.

"Yeah. I loved her."

Christine Lane runs the burn unit now. On December 28, 1986, she was an assistant there, and she remembers first seeing Michael Green shortly after he arrived.

"His injuries were devastating," she says. "We didn't know if he'd survive."

There is a ritual that is common to burn units but not to other hospital departments. It happens in cases with severely disfiguring injuries. Members of the family often do it themselves, unbidden, but if they don't, nurses sometimes encourage it. It is not for the sake of the patient so much as for the hospital staff.

Christine Lane explains: "In the first days we are dealing directly with the injuries and only with the injuries. You get the patient stabilized, resuscitate with fluids, debride dead tissue—you gently wash it away, you don't scrub it away because every cell is important. We applied salves, like silver sulfadiazine. We are dealing with amputations, drainage . . . What I'm saying is, it is easy to get lost in the job, to see the injury and not the person behind the injury."

The families seem to sense this, Lane says, so they bring in pictures to comfort everyone. They are "before" pictures.

"I vividly remember Michael's. His grandmother brought it in and we kept it next to his bed."

It was a framed portrait. It was intended, Christine says, to make sure that to the nurses Michael would be a little boy and not a . . . thing.

———

THE PORTRAIT IS STILL in its frame. It looks to be a studio shot, professionally composed. In it, Michael is about seven months old. He is in booties and a kitty-cat onesie, sitting up all by himself and looking proud of it, with a big toothless smile and the start of an earnest little Afro.

At the moment, the photo is being held out between two bony wrists. There are no hands.

"That was me," says Michael Anthony Green Jr. "But I never knew him. It's not like I miss him or regret I'm not him or anything. It's like I never was him."

The moment people first meet Michael Green is always—always—indelible. He's okay with a lingering stare, the way children instinctively react if they are young enough to be unencumbered by tact. He actually prefers that to the gape-and-quick-avert, which is typical of adults, as though something shameful or embarrassing is happening. He appreciates it when people ask him bluntly how he got the way he is, because it allays awkwardness and defuses tension and begins a dialogue. He reads these moments shrewdly. He has had all of his life to become expert in the semiotics of revulsion.

Above all, he welcomes frankness. So: His right eye is useless, a freaky-looking unblinking white marble sunk deep within a ruined lidless pink socket. He has no hands and no right ear. His skin-grafted face is leathery and seamed, as if sewn together from polygons of flesh, like a soccer ball. The surface is a spider work of veins. His nose is partly melted. His lower lip is pendulous and spatulate, which suggests stupidity, which is the cruelest and most misleading effect of all.

"This is what I am," he says simply, but there's a tacit, gritty question behind it: You got a problem with that?

WHEN MICHAEL MEETS you he preemptively extends his right wrist, so you have no choice but to take it, and that is when you realize there is some subtle articulation to the stump. He has turned his wrists into hands. There's a trigger point in each, two sweet bony spots that you can't see but that surgeons gave him, spots he can feel and manipulate, and that become the equivalent of index fingers, for hunt-and-peck. He's adroit with a smartphone. Somehow he types thirty-five words a minute on a real keyboard. The only thing he cannot do for himself, he informs you solemnly, is tie shoes with laces. This comes off not as false modesty but as a slight embarrassment. His life has been a defiant campaign to define himself as normal.

Michael says he always feels the presence of his older sister, the one lost in the fire, which is why he got his upper arm tattooed with her nickname. To show it, he must free his shoulder from beneath his shirt. It involves a quick and nimble move. It is impressive and almost mysterious to watch, like a man watching a woman removing her bra from under a sweater: Michael's elbows fly, lumps rise and fall, and as the shirt shifts you get brief flashes of his torso, which is when it becomes apparent that there are scars everywhere. He's one big scar. And these are just the ones you can see. He's gone through years of depression, social isolation, and deferred education, from all of which he has emerged, at thirty, a little late to independence and adulthood, but solidly there.

He is in the cluttered Dallas home of an aunt, with whom he has been staying while attending community college. He also has a job working as a personal assistant to a friend in the real estate business. That paycheck, and the Social Security disability payments he receives, will soon allow him the financial freedom to get his first solo apartment. He plans to finish school at a four-year college in Colorado and then go into business for himself. The nature of that career seems almost inconsequential to him as long as he is self-sufficient, which makes sense, because for Michael Green, self-sufficiency was never a given or even a likelihood.

Michael is slight and wiry. He limps a bit because he is missing toes on his left foot, which is a little clubbed, which makes it his better foot for soccer. Yes, he plays soccer. When you have a fierce will to compete but you haven't any hands, soccer is your sport. He teaches it as a counselor at Parkland Memorial's summer camp for burned kids, where he volunteers every year. His aggressive normalcy can be inspiring to children, most of whose disfigurements, while severe, are not as severe as his. Michael is the first to tell you that his soccer game is uneven—if you have only one eye, you lack depth perception, so he's offside a lot. But he plays with heartening intensity. Once he scored a goal for his high school team and got carried off the field in triumph. People love him.

It's all impressive, but it's not the most impressive thing about Michael Anthony Green Jr. The most impressive thing about him, because of the sense of self to which it speaks, is probably this: On Halloweens he works in a haunted house as a human gargoyle. He went to the management with the idea, and sold it. He'll strike a pose indistinguishable from all the manikins, mummies, werewolves and zombies and freaks, then suddenly lunge.

The tautness of Michael's stitched-together features gives him something of a flat affect, but you can find the funny in his good eye and in his words.

"I scare a lot of people for free," he says, "so why not get paid for it? I earn ten bucks an hour, and screams."

The story of Michael's recovery has two central characters, only one of whom you'll hear from here. Michael Anthony Green Sr. will not cooperate for any book that is not written by Michael Anthony Green Jr., which the father hopes will happen one day. Green Sr., a truck driver, has always had high aspirations for his son. He is a stubborn man, resolute to the point of hardness, a trait that Michael credits for keeping him whole.

"When I was little, he told me nobody was going to help me," Michael says. "It was tough love. He said it's all on me because that's just the way it is. He didn't do things for me. When I was four or five he told me I had to start walking on my own because I was too heavy. He said, 'I can't carry you no more,' and that was it. I walked."

It's hard to talk to Michael and prevent your eyes from making furtive side trips, inventorying the things he does not have or the things that are ruined. You do the best you can and it is not always successful, and when Michael catches you, he'll slyly let you know it.

"The *main thing* my father told me," he interjects pointedly at one such moment, "is that I have my brain, and that means I have everything I need."

Michael grew up with his father, not his mother, because the tragedy of the fire drove the Green family apart. The marriage had been unsteady, but what delivered the coup de grace was not so much the stress of coping with their grief and their surviving son's disability, but coping with the maddening, destructive, unnecessary, unavoidable human matter of assigning guilt.

Two theories exist about how that fire started, and they are mutually exclusive. What is indisputable is that infants had been left alone, unsupervised, in that room for at least a half hour. There had been an argument between his parents, Michael says, repeating family lore. Dad had walked out of the house, and Mom had gone to find him and bring him back.

What's in dispute is what happened next. Family tensions persist, and they color this debate. One theory is that Michael's mother, a chain smoker, left a cigarette burning. This is the contention of the paternal side of the family. Another theory involves a gas-fired space heater in the room on that chilly day, as the children dozed or played. A mischievous baby, Michael had been known to throw things into that heater, sometimes paper or other combustibles, and sometimes they ignited. This is the theory from the maternal side of the family.

The only surviving report from the Dallas Fire-Rescue Department is inconclusive. It is an antiseptic, abbreviated handwritten two-page form, with nearly as much space devoted to property damage ("Structural, $9,500, Contents, $1,500") as to loss of life and limb. As to the fire's origins, it is ambivalent. The official cause is listed as "child playing in heater," but the investigator appears to have had reservations. Under "form of heat of ignition," he scrawled: "Cig? Space heater?" Elsewhere he notes, "Mother smokes. Space heater on, but not close to bed. Somebody put something into heater, or left a cig ember." Those last five words are struck through with a single thin line, as though to create an official verdict but leave room for doubt. The entry ends: "Mother did not smoke in room, she said."

So all that is left is suspicion, which is an open wound.

Like her ex-husband, Cheri Chalmers refused to be interviewed for this book.

"It's been difficult to relate to my mother," Michael says. "We don't get along that well. She has a hard time letting go of the past. I feel she feels responsible but doesn't want to admit it."

BEFORE HE WAS FIVE, MICHAEL didn't know he was different from anyone else, but as grade school approached, his father knew he had to prepare him. So it was then that Michael learned his history and that he had become someone whom ignorant people might fear and demonize. That came to pass, with even greater savagery than most in the family had imagined. It turned out that for little kids facing the anxiety of school, it was irresistible to have a peer whom they could feel better than. It turned into a conspiracy of scorn. Today, Michael describes it as a cauterizing experience—painful, but not without value.

"When you can control yourself when kids are calling you a freak or a monster," he says, "you can control yourself anywhere at any time."

Attitudinally, he improved. But not all barriers were about

attitude. After high school, he could not get a job; it might have been more bearable had he been turned down explicitly on grounds that his appearance would disturb others. But he never was told that. What he was told, he believes, were well-intentioned lies that did not even leave him with the sullen satisfaction of nursing an obvious injustice.

At one point, as an adolescent, he had considered suicide. An ardent Christian, he figured he would do it in a passive way that would not consign him to hell: "I had heart problems, and I thought about just stopping taking my meds, and maybe God would not notice." It helped when a pastor directed him to Proverbs 3:5–6, which he quotes now from memory: "Trust in the Lord with all your heart and lean not on your own understanding; in all your ways submit to him, and he will make your paths straight." It took some pressure off.

There was another pressure release, a constant in his life, a force nearly as mighty as religion and almost as rewarding as soccer. Michael discovered that the configuration of instrumentation clusters on video game controller consoles allowed him to improvise effectively, using his wrists and thighs, which let him inhabit that world every bit as abled and competitive as anyone he was playing against. Plus, unlike most competitions, with video games you are not looking at your opponent—you're both focused on a common screen. For Michael, the games were a great leveler.

Seeing this, his father—an old-fashioned, staunchly analogue man to whom physical affection does not come easily—learned to play, too. For hundreds of hours as Michael Jr. was growing up, father and son played side by side—first Sega Genesis, and later

PlayStation, where they bonded over Tekken, a fighting game with a Gothic backstory that is not quite on point, but still oddly resonant: a scarred son's revenge upon a father who had tried to hurl him off a cliff to his death when he was an infant.

IN THE LEXICON of developmental psychiatry, *global self-esteem* is the phrase used to assess a person's overall sense of self-worth. It is quantifiable by behavioral markers. In adult survivors of permanent childhood disfigurement, this metric varies dramatically. It's a broad continuum that does not entirely conform to expectations. Love and family support matters, but not always. Ditto, financial resources. Therapy helps, except where it doesn't. It's almost as though in these cases, self-esteem hinges on something innate.

Opening Michael Green's Facebook page is nearly as startling as meeting him in person. It's full of photos of him, big ones. He favors close-ups, often with his temple pressed against the temple of a pretty woman friend or relative, and they are both smiling, and there are many different women. Here's one at a Dallas Mavericks game. Here's one at home, watching Super Bowl 50. All that's hidden are his eyes, usually behind dark glasses, but not always. For a time his profile picture was one taken at a restaurant, up close, tightly cropped, just his naked face, no glasses, that dead-fish eye, his hand stumps visible on the table, atop a fork and knife he cannot grasp. In your face. You got a problem with that?

Michael likes his women petite.

"I've dated plus-sized girls, and it didn't work out," he says.

He knows how that sounds coming from him, that it delivers a whiff of entitlement seasoned with hypocrisy. He's quick to annotate what he's just said: "It's not about looks. It's not about the girl. It's that I am a little guy." Taller and wider women make him feel less manly. "I want to be the man in a relationship."

(Of course that's still about looks. But why should Michael be held to a higher standard than three billion other guys?)

Dating, Michael says, involves a process. A woman has to get used to being with him, and if she can't, she can't. He holds no grudges and moves on.

"One of my older cousins said that if this wouldn't have happened, I would have had all the women I want. I said maybe, but I bet I wouldn't treat them right. It made me a better person. But I'm still cocky, and proud of it. I swagger. Sometimes people will be surprised, they'll go, like it's a surprise, 'Whoa, you're *arrogant*.' And I will say, 'Yes, I am, thank you.'"

ONE FRIDAY IN JUNE 2012, Michael Green went with a friend to Six Flags Over Texas, in Arlington. He'd been to the amusement park many times before, mostly for the roller coasters. On this day he waited in line for more than an hour to board the biggest coaster, the Texas Giant, a breathtaking ride with a drop of nearly 150 feet at a terrifying 70 degrees. But when Michael got to the front, the operator wouldn't let him on. It would be unsafe, he said, since Michael had no hands with which to steady himself or grip the handrail. Michael went to management. Management said no.

But there are shoulder restraints, Michael protested.

No.

But people who *can* hold on often *don't* hold on, Michael said. They let their arms fly, weightless.

Well, we don't encourage that.

But people *do* it, Michael said.

Still.

I've been here before, Michael said. You've always let me ride.

We have a new policy.

They wouldn't budge. Michael left, furious and humiliated. As a younger man, when he was still wrestling with who he was, that might have been the end of it. It wasn't the end of it.

"They had their regulations, but I had something, too," he says now, smiling, handlessly gesturing toward his chest. "I had . . . me." He phoned the local NBC affiliate. They sent a camera crew to his home. The resulting three-minute segment was powerful.

"A man who has overcome challenges his entire life tonight faces a new one . . ."

There is footage of Michael deftly typing on a laptop. Photos of him climbing a wall, riding a zip line.

"*They* don't know what I can do or can't do," Michael tells the camera. "There's nothing that I really can't do. I can cook, I can drive. . . ."

Of his treatment at the amusement park, he says, "It really hurt. It made me cry . . . it tore up the inside of me."

A disabilities lawyer told the interviewer that Michael probably has a lawsuit, if he wants one. Magnanimously, Michael said he would not do that.

It was a local TV story, but the Associated Press picked it up as a small news story. Several newspapers published it, including the million-plus-circulation New York *Daily News*.

Six Flags never relented, so Michael hasn't been back. He regrets he's lost access to that particular thrill, but the loss came with a certain frisson. He is not big on vengeance—for his own peace of mind, he's let go entirely the concept of settling scores—but he does figure that he managed to take Six Flags on a scary ride of its own, at least for a little while.

MICHAEL ATTRIBUTES SOME of his gumption and all of his empathy to the events of December 28, 1986. That leads to an unusual moment.

"Is it fair to say that, at least in some small ways, you've actually benefited by what happened?"

"They're not small ways."

"Well, I know you wouldn't say you were glad it happened, but . . ."

Fast, decisive: "I'm glad it happened."

It may be bravura or an aggressive form of denial, or it might be the literal truth. It is a conversation stopper, though, because it leaves nothing left to say.

MARCH 2016: MICHAEL Green has gotten a new full-time job. For those who do not know him, it would seem an unlikely position—one for which he might seem unqualified, one for which he would never apply. It's not as unlikely as, say, a mall Santa, but it's pretty unlikely. He's employed by a twenty-four-hour CVS pharmacy in Dallas, on the night shift, not as a clerk or a stock manager or someone who works in the back. The melted man without hands is a cashier.

"I saw a sign that said they were hiring," he said, "so I went in. I wanted to establish a record, proof that I can do this."

Proof for whom?

"Me, mostly," he says. "I'd run cash registers before, as a volunteer at the concession stands in my high school soccer games. They didn't think I could do it either, at first."

He can. He manipulates merchandise, aligns the bar codes with the scanner, bags products, makes change, gives change, engages in requisite banter, keeps up good cheer.

The late-night shift at an urban pharmacy can see a lot of suffering—people living on the margins or in the shadows, hollowed-out people, people in mental anguish, people in physical pain. CVS managers may well have known exactly what they were doing when they hired Michael Green for this particular job.

"Sometimes people tell me things," Michael says.

What things?

"One guy told me his story. Someone close to him had died, and he wanted a hug. Other people say other things."

Like what?

"Well, you know."

This isn't easy to get out when you are Michael Green, indomitable monster, relentlessly normal man.

"That I've, like, inspired them. To not give up."

———

THERE'S ONE LAST PIECE of business here, a lingering matter of fear.

Does Michael remember the fire?

Quickly: "No."

Then he looks down at that framed picture of the baby he once was. For a moment, he seems to be talking to it.

"I *know* I don't remember the fire. But sometimes I think I might. I've been having . . . dreams."

He looks back up. "There is fire all over, flames all around me, and I'm trapped in a corner and I can't get away."

The dreams bedevil him. They are terrifying on their own, of course, but what bothers him even more is that there's no way he can know for sure if this is a real memory or something manufactured by knowledge of his history and the inevitable anxieties attached to it.

He's checked it out a little. He knows adults generally remember nothing that happened before the age of three. It's called infantile amnesia. The immature brain is inept at encoding and storage. Earlier memories occur and are briefly retained, but get overwritten by newer memories at age six or seven. That's the way it's supposed to work. But what if the terror of what happened pressed it down deeper into his psyche and made it indelible, and it is just now surfacing?

This matters to Michael. He does not want this memory to be real.

Why does he care? He won't say, but consider this: The central narrative of his life, the one that has kept him sane and centered, is not a story of loss. You cannot grieve for what, emotionally, you feel you never had. He comes back to this time and again.

A memory, a solid memory, would make that first life real, on a punch-to-the-gut level. He does not want that memory. But he also wants to know the truth.

So.

Michael, there is a man you should meet someday, the fire-fighter who found you and picked you up and passed you out the window to other men. When asked about your dreams, he said right away, "He was on the floor near a window wall. Not trapped in a corner." The fire investigator's report also reflects this. He drew a crude map and marked where you were. Not a corner. So there's that.

Scientifically, research is clear: The earliest reliably real memories—specific scenes, recalled with the sort of vivid detail in yours—begin at the age of two. But in fairness, that fact alone doesn't mean your dream can't be based on your experience.

David Diamond is a professor of psychology, molecular biology, and physiology at the University of South Florida, and an expert on trauma and memory. He read this chapter right up to this line, and was asked about the likelihood that you were actually remembering the event.

There is a part of the brain called the amygdala, Diamond said, that can retain traumatic memories from even early infancy. But these are not visual memories. They are not delivered as scenes, with narratives, such as being surrounded by flames. The amygdala traffics only in feelings and emotions. The existence of this emotional memory center was predicted more than a hundred years ago by a French neurologist who had an elderly patient with advanced memory loss. The woman could remember things for only a few minutes. The doctor saw her every day, and every day he had to reintroduce himself to her, because she had no memory of his previous visits. One day, as he shook her hand, he stuck it with a hidden pin, and she cried out in pain. The next day she didn't know that she had ever seen him before and had no idea who he was, but when he held out his hand, she flinched.

The question is: Could you be remembering—really remembering—the feeling of terror, with that surviving memory in your amygdala triggering the rest of the dream?

"Ask Michael one question," Diamond said. "Ask him if in the dreams he is smelling smoke or burning flesh. There is a strong olfactory component to amygdala memories. It's what would remain."

So we're asking.

"No. It's just flames. Just visual."

In real life, does the smell of smoke or fire or burning meat particularly bother you—or even excite you?

"No."

Good. Diamond says you are reliving nothing in those dreams, Michael. They aren't memory, they're invention—no more real than a scary story told around a campfire. You can stop worrying. You're good to go.

12:05 P.M., Queens, New York City

The austere white adobe-style front wall of Our Lady of Grace Roman Catholic Church seems a bit familiar. It takes a moment to tweeze this from memory, but what it resembles more than anything else is the austere white adobe-style front wall of the Alamo.

As he walked up to the church, Ed Koch probably did not notice this architectural coincidence, but if he did, he'd have seen no irony in it. The mayor of New York had no reason to expect the siege that was coming. These were *his* people inside, working-class whites whose steadfast support had done much to put him into office three times. In a few years he'd be counting on them to win a fourth term, unprecedented for a New York mayor, an office dating back to 1665.

Today Koch was hoping these loyalists would help him defuse a volatile situation involving his bête noire, race relations. Koch was wearing a brown sports jacket, dark slacks, a white shirt, a striped red tie, and a dour countenance—something this famously feisty, happy-warrior mayor seldom displayed. He had reason to be grim.

A week earlier, late at night, a big rusty Buick Skylark containing four black men had coughed, wheezed, and hissed to a stop on a boulevard on the outskirts of Howard Beach. Dying transmission, dead water pump. While the driver stayed with the car, the three passengers left on foot to find a subway home to Brooklyn, where they would borrow another car and return with help. On the way, they stopped at a pizza joint and wolfed down some slices. As they left, they were descended upon by a dozen inebriated young white men brandishing baseball bats, a tire iron, and a tree limb. The mob called the three men niggers, and observed, unnecessarily, that they had chosen to visit the wrong neighborhood.

Outnumbered and in patently hostile territory, they scattered and ran. Two were caught and savagely beaten. One—Michael Griffith, a twenty-three-year-old part-time construction worker— was chased toward the shoulder of the Belt Parkway, a busy highway whizzing with traffic even late at night. "You *better* run, you black prick," shouted one of the mob. Buzzed on cocaine and scared silly, Griffith moved in the only direction that promised safety, for the simple reason that only a madman would pursue him: across the highway. He somehow zigged and darted across three lanes and jumped the divider, which is when his luck ran out, out there in the fast lane. He was struck by a car and thrown ten feet in the air and a hundred feet horizontally, dead on impact, his skull shattered like Limoges. The driver of the car— innocent, although initially suspected of being one of Griffith's pursuers—was the Jewish son of a New York City cop.

As things go in Gotham, you cannot get a much more fulminant set of facts.

Encouraged by a portly, pompadoured, ambitious young black Baptist minister and community organizer named Al Sharpton, street protests quickly ensued. Within days, many black people showed up in Howard Beach from around the city to protest the killing; many white locals showed up to demand that the black interlopers leave. The protesters and counterprotesters jostled and chest-bumped one another like high school boys spoiling for a fight. Racial epithets were flung. There were retaliatory attacks elsewhere in the city, both black on white and white on black. Media arrived from all over the country to cover this as the final, defining event of what had been a very bad year for race relations in the United States.

It was clearly a time for politicians of all persuasions, from all places, to rise above the ugliness and bury their ideological differences for the common good. Instead, Mayor Koch said he expected horrors like this only to happen "in the Deep South," which caused Mayor W. W. Godbold of Brookhaven, Mississippi, to say of Koch to the local newspaper: "That Jew bastard. I believe that Jews like him that get in this office don't know what they are talking about."

In short, things were going to hell, lickety-split. Like any good mayor, Koch knew he had healing work to do, and so, hours before he approached the Catholic church, the mayor had given a morning interview to Lesley Stahl on CBS's Sunday talk show *Face the Nation*. Koch had appealed for calm, compassion, and reason, and urged the appointment of a national commission on racism. The interview would ultimately show Koch to be well intentioned, well spoken and, well, tin eared—all three being hallmarks of his approach to race. It was simply who he was and had always been.

Koch had first been elected in 1977 with the support of New York's black community, which knew of and appreciated his bona fides: As a young liberal politician, Koch had risked life and limb to march with people of color in the South during 1960s civil rights protests. But as mayor, he would soon squander much of that goodwill through one of his first administrative moves, the closing of Sydenham Hospital in Harlem. The city was in a financial death spiral and the administration had little choice but to shutter money-hemorrhaging institutions; the poorly managed Sydenham was an obvious target. But it had also long been an oasis of mercy for the African American community, and one of the first hospitals anywhere in New York to hire black physicians. The new mayor was arguably right on the facts and decent in his intentions—he'd planned to replace Sydenham with more accommodating local clinics—but he had not wisely weighed the political ramifications. He seldom did. And that affront was never fully forgotten by the city's black population.

Talking to Lesley Stahl, Koch had said all the right things, pushing all the right buttons, sounding exactly like the concerned public official he was, until he committed an odd unforced error. Unprompted, he said, "Those who are racists and bigots will look to the fact that Michael Griffith had a history of involvement with the law and a bullet of several years' standing in his chest—but they didn't know that when they caused him to die. So irrespective of his background—and I don't know enough about it to pass judgment on it . . ."

It was a peculiar moment. Technically, Koch was right about the bullet, but his implication was wrong. Griffith did have a pellet in his chest, but it was not of long standing—he'd gotten it just months before his death—and it was no more a sign of a character flaw than would be a slug received by a convenience store clerk during a robbery. Griffith had been unarmed and not physically threatening when a neighbor with whom he was quarreling drew a gun and popped him. But more significantly, the mayor was disclosing a fact that was not universally known— what he'd said looked like a clumsy, cynical backhanded bit of blaming the victim.

It wasn't that, exactly. Koch was just being Koch. Unnerved by Sydenham and other early missteps, he remained sure of his judgment—he was always sure of his judgment, sometimes maddeningly so—but unsure of how to approach the complex emotional politics of race. So he tended to grasp for false equivalencies: push-pull, give-take, on-the-other-hand rhetoric designed to mollify both sides but sometimes succeeding only in offending everyone equally. As Lesley Stahl would recall thirty years later: "Generally, I was struck by how he always seemed to be straining. Every time he mentioned that whites had done something, he was trying to come up with something blacks did. He was walking a tightrope and having difficulty doing it."

And now, just after noon on December 28, 1986, Koch was tiptoeing on that same tightrope right into a white Roman Catholic church in Howard Beach, Queens.

The plain front of the church yielded to an elegant, commodious sanctuary still festooned with white poinsettias from Christmas. Koch was arriving with another push-pull message—that he didn't blame the community, but that racial prejudices existed and had to be identified and confronted forcefully. He expected acceptance and cooperation. These were *his people.*

As he moved down the aisle toward the pulpit, he couldn't help but notice something disturbing. Some parishioners were taking one look at him, glowering, and . . . leaving.

Koch didn't seem to understand a fundamental truth: that on matters of race, logic doesn't matter as much as emotion, and that a person's self-image is something he or she will jealously and fiercely guard in the face of almost any challenge, even contravening facts. Days before, Koch had publicly declared the death of Michael Griffith—still unsolved, the details still not entirely clear—a "lynching." Lynchings don't happen in nice communities.

"Go home!" someone shouted at the mayor.

"You don't belong here," someone else shouted.

"Resign!" someone else shouted.

Koch had not yet even reached the lectern.

When he got there, the mayor tried to retake control. He chose the high road. "There is a discourse that should be had more often," the mayor began, "where one can talk about the anxieties and the fears and the frustrations. That's what I'd like to talk about and to have you, if you will, respond."

They responded. The dialogue quickly degenerated into a shouting match. When Koch lectured the group about the evils of racism, it did not go well. Members of the congregation accused him of defaming their community and of using their church as a political prop.

Koch was clearly taken aback. He'd pushed. It hadn't worked. So now he pulled.

"Those people who beat and ultimately caused the death of a

black man," the mayor said, "they don't represent you, they don't. Absolutely not."

"So why are you here?" bellowed a middle-aged woman in a brown checked coat. Mary Slater had lived in Howard Beach twenty-one years. "We are not a racial community," she scolded, wagging a finger at the mayor, "but you labeled us!" Koch tried to respond but was drowned out by cheers and applause.

The mayor had struck a nerve; nothing provokes anger quite so much as venturing too close to an uncomfortable truth. Howard Beach was not, in fact, guiltless of casual racism. The neighborhood had no mayor of its own, of course, but it did have respected authority figures of a sort. New York at the time had five Mafia families, and the dons of three of them lived in Howard Beach, as did John Gotti, the don of all the dons. The American Mafia has never been a racially welcoming organization—it has a deeply ingrained contempt for African Americans—and this influence on the locals seemed to give even regular churchgoers, people who prayed and confessed and generously filled the collection plate, license to say unsayable things. And so when Slater continued, no one shushed her:

"Where are you when we women are going to work and we are being robbed and mugged, mainly from these poor, underprivileged people coming into our neighborhood?" she sneered, to more shouts of support.

"You want another racial war?" another woman yelled at Koch. "You want another sixties on your hands? Leave it alone! Leave it alone!"

Koch responded that he couldn't, that racism is like a cancer, and that black people suffer from it disproportionately "because you can single them out by the color of their skin, whereas you do not know the others." As Joyce Purnick, writing for *The New York Times*, reported, this line was almost completely lost because the mayor's voice was drowned out by boos.

Tom Wolfe's acerbically influential novel about greed and racism in 1980s New York—*The Bonfire of the Vanities*—would not be published until the following October. Much of it would be dead-on and prescient, and reflective of the times. This included the opening scene, in which the never-named mayor of New York—a man not so loosely modeled after Koch—arrives at a community meeting in an African American neighborhood during a time of particular racial tension. To the mayor's self-righteous indignation, he is treated with disrespect . . . and worse. Protesters begin shouting him down, chanting what the mayor initially hears as "Gober! Gober! Gober!" but which he eventually figures out is "Goldberg." The people, *his* people, his *constituents,* were calling him a kike.

There was a small taste of that same poison on this day with Koch in Howard Beach. He felt anti-Semitism, and the *Times* caught the briefest glimpse of it, too. One woman who had arrived with her elderly mother refused to go into the church and headed home when she saw Koch was there. She snarled to her mother, loud enough for a *Times* reporter to overhear: "Let him go to a synagogue."

And as Koch left, obviously shell-shocked and no doubt righteously indignant, he heard something else. The newspapers didn't catch it, but Koch heard it, and he told colleagues about it afterward. He said a woman hissed at him that she wanted to cut out his tongue and throw his body into Jamaica Bay.

BY ALL ACCOUNTS, Koch's appearance had been well meaning but an utter fiasco that did more to inflame tensions than to quell them. In the end, however, justice was served. Members of the mob that chased Michael Griffith to his death were eventually put on trial, and three were convicted of crimes ranging from simple assault to manslaughter. The ringleader, a sullen, baby-faced high school student named Jon Lester—he had goaded the others by shouting "kill the niggers" and never showed a moment of remorse; the judge described him as having "no redeeming qualities"—was sentenced to ten to thirty years in prison. As he left the courtroom in custody, Lester—who was seventeen but looked years younger—turned to his supporters and predicted, "I will be acquitted on appeal." In his 1990 book *Incident at Howard Beach: The Case for Murder*, prosecutor Charles J. Hynes writes that at that moment the whole courtroom, packed with white locals, gave Lester a standing ovation.

No, time doesn't heal all wounds. But it can deliver an opportunity to think and feel and reassess, even to grow. Jon Lester's appeal was denied. He served fifteen years in prison, during which time he earned a high school equivalency degree, wrote an apology to Michael Griffith's mother, learned to play the guitar, and turned that apology into a song. At twenty-five, in a prison interview, he said, "I can't stand racists . . . they're small and frightened and ignorant. . . . This is what education does. It opens the world."

After his release in 2001, he was deported to his native England, where he developed a successful career as an electrical engineer, raised a family, and committed suicide at forty-eight, tormented by a past with which he could no longer live.

And what of Mayor Koch and the legacy of time?

Koch would have been well served by an advance team before his visit to the church. They might have taken the temperature of the community and advised their boss not to make this appearance, at least not just then, or to deliver a less confrontational message. But Koch didn't always use advance teams—he tended to believe he had all the answers and all the communication skills he needed, and in particular, in matters of race, that he had long ago proved his abhorrence of racism. This was not a man plagued with self-doubt, but that meant he also was not deepened by it, made resilient by it, prodded to self-improve. Self-doubt can be a valuable tool. Koch did more lecturing than listening. That did not always work to his advantage.

What should Koch have done? A few days into the new year, in the Long Island newspaper *Newsday*, the Pulitzer Prize–winning columnist Murray Kempton offered a not-so-gentle suggestion. With Koch clearly in mind, Kempton, sometimes called the conscience of the city, wrote: "We can trace much of what has gone wrong in the Howard Beach case until now to the occupational incapacity of all parties to shut up when they ought to."

Three years later, Koch was running for that unprecedented fourth term as mayor. Race relations in the city had further deteriorated; this was the year of the Central Park jogger gang rape, a brutal crime city officials were all too ready to pin on five black teenagers—kids who turned out to be innocent. Racial tensions were so inflamed in 1989 that the borough president of Manhattan, a black man named David Dinkins, decided to challenge

Koch in the Democratic primary. Today, Dinkins said in an interview that he really didn't want to be mayor, but he felt it was in
the city's best interests, if there was any chance for racial healing.
Identity politics, if wielded benevolently, can sometimes work.

Dinkins had correctly gauged the electorate. At one point, he
was ahead of Koch in the polls by as many as 17 percentage
points, but as the election approached, the incumbent mayor was
rapidly gaining ground and might even have surged ahead. Koch
was drawing on twelve years of general goodwill, goosed by his
scrappy personality, which had always appealed to New Yorkers.
The guy was a piece of work. This was the man who, at his first
inaugural, said: "I'm the sort of person who will never get ulcers.
Why? Because I say exactly what I think. I'm the sort of person
who might give other people ulcers." Confessing to the folly of his
early über-liberal stances, he once called himself "Mayor Culpa."
His most famous line was delivered in public appearances, hundreds of times, in which he always led with his chin: "How'm I
doin'?" That sort of thing goes over well in the Big Apple.

Koch's press secretary at the time, George Arzt, remembers
what changed things. It happened on August 23, 1989. "I was in
a car with Ed when we heard about Bensonhurst, and we went
all silent. We realized everything was about to get much more
difficult."

In New York, you don't need to elaborate on what Bensonhurst means, even today. It was Howard Beach 2.0. A sixteen-
year-old black kid named Yusuf Hawkins went to that Brooklyn
neighborhood to look at a used car for sale. Whites in the area—
almost all of them Italian Americans—mistook him for a black
youth who'd had the effrontery to court a local white girl. They

descended on him with baseball bats and other weapons. They chased him and beat him. It was a bullet that killed him.

Koch had reacted the way Koch had always reacted, with infuriating certitude about his own judgment. He had learned nothing. As Arzt remembers it—and Arzt remains an admirer of Koch—the mayor made a few missteps. As always, he had refused to walk gingerly on eggshells. He waded in with hobnail boots.

Just as with Howard Beach, there had been street protests, and they were equally fractious and equally ugly. White demonstrators taunted black demonstrators by brandishing watermelons. It was *that* ugly.

During the final days of the campaign, Koch unwisely took on the popular Sharpton, criticizing him for holding demonstrations in Bensonhurst because, Koch said, such activism only inflamed tensions. Another white candidate, city comptroller Harrison J. Goldin, responded to this by calling Koch a "yahoo mayor" intent on silencing honest dissent, like southern politicians during the civil rights protests. Dinkins, shrewdly, stayed away from the fray.

Arzt remembers that the perpetually confrontational Koch directly confronted Dinkins, saying that he, the mayor, was as good as Dinkins was at "bringing people together." He wasn't, and claiming so made this deficiency seem even more glaring. Even his supporters knew that. "Once you play in another person's ballpark," Arzt says sadly, "you have a problem. It wasn't so much a problem in the African American community. It was a problem in the *Jewish* community—they *wanted* someone who could bring people together."

As the election approached, Koch was weary. In an unusually introspective moment, he told Leland T. Jones, a press aide, that he wanted to win, but that if he lost to Dinkins, he wanted to lose big so Dinkins would seem to have legitimacy with the citizenry. That sort of humility was very unlike Koch.

And if he really meant it, he got what he wanted. He lost big.

AN HOUR AFTER KOCH'S debacle at the church, a far cheerier event was playing out in downtown Pine Bluff, Arkansas. It was at the old Jefferson County Courthouse, which happened to look nothing like the Alamo. Perversely, with its clean vertical lines and steeple-like central clock tower, it more resembled a church.

Three hundred locals were gathered in and around the building. Confederate reenactors, in full regalia with Civil War–era rifles, bayonets fixed, presented arms at the command of an officer in military gray, wielding a saber. There was a drummer boy.

The pomp was dramatic, the circumstance even more so. The crowds were bearing witness to the return of a treasured local relic long thought to have been lost or destroyed.

In 1861, Jefferson County had mustered into service forty of their finest young men to serve in the army of the South as a unit called the Jefferson Guard. At that time each local company had a flag-bearer, which meant having a flag. That job was given to a young woman named Etta Bocage, daughter of Judge William Bocage, the most important man in Pine Bluff. Etta became Jefferson County's Betsy Ross. She spent three months embroidering the flag on a field of blue silk, bordered in golden silk.

It was an impressive thing, though not recognizable today as anything remotely representing the Confederacy. The familiar starred blue X on a red field had not yet been adopted, and at any rate, there was nothing official about this: Arkansas had not yet seceded, though the rebel sentiments of the citizenry were clear. Thus there were no rules. This flag could have been absolutely anything, and basically it was a little bit of everything.

It was four by eight feet. On one side was a Latin slogan, *Fiat Justitia Ruat Coelum,* meaning "Let Justice Be Done Though the Heavens Fall." On the other side was the only illustration: a green, white, and brown cotton plant, topped by fifteen crude stars—a number no more easily reconciled with the Confederacy than the design itself. Beneath this was *Regnant Populi,* which is the Arkansas state motto. It translates to "The people rule." It all meant what it meant, whatever that was.

Etta herself had shyly presented it to the troops, gathered in Tennessee, shortly before they rode off to battle. The moment was chronicled by a Memphis newspaper in the flowery, war-besotted argot of the day:

> The fair donor of the flag, Miss Bocage . . . is one of the loveliest women it has been the good fortune of those present to gaze for a time whereof the mind runneth not to the contrary. Tall, dark eyed and dark haired, graceful in every movement, it was not surprising that the soldiery greeted her with so much joy and enthusiasm . . . Captain Carlton, as brave and handsome a soldier as can be found in any corps, received the beautiful gift.

With the flag, amidst the pomp, the men rode off. They fared well for a time, and then dreadfully. One of their eventual destinations, in April of 1862, was Shiloh, where they were slaughtered like rabbits. Other defeats followed. Of the forty men who left Pine Bluff, only eight would return. The flag was not with them. It had evidently been seized from Captain Carlton, who had been captured by the 15th Illinois Cavalry in 1864 and served out the rest of the war as a prisoner. As far as he knew, the flag was either destroyed or carried off to parts unknown.

And that would have been the end of the story, but for some sharp detective work in 1984 by James Carter Watts, a local amateur historian in Pine Bluff. Working on a history of the Jefferson Guard, Watts traced the flag a thousand miles to the north, to Illinois, where it had been kept for 120 years at the Springfield Armory, rotting, wrapped in newspaper. He traveled there to take a peek. Yep, same flag.

Arkansas state officials—led by ambitious young governor Bill Clinton—politely requested its return. Illinois state officials politely declined; apparently, the state regarded spoils of war as, well, spoils of war. Things got a little strange. In verifying the location of the flag, Arkansas historians noted that Illinois still was in possession of the handsome wooden leg of the Mexican general and dictator Antonio López de Santa Anna, who was, depending on your nationality, either the hero or the villain of the siege of that selfsame Alamo. The leg had been seized by a company of Illinois soldiers in 1847 during what, depending on your nationality, was either the Mexican War or the Invasion of Mexico. The Illinois soldiers surprised the Mexican general at camp and he fled in such haste he left the prosthesis behind. Apparently both Mexico and Texas had wanted the leg returned for decades but had never got anywhere with their requests. If a sovereign nation and a huge and powerful state failed to persuade Illinois to cough up confiscated property, what chance did a pissant little chicken-farm hick state like Arkansas have?

Somewhat better, it turns out, because the chicken-farm hick state had Bill Clinton as its governor, and, by 1986, Illinois had Big Jim Thompson as its governor, and these were two of the finest schmoozers this glorious republic has ever produced. Both by themselves and through intermediaries, they schmoozed. They hondled. Political implications were weighed. Accommodations were made. Skids were greased, and the deal was done. The flag would be returned "on loan" and put on display in the Jefferson County Courthouse to celebrate Arkansas's sesquicentennial.

So after a restoration project, here it came marching downtown on December 28, 1986. The ceremony managed to be both festive and solemn, which was an achievement. Huzzahs were raised. The banner was unfurled. Oohs and aahs. Dignitaries speechified. The main speaker was historian David Perdue, a courtly man who, with Watts, had done much to get the flag back.

This was 1986, long before serious controversies would erupt over the meaning of the Confederacy, the nature of treason, the ghastliness of slavery, and the appropriateness of retaining and celebrating Confederate monuments and mementos. But Perdue was not blind to the historical complexities here, and as a serious historian, he was not about to ignore them. However, he was also no one's fool: This was a joyous occasion and he did not want to be the guy spraying the shit mist. So he mapped out a judicious, eloquent middle ground within which he could live. It was not daring, but it was at least ambiguous:

"Preserve it always," he told the crowd, "and let it serve as a precious relic of a bygone era, a memorial to those who died while carrying it, a lesson in history for our children of a dark and bloody time."

Perdue ended on a note of harmony, solidarity, and optimism. He said he believed the brave members of the Jefferson Guard would have wanted the people present to not only appreciate their flag but also Old Glory. "We are one nation now," Perdue said, "and we are whole and healthy."

This fine sentiment was immediately, if jocularly, undercut. A state government official—an emissary of Clinton's—noted in a speech that although the flag was technically a loaner, he figured Illinois would have a hard time if they tried to retrieve it. "They'll never get it back," he said, and pointing to the armed Confederate reenactors, added, "If they try to take it, we'll load up those muskets and blast them out of the courthouse."

Cheers and laughter. And then the event was over.

If anyone noticed the two ghosts at the courthouse that day, no one talked about them, and no one wrote about them in the newspapers. But they were there, looking on. Their names were John Kelley and Culberth Harris.

If you google "Jefferson County Courthouse" and "lynching," you learn what had happened there, in that later spot of celebration and pride, on February 14, 1892. A mob of three hundred men from Pine Bluff met a train carrying Kelley, a black man who had just been charged with having killed a Pine Bluff businessman a few days before. The mob grabbed Kelley from authorities and frog-marched him to the Jefferson County Courthouse, where a crowd of a thousand had assembled. He was brought to the same front steps of the courthouse where the flag celebration would take place nearly a century later. The terrified Kelley was given a moment to defend himself, and he said he was innocent. Then the mob hanged him from a telephone pole across the street. As he strangled, they used him for target practice. A hundred shots were fired.

Then, the mob descended on the jail and demanded the release of a second black man who was accused of being Kelley's accomplice. Culberth Harris was also given a chance to defend himself. He said he was nowhere near Kelley and knew nothing of the crime. Then he was hanged from the same pole, his body riddled with bullets from the same guns.

In Jefferson County, as with some other places in the South, the war had not really ended with the surrender at Appomattox. The legacy of all this was complex, perhaps best summarized by a somewhat disturbing passage in the *Pine Bluff News* dissecting the mood of the crowd on the joyous day in 1986 that the flag was returned: "What might be harshly viewed as simply a decorated piece of cloth by some brought forth stirrings of loyalty and pride within the audience members. It was as though a part of themselves had been returned after being sacrificed in defense of their principles." Exactly which "principles" remained unspecified.

Also unstated was a certain obvious fact that no local newspaper seemed to have immediately noticed—or if they did, they did not seem to think it worthy of mention.

Pine Bluff in 1986 was a vibrant and diverse small city; 40 percent of its population was African American. And yet it took two days before Pulitzer Prize–winning editorial writer Paul Greenberg—a man accustomed to stating difficult truths— observed this in his article in *The Pine Bluff Commercial*:

"Amidst all of the hundreds of people crowding the courthouse Sunday afternoon, there was not a single black face."

THIS WAS NOT THE CASE at 6:30 P.M. on December 28, 1986, when large buses carrying large men converged on a large steakhouse in Scottsdale, Arizona.

Some of the buses were filled with clean-cut white guys, mostly—the sort of well-mannered gents who addressed their elders as *sir* and, especially, *ma'am*. They were wearing suits and ties. The other buses were filled with sullen-looking urban black guys, mostly—the sort of guys who are aware of how they are stereotyped as thugs by much of white America and aren't entirely displeased by the discomfort this brings. These men were wearing black sweatsuits, which at a critical moment some planned to theatrically unzip to reveal combat fatigues underneath. Ergo, this means war. We will kill you.

These were, respectively, members of the Penn State Nittany Lions and the University of Miami Hurricanes, the two best college football teams in the country, each undefeated. In a few days they would meet in Tempe in the Fiesta Bowl in a battle for the undisputed national college football championship. The game would set new records for TV viewership of any college sports ever, in large measure because of the collision of cultures and colors. It was a compelling story line, if a disturbing one for its racial overtones, but it also seemed to crystallize the restive, polarized racial mood of the country. Even when some sportswriters were offensively calling the impending game a showdown between good and evil, both teams seemed to revel in those roles. The public was gobbling it up.

Much of this was deliberate hype, but the fact is, there *were* stark differences in culture between the two teams. The Hurricanes *did* cultivate their outlaw, badass image. They *did* talk trash, taunted the other team after touchdowns, ran up scores to humiliate their opponents. They broke penalty yardage records for dirty play. Their most fearsome defensive player, three-hundred-pound lineman Jerome Brown, age twenty-one, *did* have a four-year-old son and *did* carry a gun on campus. *Sports Illustrated*'s Rick Reilly wrote that the team was known for "fights and fraud and unsavory shenanigans. . . . Miami may be the only squad in America that has its team picture taken from the front and from the side." *Sports Illustrated did* vote the 1986 Hurricanes the all-time "most hated team in sports." Badass.

The Nittany Lions *did* cultivate a goody-goody, fuddy-duddy image. They *did* stress the importance of team over individuals, of modestly not calling undue attention to oneself; pointedly, their uniforms didn't have the players' names on the back. *Sports Illustrated* had just named their coach, Joe Paterno, Sportsman of the Year—a tribute, mostly, to his unchallenged image as a builder of fine, upstanding young men. It was football gospel that Paterno's teams won not because they were filled with great individual players, but because they were filled with people of character and self-discipline who were obedient to team strategy. *Good* boys.

The Hurricanes, led by the slick, flamboyant, flagrantly permissive Jimmy Johnson, were loaded with colorful individuals with huge egos. Many of them were future NFL stars, including Brown, and Hall of Fame wide receiver Michael Irvin, and quarterback Vinny Testaverde, who had just won the Heisman Trophy and was about to be picked first overall in the NFL draft, and who would be headed off to a twenty-one-year career in the NFL. Meanwhile, the quarterback for the Nittany Lions was some noodle-armed guy named John Shaffer, who would never don a pro uniform and would eventually become an executive at Goldman Sachs.

(Some of the agreed-upon generalities about these teams were too facile: Penn State had more than a few black players, and Paterno's team was cited for plenty of unsportsmanlike conduct penalties of their own. They played rough, too. But this was about appearances and public imagery, and the images were rock solid.)

AS THE GAME APPROACHED, the Fiesta Bowl committee was doing its best to take this collision of stereotypes and exploit it. On this evening they had arranged for the teams to sup together at a steak fry and then asked them to offer good-natured skits and roasts of the other team.

A roast! What could possibly go wrong?

After dinner, it was time for all that good-natured fun. Nittany Lions punter John Bruno, a white guy, was among the first to speak.

Bruno was by most accounts no racist; his black teammates liked him. But he was trying to navigate very, very treacherous terrain, the no-man's-land of race. And he gamely tried to do it with humor, which required a deft touch he did not have. Literally within seconds he'd bumbled into a trip wire.

Ostensibly bragging about the healthful state of race relations at Penn State, he said "We've come a long way in twenty years. We even let the blacks eat with the whites."

This did not go over well. Ominously, Jerome Brown stood up. He unzipped down to the combat gear, as did some of his teammates.

(This was deliberate provocation. The team had first appeared in these uniforms when they descended from the plane upon arriving in Phoenix. They said they were "on a mission." It had caused a stir. Now they were doubling down.)

Brown growled: "Did the Japanese sit down and eat dinner with Pearl Harbor before they bombed them? We're outta here!"

And they were. The entire team rose as one and bulled their way out into the night. The moment was captured in a photo in the next day's *Miami Herald*, a head-on shot of five angry men. With the rest of the team behind them, Brown and four of his African American teammates are in the foreground, striding purposefully forward, dour and determined, looking as though they are about to kill and eat the photographer. Some are in combat fatigues, some are in leather jackets, and almost all, for some reason, wear big, floppy cowboy hats. In a separate photo we see Brown next to a glowering Vinny Testaverde, who is dressed in camo, black gloves, and wraparound sunglasses, out there in that almost-moonless night. He is apparently trying to look—as best a palefaced white man can—angry and black.

At this moment, back in the steakhouse, a brief shocked silence prevailed. It was broken when John Bruno found his voice and deadpanned to delighted teammates: "Didn't Japan *lose* that war?" The media ate it up.

"When they walked out," said Tim Johnson, a black defensive lineman for Penn State, "that was the moment where the heat turned up one hundred percent. I was ready to go find our locker room, suit up, and play right now. It's on. It is *on*."

In truth, no one could quite explain what had actually happened. There had been, obviously, a grotesque failure of communication— a clumsy effort at cross-racial camaraderie had backfired. But was it *that* bad? Bruno was obviously not serious; after all, his black teammates like Tim Johnson were in the room, too, and they said they took no offense. Was the reaction faux outrage, merely a bit of street theater—essentially a publicity stunt? Miami players later conceded they had been planning a walkout of some sort.

But part of it was deadly serious. Brown made that clear with the next thing he said, outside the steakhouse, near the buses. It was blunt, even cruel, and it seemed to preclude any possibility of anyone anywhere taking any of this as a joke: "One thing I really question? I question the intelligence of the black players on the Penn State team," Brown said. "How can they take a racial slur like that?"

FIVE DAYS LATER came the Game. Miami went into it as seven-point favorites. They not only didn't cover the spread, they lost the game. Final score, 14–10, Penn State.

Good defeated evil!

Not so fast. Appearances can deceive. Some of the bad boys turned out not to have been so bad after all. Miami's star running back Alonzo Highsmith is now the widely respected vice president of player personnel of the Cleveland Browns. Free safety Darrell Fullington contributes his time to the Muscular Dystrophy Association. Many of their teammates went on to successful, scandal-free NFL careers.

And on the other side of the ball? The undisputed hero of the game was not even suited up to play. He was stalking the sidelines. This was Jerry Sandusky, Penn State's brilliant, bucktoothed defensive coordinator. In preparing for the game, Sandusky had had an inspired thought: He guessed Miami would want to showcase Testaverde's passing prowess to make him more attractive in the upcoming draft. Moreover, Sandusky had also heard Testaverde was color-blind. He figured that, if under pressure and facing complex, shifting coverage, the kid might get confused by which uniform was which.

So Sandusky decided to drop as many as eight defenders into pass coverage, daring Miami to run the ball. As he had predicted, they didn't: This was going to be a Testaverde highlight reel, by God, and handoffs to tailbacks don't make for compelling video. So Vinny kept slinging the ball into that crowded, crisscrossing mess downfield, and—unsurprisingly—was intercepted five times, the last one with eighteen seconds left on the clock, sealing the win.

It turns out that the hero of the game, to put it diplomatically, did not represent the forces of good. In 2012, Jerry Sandusky, at age seventy-four, was convicted of raping several young boys over a period of at least fifteen years. Some were twelve years old or younger. Sandusky's thirty-to-sixty-plus-year sentence means he will never leave prison. And Paterno, the builder of fine upstanding young men, would later die in disgrace when it became clear he had abetted his defensive coordinator's predations. Paterno had been alerted to them in 1998—and possibly as early as 1976—and did next to nothing.

The issue of race that was fought out ineptly and inconclusively and pointlessly on the day of the steak fry was, of course, universal. But in this case it was conducted in microcosm, as single-warrior combat between two headstrong young men.

One more fact underscores the emptiness and the pointlessness of the events of that evening. Six years after the steak fry, both Penn State's Bruno and Miami's Brown lost their lives. They died within two months of each other, each at twenty-seven. Bruno lost a battle with metastatic melanoma. Brown lost control of his Corvette ZR1 and hit a utility pole. He'd been driving at badass breakneck speed, as he often did.

THE FINAL WORD HERE belongs to Ed Koch, the earnest, indefatigable New York City mayor with that notoriously tin ear on race. December 28, 1986, had been a dramatic experience for him—humiliating, and no doubt infuriating. His ordeal got into newspapers all over the country. This was the portentous dilemma of America in the mid-1980s, individualized for one aging New York Jew: racial resentment, the tribal instinct to dehumanize and attack. It must have been as scarring an experience for Koch as it had been, and would continue to be, for the nation as a whole.

Koch wasn't a bad man. His intentions were decent, even noble. So maybe there's something the rest of us can learn from the quarter century he spent stewing over the unforgettable events of that day, the beginning of the end of his political career. Had he rethought his actions? Did he have any insights to share now, at the age of eighty-eight? What did it all teach him, ultimately, that would help the rest of us stop remaking the same mistakes?

He was asked about that in an email on January 22, 2013, twenty-seven years from the day it happened.

His answer in its entirety, delivered the following day by email, read:

I honestly don't have a recollection of that church appearance.

He didn't mention that he was typing from a hospital bed, where he was still lucid but gravely ill.

Ten days later, he was dead.

1:58 P.M., Miami, Florida

The parade was about to begin, and he was at the front of it, seated on the back of an open-top convertible, test waving, ready to roll. If he was nervous, it wasn't showing. A Vietnam veteran with combat experience, Prentice Rasheed prided himself on his sangfroid.

Nobody *expected* trouble, exactly. Miami seemed to embrace the man. But it was impossible to ignore that this was a motorcade, with all the forbidding historical implications. It would be a slow-moving procession through downtown, with plenty of rooftops and narrow casement windows and big spatulate palm fronds that could provide cover for a sniper. Exactly three months earlier, Prentice Rasheed had fried a man to death. Did the dead guy have friends? Would they be out there?

The King Mango Strut was a yearly parade in the funky Miami neighborhood of Coconut Grove, first organized four years earlier as a thumb in the eye of Miami's city fathers. The Strut lampooned Miami's annual spectacle known as the King Orange Jamboree, a garish, overhyped, overdone, overfunded, corporate-sponsored, pompous, chamber-of-commerce-driven, big-name-drenched, New

Year's Eve parade advertising the upcoming Orange Bowl by celebrating the tony and glitzy image of itself that the city liked to
project. It was nakedly boosterish. Seats in the reviewing stand
were by invitation only, and invitations only went to the city's elite.

At the Strut, there was no reviewing stand. There were no
corporate sponsors. There was nothing "nakedly" anything about
it, except as the adverb that might be applied to the occasional
overly exuberant participant. The King Mango Strut was all goof
and spoof; cheese and sleaze; camp, vamp, and tramp. And it was
always pushing the boundaries of taste. Miamians, a fun-loving
people, fun-loved it. Thousands showed up each year to watch
and cheer, and often to drink.

On this day, assembled behind the lead car, were the World's
Greatest Jewish American Princess, who would ride on the back
of a canary-yellow Cadillac Eldorado, tossing emery boards to
the crowd while sipping Tab; a troupe of "cocaine cowboys" brandishing wads of play money, with bags of white powder stuffed
into their holsters; a cadre of tightly uniformed stewardesses who
would hand out "in-flight snacks" of Alpo and dog biscuits, vow-
ing to make you feel like you never left the ground "because we'll
treat you like dirt"; a faux chamber of commerce, men and women
dressed as pimps and prostitutes; an African American woman
in a sequined dress, introduced as game-show hostess Vanna
Black, marching beside a poster with *Wheel of Fortune* lettering
spelling out *airhead*; a live pig that swilled Budweiser from the
can; and as in previous years, the Marching Freds, a strutting
contingent composed entirely of people named Fred. All these
and others were accordioned in place and ready to go behind that
lead car containing the grand marshal, who, in the subversive

and merrily cynical spirit of Miami's most alternative event, was the city's most famous killer.

On the morning of September 30, 1986, when Prentice Rasheed arrived at his modest African-themed clothing and general goods store on Seventh Avenue in the city's blighted Liberty City neighborhood, he confronted the body of a man partly dangling through the ceiling. It was a burglar who had been caught and summarily executed while committing a crime so common in Miami that local cops had coined a term for it: a "roof job." A thief would enter a store by smashing a hole in the roof and slithering inside, thus avoiding the ubiquitous anti-theft security gates that protected downtown businesses' doors and windows. This particular burglar, a twenty-seven-year-old two-bit criminal named Odell Hicks, had done time for both larceny and rape. Hicks had climbed a tree, leapt onto the wood-and-tar-paper roof of Rasheed's store, battered through it, and dropped down onto the floor, right near the display of ultra-sheer pantyhose.

He looked around, grabbed some $5.50 shoes and $12 blue jeans, and pushed them out into an alleyway through the bars in the locked back door, to be retrieved momentarily. Then he climbed back through the ceiling to make his escape, carrying his final bits of swag: a bunch of cheap watches stuffed into his pockets and a $110 boom box under an arm. He was sweating. His skin was salty when he scrabbled up against the two grids of metal mesh, positioned inches apart and bolted to the top surface of the ceiling, each grid attached to one of the two split and stripped wires of an extension cord, which led to a 115-volt wall outlet. He was still clutching the boom box as he died, thrashing.

The jury-rigged booby trap had been installed by Prentice

Rasheed himself, in exasperation, after suffering his eighth or tenth or thirteenth burglary that year alone (the exact number was in dispute, but was gargantuan in any case).

Rasheed, forty-three, was arrested and charged with manslaughter on the arguably reasonable principle—dating back to seventeenth-century British common law—that a person may not use lethal force to protect property alone. But that was not the end of the prosecution's case against the merchant. For certain criminal charges in Miami, arrests come first, but they must then be ratified by a grand jury.

In this case, the jury got a little help from the dead man himself. Odell Hicks, it turned out, had been a particularly unsavory individual.

The media located Ellen Morphonios, the colorful and outspoken circuit court judge who had sentenced Hicks in 1977 on a charge of rape, and who was unhappy when he was released on parole. She was more than happy to express an opinion on this new case. She said she was not at all sorry that Hicks was dead. She told Barry Bearak of the *Los Angeles Times*:

> He wanted the world to know he was the friendly neighborhood rapist. He bragged that he had raped 75 or 100 women . . . He went to a wash house and he got one woman's laundry and he spread it out like you'd spread out bread crumbs for a duck. The woman went along picking it up. When she got to a bushy area, he grabbed her.

The grand jury vacated Rasheed's arrest and cleared him. Their generous reasoning was that he had not deliberately used lethal force because he did not know, and had no reason to know, that a simple household current—the type that delivers a nasty but nonlethal shock to many of us from time to time while we've changed a lightbulb in a compromised socket—could actually kill a man.

All of this made Prentice Rasheed something of a national celebrity. He hired an agent. He went on Oprah. He went on *Larry King Live.* He did NBC's *Today* and ABC's *Nightline* with Ted Koppel. He was America's poster boy for the virtues of urban vigilantism.

And here, at the King Mango Strut just three months after he electrocuted a guy, Prentice Rasheed was out in front of a parade.

A tall, slender, gentle man with a neatly trimmed beard that he tended to stroke professorially as he spoke, Rasheed was dressed conservatively—for the Strut, at least—in a sports jacket, slacks, and an open-collared shirt. Always the businessman, he wore a purple baseball cap advertising his commercial mission: AMCOP, which he said was a sparse acronym for his plans, looking ahead: "The American-Muslim Committee to Purchase 100,000 Commodities Plus."

Thirty-two years afterward, in an interview, Prentice Rasheed would look back on the day and say that he was not concerned for his safety, but he was worried about his dignity. He was a complicated man, in a complicated situation. "Rock and a hard place," he said. "That's where I was."

Rasheed felt genuinely sorry for the man he killed, but not guilty that he'd killed him. Odell Hicks, he reasoned, was a criminal who knew the risk he was taking—if not from a hidden trap, then from a different fed-up merchant, in the shadows,

protecting his property with a rifle. But to Rasheed, the whole
thing was odd.

In Vietnam, he said, he'd return from a mission, and he and
his buddies would be congratulated for their kills: "They'd tell
us, 'You all got seven!' or 'You all got twelve! Yay, hooray, keep
your spirits up! *They* would have killed *you* if they could have.'"
Yet here there was one death, and it was deeply controversial, the
morals of it meticulously parsed and relentlessly debated by a
civilian world. The ACLU was basically calling him a murderer.
Others were calling him an urban avenger, a hero.

Rasheed knew the public could be fickle. Two years earlier, a
high-strung white man named Bernhard Goetz had whipped out
a gun on the New York City subway and shot four young black
men who were hassling him for money. He injured them severely;
one was paralyzed for life. Initially, Goetz's act was celebrated by
many crime-weary New Yorkers, but in time—as the details began to coalesce about his cold-blooded reaction to what amounted
to run-of-the-mill bullying—a lot of the support disappeared.
People resented the fame that would come to Goetz for what was
seen by many as an act of racism and brute vengeance. Would
something similar happen here?

In this case, at least, racism was no issue—both Rasheed and
Hicks were black men. But Rasheed understood that his appearance at the cocky King Mango Strut parade was a bit crass, and
at least borderline tasteless. Maybe, he thought, it was not even
borderline at all. He had agreed to do this on the theory that all
publicity was good. But was it?

So, Prentice Rasheed says today, he was not worried about
bullets. He was worried about boos. That's what he was thinking

about when his convertible pulled forward into the cheering crowd, trailed by the nail-filing JAP and the dog-food flight attendants and the drunk pig and the pimps and the whores and the guys named Fred.

What would happen next was unknowable, but it was hardly unpredictable.

In the 1970s and 1980s, Miami became the unfortunate bellwether for crime in the United States. What would happen later elsewhere would happen first and worst in South Florida. In the initial years of operation of the notorious Medellín cartel, Miami and its environs were inundated with powder cocaine—and the violent crime wave that accompanied it—long before the scourge metastasized in other cities. Terms arose in South Florida that would soon become universal: Miami drug enforcement agents coined the expression *square grouper* to describe the new sort of "fish" washing ashore—bales of marijuana jettisoned by planes or boats that had come under police pursuit. Square grouper often had a waterproof package of cocaine tucked into the center.

The single most successful drug-sniffing dog in the United States—and possibly the world—was a big Labrador named Moose. "Officer Moose" patrolled South Florida's seaports and airports. He alerted on literally tons of stuff. (Headline in *Tropic*, the Sunday magazine of the *Miami Herald*: "Officer Moose Nose His Job.")

And then around 1985, crack arrived. The concentrated, smokable form of cocaine delivered a short but extraordinarily intense high—many first-time users reported spontaneous orgasms—and when that brief brain blast dissipated, there was an almost unendurable hunger for more. If there was no money for more, and because of a form of psychosis crack sometimes created, "crack frenzies" would often ensue: unplanned, un-thought-out burglaries and robberies. In 1986, crime in Miami alone had risen to previously unthinkable levels: There were 12,000 criminal incidents that year per every 100,000 people—roughly 1 in 8 Miami residents was victimized by crime—a rate that surpassed all other cities except Detroit. (By 1989, the figure would leap to 13,500, at least briefly making Miami the most lawless city in the country.)

It surprised no one when Odell Hicks's autopsy revealed he was stoned on crack.

By 1986, the crime wave had begun to spread to other cities, playing out in hellish scenarios. In Washington, D.C., on December 28, it had led to an excruciating, pathetic drama. The family of a young woman named Nancy Gardner was beginning to circulate petitions urging the city to take her death more seriously than they were taking it.

Exactly one week earlier, on Sunday, December 21, Gardner had been standing at a bus stop at Sixth Street and Pennsylvania Avenue SE, six blocks from the U.S. Capitol, when a hand reached out from a passing car and grabbed her handbag. Gardner, twenty-four, hung on or was trapped by the strap. The car sped off, dragging her twenty-five feet until she lost her grip and fell head down onto the pavement. She died of blunt-force trauma.

The city of Washington assigned the case not to its homicide division, but to traffic enforcement, in effect assuring that it would be put on a back burner. The city's apparent motive? Homicide stats were rising, and they didn't want to add another to the total.

That's what the family was protesting, to no avail. (It would not be until March of 1988 that the city finally officially listed the crime as a homicide. Not surprisingly, the murder has never been solved.)

That was the climate in the United States on December 28, 1986—increased fear of crime coupled with increased doubt about authorities' determination to fix things—when Prentice Rasheed, urban vigilante, led a parade.

He heard not a single boo. He was so comfortable, and the crowd so enthusiastic, that he dismounted at one point and gave an interview. He was famous enough that the local TV station didn't even bother to identify him in its clip. Rasheed tells the cameras, somewhat puzzlingly: "This is a democratic society. We should show our humor in the bad times as well as the good times."

The crowd cheered.

EPILOGUE:

Odell Hicks had a brief funeral. Two people attended. There were no flowers. His family had wanted to cremate him, but could not come up with the required $100. The records show he was buried in an unmarked pauper's grave, in a trench 416 feet up Row No. 610.

For many months after Hicks's death, Rasheed slept in the store most nights and carried a gun. He was burgled at least once more. He ran unsuccessfully for a seat on the Miami city commission. He also announced plans to market a nonlethal "electrified curtain" that would give intruders a shock equivalent to a stun gun—which he claimed had been his aim all along. He never got the financing to proceed.

A final note:

The King Mango Strut lives on as a Miami institution, a raised middle finger to the corporate and bureaucratic elite. It has never lost an ounce of its seditious, antiestablishment voice.

And what of the King Orange Jamboree parade, the civic-booster extravaganza that the Strut was created to lampoon? It's gone. It died in 2002, a victim of dismal ratings and just plain irrelevance.

2:10 P.M., Takoma Park, Maryland

Joel Resnicoff drew a shallow, final breath. Beside his hospital bed, a heart monitor stammered, beeped, then flatlined. The brilliantly mischievous commercial artist was thirty-eight. The death certificate would diagnose what killed him: acquired immunodeficiency syndrome, or AIDS.

Exactly twelve hours earlier to the minute, just ten miles away in a handsome row house in Washington's fashionable Dupont Circle neighborhood, Terry Dolan drew a shallow, final breath. The brilliantly ruthless conservative political operative was thirty-six. The death certificate would diagnose what killed him: heart failure caused by cardiomyopathy. That was a lie. It was a genteel, well-intentioned lie, based on a doctor's solemn promise to his patient, but it was a lie just the same.

Nineteen eighty-six was a dreadful year for gay men in America. It was the year that the U.S. Supreme Court formally gave its imprimatur to homophobia, deciding in the Georgia case of *Bowers v. Hardwick* that governments can prosecute acts of sodomy—anal or oral sex—between consenting adults. The Georgia law ostensibly applied to everyone, but had been enforced only for homosexuals. That Supreme Court ruling—essentially, the Dred Scott decision for gay America—would stand for seventeen more years before being overturned in 2003.

Nineteen eighty-six was also the year that the microbe that causes AIDS was given its iconic name—the human immunodeficiency virus, or HIV. It was the year infections and deaths climbed so precipitously that public health experts began to whisper the word *pandemic,* even as the Reagan administration was enforcing what journalist Randy Shilts would later call a policy of "ritualistic silence."

Nineteen eighty-six was the year that Ricky Ray, nine, and his two younger brothers, all hemophiliacs, were thrown out of their public school in Arcadia, Florida, because they had AIDS. Their parents successfully sued to have them reinstated, against virulent community protests. But after their first week back the family would be forced to flee the town when the Rays' house was burned down by an arsonist.

For an exponentially increasing number of gay men outed not by choice but by the undisguisable symptoms of a disfiguring disease, 1986 was a year in which they were forced to deal not just with mortality but also with stigma, shame, and public hysteria. Some, like Joel Resnicoff, embraced who they were and died in peace. Some, like Terry Dolan, embraced little and died at war with themselves.

Dolan was hardly alone in his public duplicity. Fashion designer Perry Ellis said he was suffering from "sleeping sickness." Piano virtuoso Liberace claimed he'd been knocked for a loop by the effects of an ill-advised all-watermelon diet. And most famously, celebrity lawyer-fixer Roy Cohn, acid-tongued mouth-

piece for Joe McCarthy and later consigliere to Rupert Murdoch
and Donald Trump, succumbed to the disease in the summer of
1986. He died gaunt, hollow-faced, and yellow-eyed, snarling to
the very end, to whoever dared to inquire, the lie that he had liver
cancer.

NEAR THE END, on Friday in his second-floor room at Washington
Adventist Hospital, beside his mother, Blanche, and his older
brother, Arnold—a rabbi who would walk two and a half miles
home that night and who would walk back the next morning
because he could not drive on the Sabbath—on that Friday, Joel
Resnicoff decided to die. He'd held off gamely for months as his
weight plummeted and skin lesions took over. He accepted the
explosive diarrhea and the other humiliating symptoms with
characteristic grace and even humor. He gasped through pneu-
monia. But when he finally went blind from AIDS-related retini-
tis, he could think of no reason to continue living. Neither his
mother nor his brother even considered dissuading him. To be a
visual artist without eyes? Unthinkable.

You might well recognize Resnicoff's art, even today. It survives in old designs of Esprit, the international fashion company,
and in shimmery rayon vintage Joel Resnicoff scarves, skirts,
aprons, and T-shirts, many of which have been treated so lovingly
over the years that they look brand-new today when offered for
sale on eBay, which happens a lot. A thirty-five-year-old Resnicoff scarf can go for eighty bucks.

In the mid-1980s, Joel Resnicoff's paintings, drawings, and
sculptures were everywhere. He had spreads in *Women's Wear*

Daily. He crafted 3-D mannequins into traffic-stopping window displays in Macy's and Bloomingdale's. He drew ResniCards, cartoony greeting cards that he marketed himself, and that sold briskly.

Most of his work was infused with whimsy, alive with primary colors and pastels. He trafficked playfully in extremes. His fashionable men were mammoth-shouldered and zoot-suited. His fashionable women had triangulate, mantis-like faces with spiky hair and the knobby-kneed, tweezer-legged, emaciated breastless bodies of the Studio 54 cocaine crowd. His unfashionable women were more fun—often a good-natured version of the dumpy, middle-aged, big-honkered, affectionately pushy-Jew stereotype, something that only a proudly Jewish artist with an emphatically Jewish surname could have gotten away with. He would even name some of these women after his beloved ma. Here is a poster of one of them in swimwear, looking none too good. "Beach, beach, beach, Blanche," kvetches her long-suffering husband, "that's all you ever do." Here is a ResniCard: A hideous-looking woman in a dress, high heels, and gaudy jewelry is saying, "Birthdays don't have to be a drag!" She is clearly a fat, hairy-armed man.

Resnicoff worked within the genre pioneered by Andy Warhol—the collision of fine art and commercial art, which both artists considered a distinction without a difference. Resnicoff's work had balloony, cartoony echoes of Roy Lichtenstein and perspective-bending elements of Picasso, and certainly the impromptu feel of Keith Haring, the 1970s graffiti artist turned pop icon. Resnicoff and Haring were contemporaries; among the things they shared were New York City and AIDS. Haring lived four years longer. His work still sells briskly. The truth is, the far more famous Haring was not nearly as inventive or versatile as Resnicoff.

Like Haring, Resnicoff had briefly been a street artist, and like Haring he carried that exuberant sensibility with him into the studio. He'd lived in the East Village, worried always about rent because money scorched his pocket. He once got a commission of ten grand and blew it on a piece of jewelry for his mother.

Resnicoff was proverbially tall, dark, and handsome. He had piercing, twinkly eyes; superficially, he resembled the magician David Copperfield. In high school the girls pursued him, with predictably unsatisfying results. The artist came out in college in the mid-1960s to both friends and family during a hedonistic year at the hedonistic University of Miami.

He was always restless, constantly changing his appearance, always experimenting. Sometimes he'd have shoulder-length hair, aggressively poufed out. Sometimes he'd get a buzz cut down to his skull. Sometimes he'd be clean-shaven, but other times he had a mustache, a beard, or both. While his clothing was often daring and modern, sometimes he seemed contentiously counter-fashion, a precursor of the hipster—he'd wear the ultimate uncool footwear of sandals with socks. His experimentation extended to drugs, including intravenous narcotics. In his final years it wasn't entirely clear to his friends and family whether he had contracted his disease in the bedroom or the bathroom.

He'd introduced his lovers to his mother, and she accepted them warmly and generously. In the end, in the hospital, in a section filled with young men dying of AIDS, Blanche Resnicoff would love them all. She mopped brows and performed more intimate services as well. Some of the men had been jettisoned by their families. She became their mom.

And then Joel went blind, and that was that. Somehow it extinguished his fear because, ironically, his lack of vision brought clarity. Before, he'd had a choice—drag this out as long as possible or cut it mercifully short—but now the choice, in his mind, had been taken out of his hands. Only one perspective made sense, and he welcomed it. He had lived an exciting, influential, honest life, and now it was over. His eyes, deadened of their twinkle, told him that.

He had one last thing to do. He spoke to his doctors and assured them that despite what was about to happen, he knew they had not failed him.

In that hospital room, at the desire of the patient and with the concurrence of loving family, the order was given: increased palliative care. That is a common medical euphemism in the world of the dying. Essentially, doctors stopped the blood transfusions and increased the pain meds, inducing a coma from which Joel would not emerge.

For weeks Joel Resnicoff had hardly slept—he was in agony from insomnia—and now he was snoring. There was comfort in this. At the end, with the heart monitor flat and beeping, brother and mother cried but also could not suppress a smile, like sun on a rainy day.

DAYS AFTER THE DEATH of Terry Dolan in his Dupont Circle townhouse, there were two memorial services held for him in Washington. The first was a very public ceremony at the Dominican

House of Studies, attended by some of the most influential Republican politicians in the country. U.S. Senator Orrin Hatch spoke. Senator Paul Laxalt was there, as was Patrick Buchanan, former White House director of communications and future presidential candidate.

It was a celebration of a potent political life ferociously lived. At a young age, Terry Dolan had become one of the leading voices of the modern conservative movement; for a time, he was perhaps its mightiest facilitator. In 1975, Dolan had cofounded NCPAC, the National Conservative Political Action Committee, and in that capacity became a startlingly successful fundraiser and political hit man in the take-no-prisoners style of his contemporary Lee Atwater. Many of the candidates Dolan financed, and whose elections he helped engineer, were opponents of, or indifferent to, gay rights.

The second memorial service for Dolan was held two days later, three miles away in St. Matthew's Cathedral. This one had a smaller, less illustrious crowd. A few of the attendees from the first ceremony were there, but mostly it was others—personal, not political, friends of Terry Dolan. The attendees were largely male and young. People in the know speculated there would have been a significantly bigger turnout, but that many men were afraid to attend, lest the media—or people from rival political camps—started taking pictures, allowing people to link faces to jobs in Washington, drawing conclusions, assassinating reputations, gaining political leverage.

The people at this second service were mostly men Dolan knew from the gay nightlife in D.C. This was his big secret, the one he kept from almost all of his professional associates and even his immediate family. It was the secret he'd asked his doctor, Cesar Caceres, to keep. Caceres was the man who signed the death certificate. Even today the doctor won't confirm what killed Dolan; he considers his promise to his patient to be sacrosanct and timeless. But he gently concedes that Dolan did not die of heart failure, except in the sense that, at death, most everyone's heart fails.

Terry Dolan's death, like Terry Dolan's life, became a matter of politics. Some news organizations reported that he had died of complications from AIDS. Others did not. Brent Bozell, the conservative spokesman writing Dolan's obit in the *National Review,* stubbornly went with the busted-heart story. NCPAC officially said he had succumbed to "diabetes and pernicious anemia."

Terry Dolan had in fact died of AIDS, as most of the mainstream media eventually acknowledged. In May 1987, *The Washington Post's* Elizabeth Kastor stated it as fact in a riveting five-thousand-word piece titled "The Cautious Closet of the Gay Conservative." It was a nuanced story, sensitive and sympathetic to the dilemma of gay men like Dolan, whose public and private lives collided so stridently and painfully and, arguably, encouraged hypocrisy. Kastor quoted Dolan's priest, who served Washington's gay and lesbian community: "It's not easy to be a gay man or woman. If you're Irish, Catholic, and Republican, it makes it even more difficult."

The secret was officially out. And yet eleven days later, something remarkable happened, even for Washington, the epicenter of bitter political contention.

Anthony Dolan, Terry's older brother, took out a two-page ad in the conservative *Washington Times* headlined "What the

Washington Post Doesn't Tell Its Readers." Anthony Dolan happened to be Ronald Reagan's chief speechwriter. In the ad, he declared that Kastor's story had been an abhorrent libel dishonestly prosecuting a political agenda: "The greatest and most malicious falsehood in this story," Anthony Dolan wrote, "was its entire thrust, its basis: the claim that my brother lived and died a homosexual."

John Terrence Dolan was a slim, small-statured, high-energy political player who campaigned for Richard Nixon at the age of nine, honed his political skills as a national college Republican leader, then, on the national political stage, sharpened them to the point of an ice pick. In the end, as his politics drifted further rightward, Dolan soured even on Nixon, denouncing him, with dubious authority, as "the most liberal President we've ever had."

Dolan's style was button-down dapper, but he seemed always to be hiding an impish smile. His mustache was bushy, like Ned Flanders's in *The Simpsons*. Dolan gave the impression of the popular and dedicated 1970s high school civics teacher who would invite students over to his house for a study group and then pass out the joints. People who liked Terry Dolan liked him a lot. People who disliked him detested him.

One day in 1984, the famously prickly gay playwright Larry Kramer, author of *The Normal Heart,* the first mainstream play about AIDS, walked up to Dolan at a cocktail party in D.C. and dashed a glass of water in his face. At the time, Dolan was known in gay circles to have just ended a relationship with a male epidemiologist in New York and was actively partaking of the gay party scene in Washington.

Among AIDS activists it had become a truism: The greatest

impediment to getting better attention for the terrifying national
health crisis was not the outspoken homophobe. You could mar-
ginalize that guy; you could call him out for what he was. The
bigger impediment was the closeted gay person who is in a position to help but is afraid to.

"How dare you come here?" Kramer shouted at Dolan, whose face
was impassive and dripping. "You take the best from our world and
then do all those hateful things against us. You should be ashamed."

The anecdote was first reported in Randy Shilts's book *And
the Band Played On: Politics, People, and the AIDS Epidemic.*
Today Kramer confirms it. He says Dolan just smiled and ambled
away into the crowd, and the crowd looked at Kramer like he was
nuts for making a stink. Many of them empathized with Dolan.
"Gays in D.C.," Kramer remembers, "were very closeted in fear of
losing their jobs with the government."

Nineteen eighty was a tremendous year for Republicans. It
was the year the Ronald Reagan landslide redrew the political
landscape in the United States. Some iconic Democrats who'd
seemed unbeatable lost their jobs, including George McGovern
in South Dakota, Frank Church in Idaho, and Birch Bayh in Indiana. They'd been specifically targeted by NCPAC, which spent
millions of dollars in advertising against them—empowered by
loosened court interpretations of post-Watergate spending regulations that placed no limits on the amount of money an independent organization could spend on a political campaign, so long as
it had no direct affiliation with the candidate.

Terry Dolan took that broad license and brandished it jubilantly. In a remarkably candid (and prescient) interview with *The
Washington Post,* he'd said this about his new freedom:

Groups like ours are potentially very dangerous to the political process. We could be a menace, yes. We could say whatever we want about an opponent of a Senator Smith and the senator wouldn't have to say anything. A group like ours could lie through its teeth and the candidate it helps stays clean.

Later, Dolan would claim he was not speaking about *his* organization—he was talking about potential abuse by *other*, unspecified, presumably less scrupulous PACs.

And yet NCPAC was on the forefront of profoundly negative, dubiously accurate advertising, long before "profoundly negative, dubiously accurate" became a standard tactic. In the 1980s some TV stations refused to run NCPAC ads.

It was NCPAC that bought ads describing George McGovern as a "baby killer" for supporting abortion rights. (Even McGovern's opponent, James Abdnor, who would win big, renounced that attack.) Another NCPAC commercial falsely accused Frank Church of having voted for an increase in his own Senate salary. That one was actually withdrawn after complaints. The NCPAC ads crushed both men.

Both Church and McGovern were sympathetic to gay rights; their opponents were not. (For Church, the issue was deeply personal. His gay brother, a closeted Navy admiral, had taken his own life in the 1960s after being targeted in a sexual blackmail scheme.)

Dolan clearly walked a fine line in his public life, and his public statements did not always jibe with his public policy. He once gave an interview to *The Advocate*, the national gay magazine, saying he opposed laws that discriminated against homosexuals. And yet his organization had recently sent out a fundraising letter signed by U.S. Representative Daniel B. Crane of Illinois saying: "Our nation's moral fiber is being weakened by the growing homosexual movement and the fanatical ERA pushers (many of whom publicly brag they are lesbians)." In the interview with *The Advocate*, Dolan apologized for this ad, claiming he hadn't personally approved it.

But it had done its job. It pulled in significant money for Crane, who won his election and remained a congressman until defeated after it was revealed he'd had a sexual relationship with a seventeen-year-old female House page.

Perhaps there is no better evidence of Dolan's willingness to manipulate the truth for his own ends than his preface to a 1984 book he wrote with Greg Fossedal, *Reagan: A President Succeeds*. The book apparently was never released, but a publisher's proof copy was issued and circulated to interested parties. It's still around. The book is mostly a paean to the first Reagan presidency. The dedication page reads like this:

> This book is dedicated to the many patriotic conservative Americans who made the election of Ronald Reagan a reality in 1980. Before Mr. Fossedal and I wrote even the first word of this book, I had all of the following people in mind. Now, in the 84 campaign to reelect our president, I call these people "American Heroes for Reagan."
>
> (With your written permission your name will appear here, along with your designation as director, patron, or sponsor.)

Dolan died three days before Ronald Reagan delivered his annual New Year's speech to the people of the Soviet Union.

Anthony Dolan's office wrote that speech, which was in part an eloquent defense of human rights, if tone-deaf to the irony of America's persecution of people who were dying by the hundreds of a disease their administration was failing to take seriously.

"The American people are deeply concerned with the fate of individual people," Reagan told the Soviet people. "We believe that God gave sacred rights to every man, woman, and child on Earth. . . . Respect for those rights is the bedrock on which our system is built."

AT SOME TIME IN THE AFTERNOON, around the time Joel Resnicoff was breathing his last, a New York entertainment lawyer and Broadway entrepreneur named John Breglio arrived at a stately, spacious ranch-style home in the suburbs of Tucson, Arizona. It was at the foothills of a mountain range outside the city, and the view was spectacular.

Breglio had been summoned to Tucson by his friend and client Michael Bennett, the choreographer. Bennett was the gifted, driven, elegant, wildly innovative genius behind the 1975 smash Broadway hit *A Chorus Line,* which he conceived, created, choreographed, and directed. Over the years, Bennett had won five Tony Awards for choreography; only Bob Fosse has more.

Bennett was very ill. He'd be dead in a few months, at forty-four, of AIDS-related lymphoma, and on this day he knew the probable timetable. There was something he needed to get done first.

Like Joel Resnicoff, Michael Bennett was comfortable with his sexuality. But like Terry Dolan, he had lied about why he was sick.

Bennett was bisexual and had made no efforts to hide that.

He'd been briefly married to the dancer Donna McKechnie, who created the role of Cassie in *A Chorus Line*. He had also had numerous relationships with men; in accepting his 1976 Tony, onstage, Bennett unhesitatingly kissed Bob Avian, his friend and co-choreographer, on the mouth. But when Bennett's health began to fail, like Dolan he equivocated. He told people he had heart trouble. His reasons for the lie were complicated.

At the time of his diagnosis, Bennett's name was everywhere. He was involved in a half-dozen high-profile productions and felt he had a financial obligation to protect his reputation—both for himself and for others. "He didn't want to become a poster boy for the disease," Breglio says today.

It was understandable, if less than fully courageous. There was at least one precedent for a famous man risking his reputation for the greater public good of AIDS awareness. When Rock Hudson finally disclosed his disease in 1985, he did it with this generous statement, read by Burt Lancaster to a silent, shocked audience at a huge Hollywood charity dinner: "I am not happy that I have AIDS. But if that is helping others, I can, at least, know that my own misfortune has had some positive worth."

But Bennett told *The New York Times* he had angina; when others reported that he was suffering from heart problems, he kept quiet. And yet Bennett was a fundamentally principled man, and all this seems to have been weighing on him. He never quite articulated that, but his business meeting on December 28 was evidence enough.

Bennett had moved to Tucson from New York months before to be near a doctor who was treating his illness.

He was having some cognitive troubles. His longtime dalliances with Quaaludes and alcohol did not sit well with a fatal disease. He became occasionally confused and paranoid.

But on the day lawyer John Breglio arrived at Bennett's house, his client was lucid and thinking clearly. He told Breglio that he had decided to add a codicil to his will. He was going to leave 15 percent of his $25 million estate to help fund AIDS research and treatment. The two men worked it out.

The money went to several charities, some of which—like amfAR—were directly involved in research. Others, such as God's Love We Deliver, specialized in bringing psychological comfort and free food to the critically and chronically ill.

As it turns out, Bennett's final generosity was literally bottomless. His bequest was permanent, meaning that for the last thirty-odd years, as residuals kept pouring in from all over the country from the hundreds of small and large and amateur and professional performances of *A Chorus Line* and *Dreamgirls* and other famous Bennett works, a percentage *still* goes to AIDS research and to comforting the afflicted.

ON PASSOVER 2018, Rabbi Arnold Resnicoff presided over a seder in his Washington apartment, as he does every year for about twenty-five people. It's a joyful affair, devoted, as seders are, to a celebration of the story of the Israelites' escape from slavery in Egypt. A graying, patrician-looking man with a military bearing, Resnicoff is a gifted storyteller, so he peppers his historical lesson with intriguing, occasionally unsettling trivia. (Q: Why, for

hundreds of years, did Jews tend to have only white wine at seders? A: To avoid being seen by a goy and being accused of the
"blood libel"—drinking the blood of Christian children.)

Joel Resnicoff's name didn't come up in any of this. It didn't
have to. He was everywhere. The big brother's apartment is a shrine
to his younger brother's art. There is some of it on every wall, more
than two dozen pieces in all, and they are as eclectic as Joel was.
Here, as you come in, presiding over the entrance almost protectively, like a mezuzah, is a gaily colored Joel Resnicoff scarf. (Arnold
Resnicoff buys them on eBay, when he can.) There's a silk screen of
way-too-fashionable people with their way-too-fashionable dogs. A
bed is covered with a huge beach towel Resnicoff designed for
Bloomingdale's: twenty-one young people looking impossibly hip.

There is a ResniCard: Two older ladies, wildly bejeweled, overly
made up, overly broad in the beam, observing a wasp-waisted
fashion-model type, and trying, as best they know how, not to be
judgmental. "Maybe," theorizes one, "she doesn't like food."

Here's a small self-portrait in the foyer, done early in Joel
Resnicoff's career. It's straightforward. He's deeply tanned, thick
of neck and resolute of mouth, a young man determined to grab
the world as his own. Here's another self-portrait, a larger one, in
the dining room, painted much later, possibly after his diagnosis.
It's more surreal: Picasso triangles and Van Gogh colors and perfect almond eyes, a stylized young man with a stylized look of
ineffable sadness. He is wearing a necktie, which Joel never did,
and looking strangled by it.

Part of Joel's bigger legacy is in fact his older brother. Arnold
is a retired Navy chaplain. He was enticed into the clergy as an
ensign in Vietnam in 1969, when an Episcopal priest realized he

had no one to minister to Jewish soldiers in the Mekong Delta and deputized the lay Resnicoff into service.

Joel's life and death had a profound impact on his brother. As a military rabbi, he risked censure by railing against the "Don't Ask, Don't Tell" policy that compelled gay service members to hide their sexual identity. Resnicoff called it "immoral," saying that it "forced people to hide who they were while at the same time we were promoting core values that included honesty." Resnicoff had been so outspoken and passionate on the subject that he was asked to deliver the invocation at the 2010 ceremony where Barack Obama signed the repeal of the policy. Resnicoff says today, "I think Joel was watching. I could feel his pride in me."

ANTHONY DOLAN, TERRY'S brother, still lives in the Washington area. A former journalist, he once won the Pulitzer Prize for an exposé on public corruption, and then made the move into politics, where he found even greater fame and influence as Reagan's hardline, anti-Communist speechwriter. It was Dolan who wrote Reagan's "ash heap of history" speech delivered to the British House of Commons, and, later, it was Dolan who persuaded the president to refer to the Soviet Union as an "Evil Empire." He is not an insignificant cog in the machine that ended the Cold War. At seventy, Dolan remains an icon of the national conservative moment.

He declined to be interviewed about his brother, and with characteristic bluntness, gave his reason: He didn't want to take questions from someone working for a newspaper he dislikes, someone who is, he has decided, "a spokesman for the gay agenda."

4:25 P.M., Matlock, Washington

D aylight was slipping away. The helicopter, a runty three-seater, lifted off into the soupy mist of a sudden fog. The veteran pilot knew he was racing both darkness and diminishing visibility. Still, he was a mere ten minutes from home, and he had taken measures against the elements. Five feet off the ground, he tipped the vehicle forward to begin his ascent. Neither he nor his passenger had any idea, any slender premonition, of what would befall them not two seconds later . . .

WHEN YANKED FRESH from remote rivers in the Pacific Northwest, steelhead trout make some of the most succulent meals taken from any waters anywhere in the world. That is why Brad Wilson and his friend Bob Boelk had set out from their homes in Shelton, Washington, just after daybreak on December 28, and headed west.

They'd taken Brad's helicopter, a small, no-frills Hughes model 269B, because a car or truck would not have done the job. The rivers that Wilson and Boelk sought out were inaccessible by wheels. They wanted waters that were virtually unfished, and

this copter was perfect for the job, if barely big enough to accommodate the two men, their gear, and the cornucopia of fat trout
they hoped they'd be returning with.

It was icy cold, but neither man minded. Wilson, thirty-six,
who owned a construction company, was a toughie. Boelk, twenty-
nine, an electrician for a lumber mill, was even tougher. His nickname was "The Iceman," a moniker bestowed on him once by an
Indian guide who swore Boelk would stay outdoors with a rod in
his hand even if the river froze solid.

The flight to their destination took Bob and Brad fifty minutes.
The two friends touched down and walked out into the waters in
their hip waders. Things went splendidly as they fished for hours
without seeing another human. By the end of their day—around
three P.M.—they had nine fleshy steelhead, maybe seventy pounds
of fish, sardined into the copter's two small outside cargo racks.
And then they took off for home. The weather was dreary and wet
and cold, and getting colder.

Once they were airborne, the outside temperature plummeted
until it collided with the dew point, which was not good; this results in an uncommonly thick mist. The copter's windshield—
made of plexiglass, which is particularly susceptible to atmospheric
fluctuations—began to fog up. Visibility became perilously limited. Wilson found himself navigating like Mr. Magoo, squinting
treetop to treetop, a bitch of a way to fly.

Small-craft helicoptering is notoriously dangerous, and dealing
with adversity often involves improvised, seat-of-the-pants tech-
niques. In conditions like these, the pilot of a copter is sometimes
urged to set down and remove the driver's side door, give it to the
passenger to hold, then take off again and sight-navigate—not

through the foggy front window, but out the open door, moving sideways like a crab.

Wilson peered down for a place to land and found a hospitable one, in a clearing in the middle of a big lumberyard, on a huge expanse of discarded tree bark. Not an upright tree in the area. The landing on the soft bed of bark was gentle, as expected. Boelk took the door in his lap. Wilson throttled up the rotor and the helicopter rose slowly. What would happen next involved a confluence of factors so unlikely no oddsmaker would touch it.

Wilson didn't know it, but a rivet had popped loose on the rear of his left skid. The rivet had held the skid to the skid shoe, a tough metal plate designed to protect the skid during landings, like a tap on the heel of a person's shoe. Because of the loose rivet, the shoe had separated from the skid by a fraction of an inch—just space enough for a thin metal band to wedge into. Which is, alas, exactly what had happened.

When being transported, lumber is held together in bundles by long metal bands. One of them happened to be in that pile of discarded bark. One end of it was sticking up free; the other end, forty feet away, was pinned to the ground by a huge horizontal tree trunk. Improbably, the free end of the metal band found the slot in Wilson's damaged skid. The devil had decided to thread a needle.

Brad Wilson's chopper reached a height of five feet, and then Wilson tilted the nose down and the tail up, to achieve greater airspeed, get greater lift, and set a direction. The copter nosed up and forward. At about twenty feet in the air, the metal band that was now tethering the copter to the ground ran out of slack. The tree trunk did what tree trunks do: nothing.

Wilson knew none of this at the time, of course. He just knew that at twenty feet, in pilot talk, the copter "inverted," meaning it flipped clean over like an egg from a skillet. The rotor was still roaring, and it was augering the tiny vehicle straight down to the ground, at almost 90 degrees. Neither man remembers saying anything; there was no time. Wilson does remember thinking: This is not survivable.

BRAD WILSON'S HELICOPTER inversion was one of three aviation accidents reported to the FAA on this day. Each was dealt with briefly in the agency's daily summary, described in the same emotionless, matter-of-fact professional language. In the first, a pilot of a small plane had had his right wing scrape the ground while practicing touch-and-go landings, causing the plane to veer 90 degrees off the runway. In the second, a small commercial Cessna flight had careered out of control on landing and a wing hit a "small pine sapling."

Finally, there was this one. Number three. The FAA report accurately described the general facts. It didn't even begin to capture the drama. Or the humor.

BRAD WILSON'S HELICOPTER slammed into the ground, upside down, the rotor blades churning themselves into a tangled mess in the tree bark. ("Helicopters make lousy rototillers," Bob Boelk would wryly note thirty-plus years later.) Then the machine shuddered silent. Wilson and Boelk surveyed each other. Both were alive. Both were dangling in the air, suspended at the belly by their lap belts, like marionettes undergoing the Heimlich maneuver.

"What the hell just happened?" gasped the pilot.

"You're asking *me*?" croaked his passenger.

"We gotta get outta here," Wilson concluded, reasonably. "This thing could blow up or something."

Simultaneously, as though they were synchronized swimmers, both men unbuckled their belts and fell unceremoniously through the shattered Plexiglas roof of the helicopter, thudding onto the mangled machinery in the mangled bed of bark, below.

Bob hit the ground running.

"*You're far enough away*," Brad called after him. But Bob didn't stop for a bit. After he returned, Brad got philosophical. They'd been extra lucky, he figured.

"Why?" Bob asked.

"On account of when rotor blades stop all of a sudden like that, and you are upside down, sometimes the core of the rotor snaps off and comes roaring through the cabin and cuts you in half."

"Oh," Bob said.

The fact is, neither man was at all injured, beyond a small bloody scrape on Brad Wilson's forehead. Thirty-plus years later, parsing the odds, Wilson would say that he believes their lives were saved because they'd drilled down into a bed of soft mulch, making for a peculiarly cushioned landing, considering. The impact itself had been bone-rattling but survivable. Nothing snapped off and became a flying body-severing buzz saw. Had they landed on hard dirt, he figures, they'd have been significantly injured.

Had it been wood beams or logs or cement or tarmac, they'd have been significantly dead.

A truck pulled up. Bunch of guys inside. They'd been target shooting or maybe cutting firewood—the two survivors disagree on this—and had seen the crash. They offered to drive Boelk and Wilson to a phone.

Hang on, Boelk said. He wanted to retrieve the fish.

"Forget the fish," Wilson growled, pointing out that he had just lost a $100,000 uninsured helicopter and they had both barely escaped with their lives. His tone must have carried some weight. The Iceman actually agreed to forget the fish.

The woodsmen drove them to Matlock, which consisted of one grocery store with gas pumps out front. Fortunately, it had a pay phone. Unfortunately, when Wilson called home and explained to his wife what had happened and that he needed a lift home, she informed him that he'd gotten into this mess by himself and he should get out of it the same way.

Their relationship had lasted ten years and produced three children. It had never been easy—riven from the start by certain anxieties and tensions—but Wilson says today that it wasn't until he heard the click on the other end of the line that he realized his marriage was over. As it happens, he was right, but, as it also happens, he was seriously underestimating the pain to come.

The two men cadged another ride home. As they waited for it to arrive, the Iceman got to thinking. He wanted those fish, and by God, he was going to get them. A disgruntled Brad wanted no part of this, so the Iceman got a ride back to the wreck and happily harvested them all. Thirty-plus years later, in an interview

for this book, Bob Boelk reconsidered the numbers: There must
have only been four fish, he concluded, because state fish and
game laws allowed only two steelhead per fisherman. So he em-
phasizes, for the record, that he took *just the four fish* home.

The following day Brad Wilson set off to the site of the crash
in his little crappy blue diesel Chevette, trailed by a tow truck,
which was going to bring the helicopter carcass back to be sal-
vaged in any way possible. But on the way out to Matlock, a tie
rod blew out in the steering column of the crappy diesel Chevette, and at 55 miles per hour, Wilson lost complete control of
the car. It was on its own. On its own, it swerved sharply, nearly
clipped the end of a twenty-ton logging truck, which would likely
have been fatal, and crashed headlong into a ditch, which could
also have been fatal but wasn't. Wilson was intact, though his car
was not. The tow truck driver just hitched the car carcass to the
back of the truck—all in a day's work—and, with the shell-
shocked Wilson now in his cab, they continued out to the site of
the copter crash.

That afternoon, the tow truck returned to Shelton with Brad's
pretzeled helicopter on the platform of the truck, and Brad's
crumpled Chevette towed behind it. This entourage moved
slowly through town, Brad in the passenger seat of the tow truck,
trying to disappear. He got ribbed by friends about his wrecked
vehicles for *weeks.*

And his wrecked marriage? That phone call on December 28,
1986, was indeed the beginning of the end, but it was the sort of
end Wilson had not anticipated. How could he have?

Wilson and his wife had a good, prosperous life, but they also
had a problem that was gradually becoming apparent. Its official

cause would not be given a name until the divorce and custody proceedings, just before the abductions and interstate flight, the new identities on the lam, the federal fugitive warrant, just before the start of the seven-year period that the three Wilson children would have their faces on milk cartons, aged year by year through computer enhancement.

During the initial custody battle, in a court-ordered test, Brad's wife was diagnosed with borderline personality disorder, a complex psychological condition that, in retrospect, explained a lot, including her perpetually fragile emotional states.

Following her diagnosis, Brad Wilson was awarded sole custody of the children, ages three, six, and eight. His now ex-wife was outraged. On Friday, September 6, 1991, she picked up the kids from school midday and was gone. It would not be until early 1998 that the FBI found her, living in Ann Arbor, Michigan, under an assumed identity. She was arrested and eventually pleaded guilty to custodial interference. The kids were brought home to Brad.

The youngest child, Nathaniel, who now was nine, was horrified. He had no clear memory of his father, no idea who he was.

"So I guess you could say I missed their childhoods," Wilson says, simply.

THAT'S NOT QUITE the end of the story of Brad Wilson and his helicopter. It has two more small chapters. The man who had escaped death twice in twenty-four hours had been given a gift of life. What, if anything, would he do with it?

Wilson never asked himself this. He is not the sort of man to agonize over the mysteries of fate, or the obligations of good fortune, or the nature of karmic reciprocity. But he is a man of action and gumption, and, consistent with his abilities, quite without meaning to, he found a way to even things up.

It was early September 1995 when two young women—Shari Rubin, thirty-one, and Karen Starke, thirty—were hiking in Olympic National Park, a sprawling 920,000-acre wilderness area on the Pacific coastline. It was the last day of their weeklong fifty-mile backpacking trip when they took a wrong turn, compounded the mistake with another wrong turn, and were lost. They did not come home the day they were supposed to, or the next.

Rangers began looking for them. The search came up empty. It was cold out there.

On the third day, Brad Wilson and a friend—both unaware there were missing hikers—decided to take a sightseeing excursion over the Olympic Mountains in Brad's copter. They'd been in the air about an hour when they spotted something odd on the ground: a huge, crude *SOS* etched into the snow with rocks. Beside it was a huge crude snow-and-rock arrow pointing to the right, toward a creek bed. Almost out of gas, Wilson returned home and phoned rangers. That's when he learned that there were missing women—and also, from what the rangers told him, that they been searching waaay in the wrong place. They might never have located them.

Wilson gassed up and returned to the *SOS*. He then followed the big arrow until he saw a woman down there, near the creek bed, frantically waving a red shirt. He phoned in his location and waited for the rescuers, who had far bigger copters. It turns out the two women had remained impressively calm, but were more than a little worried. They'd been rationing their food. They were running out.

That was two lives for Brad Wilson, and counting.

IN JULY 1997, Wilson was fishing alone in the rivers near the Olympic Mountains and dropped in on a grocery store for a Pepsi. Seeing his copter, the grocer asked if he was part of the search party for the two rafters.

What two rafters? he asked.

A man and a woman. They'd been lost for six days, somewhere on the Wynoochee River near the Olympics. The search was about to be called off.

Hell, Wilson thought. *If they're still alive, I know* exactly *where they are.* He'd fished the Wynoochee. Rafted it, too. There was only one place they could be. It was a choke point at the bottom of a deep gorge, near a big rock outcropping. He had once lost one of his three rafts there—alas, it was the one carrying all the beer.

The spot was perilously near a small but churning waterfall, and—more to the point—it was miles downriver from where the searchers had been looking.

Wilson hopped back in his copter, flew straight to the spot, and there they were with their deflated raft, stranded on a rock quite near the falls. The narrow gorge rose a hundred feet above them, topped by two-hundred-foot trees. Top to bottom, it was the length of a football field, a straight vertical drop, to get to them.

What would happen next would earn Brad Wilson an award for heroism from the regional Red Cross.

Wilson could not get cell phone service. He knew the couple below had been out there for days, and didn't know their physical condition or how much longer they could hold on. He decided to attempt the rescue himself, alone.

He set down on dry land and removed both helicopter doors to shed weight for the arduous climb back up from the gorge with passengers, then re-approached the area. Centering himself between the ravine walls, he dropped straight down. The space was so narrow that the rocky walls were less than ten feet from Wilson's rotor blades on either side. He could not land on the small rock where the rafters stood, so he lowered his helicopter perilously close, tipped his right skid down to the rock, and had one of the rafters climb onto the skid and then into the cabin. Up again, then across to a rock quarry, to drop off his passenger. Back to the gorge for the second rescue.

The couple told him afterward that they'd given up hope. They were hungry and exhausted and suffering from exposure, and they said they'd decided that the next day if there'd been no rescue, they'd jump into the water and take their chances. Their chances would not have been good, down there near the falls.

Those were lives three and four, for Brad Wilson.

And counting?

"You never know," he says. He's sixty-eight now, with a touch of Parkinson's, and doesn't fly anymore. "But I spend a lot of time outdoors on rivers, and people are still putting themselves in peril."

Perhaps, in some spiritual, otherworldly way, he was meant to do this? Maybe this was ordained, somehow? Maybe this carries the thumbprint of something bigger than all of us?

"Naw," says Brad. "I just spend a lot of time outdoors."

5:05 P.M., Washington, D.C.

The two-man backfield shifted, Knute Rockne box-step style, then came set. Hunched over center, calling signals, was the Los Angeles Rams rookie quarterback Jim Everett. It was second and eight, with the ball on the Washington Redskins 28-yard line. Ten minutes and three seconds were left in the second quarter of this wild-card play-off game between two venerable franchises having unexpectedly good seasons. The Redskins were ahead 10–0, but the Rams were driving.

Everett took the snap, dropped back five steps, head-feinted downfield, then turned to his left, where tight end David Hill was breaking wide. Everett lofted the ball toward Hill on a high arc, but the throw was a little too stingy to hit him in full stride. Hill had to do a half-hitch stutter and pivot to face the ball, slowing him just a bit. He made the catch off-balance just past the line of scrimmage, with Redskins linebacker Monte Coleman closing on him, fast.

Freeze the frame for a moment.

The events of the ensuing few minutes at Robert F. Kennedy Memorial Stadium would find a small but important place in football history, not because of what happened on the field so much as what happened forty feet above it in a cramped booth on the press-box level. On this day, a grand experiment would almost die, killed by conscientiousness.

RFK was an old-fashioned building, perfectly round, homely, and utilitarian in its basic design but crowned by a futuristic concrete roof over the seats—a brash, undulating swoop designed in 1960 with the obligatory nod to space-age sensibilities. The jarring collision between old and new—Flintstones meets Jetsons—would turn out to be appropriate to the moment, as a hundred-year-old sport came face-to-face with both the possibilities and the perils of technology.

So-called instant replay—essentially, split-second turnaround of game film—had been invented nearly a quarter of a century earlier by a twenty-nine-year-old television director named Tony Verna, who first used it during the broadcast of the Army-Navy game on December 7, 1963. It was a dramatic game, held just two weeks after the assassination of John F. Kennedy, and only with the blessing of the president's widow.

On third and goal from the 1-yard line, Army quarterback Rollie Stichweh faked a handoff and plunged over the line. Fifteen seconds later, the TV audience watched the touchdown dive again. The sight was so peculiar, so foreign to anything anyone had ever seen, that announcer Lindsey Nelson felt the need to say, "Ladies and gentlemen, Army did not just score again."

Within three years, instant replay was commonplace as a tool of the TV networks. It was a no-brainer, an enhancement of coverage that took nothing away from the game. But it was not until twenty-three years after that, the beginning of the 1986 season, that the NFL approved its use as a diagnostic tool to second-guess calls on the field.

In that first regular season, review by instant replay had been deployed judiciously, and only at the discretion of the officials; coaches could not request it. By December 28, there had been roughly 35,000 plays called in regular season games, only 1 percent of which had been looked at a second time. And in only 10 percent of those—38 plays, total—were the on-field rulings overturned. The caution was understandable. Money was at stake.

Football was in a war with baseball for the hearts and wallets of American sports fans, but the playing field was not entirely level. Each sport claimed a certain psychological turf. Baseball was the genteel pastoral game that clung stubbornly to tradition, eschewing innovations that might streamline the sport at the expense of "authenticity"–even at the cost of accepting the element of human error. Football was different. It was fast and violent and modern, and the people who ran it had always been more willing to embrace technology, including computer analyses of the opposition's offensive formations, and later, helmet microphones to connect coaches to players. But those innovations were safe. They did not threaten to drive away fans.

At the start of the era of shortened attention spans, football team owners fretted about anything that could further delay games. Delay was already imprinted into the DNA of the sport; it had even been quantified. In 1986, NFL owners were bootlegging a daunting statistic that they knew but didn't share: Though the average game lasted more than three hours, the ball was in play for just about eleven minutes. The rest of the time was parceled out to commercial messages during time-outs, to halftime, and largely to the pace of the game itself, in which significant play was maddeningly and microscopically episodic. Between seconds-long bursts of action, there were endless shots of men tearing themselves off the turf, men standing around, men walking back to the huddle, men in the huddle, and older men pacing sullenly on the sidelines, looking aggrieved.

With a players' strike looming—1987 would become the year that scabby, largely inept "replacement players" were used for three games, deeply scarring the NFL's reputation—team owners were concerned about not squandering fan loyalty.

On the one hand, they knew football fans in particular valued accuracy—they hated the element of human error in officiating. And they knew that the networks' use of instant replay (with its slo-mo capabilities) had infuriatingly magnified errors, showing them again and again from different angles—errors that were, under the rules, unreviewable. This delivered a hit to the basic covenant between a sport and its fans. So owners knew that as a tool to reverse errors of judgment, instant replay could potentially make the game more enjoyable. But at what cost? How much finger-twiddle time would it add to an already overlong game? How much more downtime could the game endure? What was the breaking point?

When the lords of football approved the instant replay plan, it was with trepidation, and for 1986 only, a one-season experiment to be instantly reviewed in early 1987.

(Baseball executives would stubbornly resist the full use of replay challenges for another twenty-four years, until a particularly ghastly error forced their hand: A would-be perfect game— among the rarest of all baseball accomplishments—was ruined by an obviously bad call at first base on what should have been the last out. There was no procedure to permit a review of it. Clinging to baseball's religion of embracing human error, the commissioner declined to make an exception.)

By December of 1986, the NFL's grand experiment had shown fairly good results. Because replay review had been used sparingly, delays had been manageable, and most had been of reasonable length: a two-minute maximum was the goal, and it was mostly achieved. But the technology had not yet been employed in the postseason, with its huge TV audience. Fingers were crossed.

That was the state of affairs at 5:05 P.M. on December 28, 1986, when Dave Hill hauled in the lob pass, with Monte Coleman literally at his heels.

ALMOST INSTANTLY, Coleman hit Hill from behind and bear-hugged him to the ground. They landed hard.

Up in the broadcast booth, CBS play-by-play announcer Pat Summerall—the man who had coined the term *instant replay*—thought the play was over, good for a two-yard gain. But at that moment, the camera and Redskins linebacker Neal Olkewicz simultaneously discovered the ball lying on the turf two feet from the entangled receiver and defender. Olkewicz dived on it, bounced up, and started sprinting toward the Rams goal line, picking up an entourage of blockers. The crowd yawped and roared.

"It looks like it must be a fumble!" Summerall exclaimed. "No one has indicated otherwise."

In fact, someone had. Side judge Al Jury was back near where the tackle was made, stolidly pointing to the ground. No one saw him; the action was elsewhere.

Olkewicz was finally brought down around the Rams 35-yard line. And that is when things went to hell.

The officials sent the teams back to the point of the tackle, and announced that Hill's knee had hit the ground before he lost possession of the ball, meaning he was "down by contact." No fumble had occurred. The Rams would keep the ball. The stadium thundered its disapproval.

But line judge Jack Fette stepped in to talk to the others. He'd seen it differently. There was some discussion, and then the officials announced they would be going to review by instant replay.

Up in a small booth far above the field, NFL official Joe Gardi swiveled to face a nine-inch screen, designed not as much for fidelity as for physically fitting into tight stadium spaces.

Gardi, forty-seven, was a sad-eyed old-school former assistant coach in the NFL, widely respected for his integrity and, particularly, for his attention to detail. He was a meticulous man who liked to get things right. Squinting into the pygmy screen, he watched the play twice from a distance, stopping and starting the action, then switched to a second nine-inch screen with a different camera angle, closer to the play.

One minute passed, then two, then two and a half.

On the field, Redskins defensive end Dexter Manley decided to hooch up the crowd. Manley was a fan favorite, nicknamed the "Secretary of Defense." (Tragically, no one had thought to yoke him together with fellow lineman Charles Mann and call them the "Manley-Mann" pass rush.)

On the field, Manley was bouncing up and down, waving his arms as though he were conducting a symphony. A master of manipulation, Manley was also secretly into crack cocaine, an addiction that would eventually get him thrown out of football for good and lead him to the brink of suicide before he found sobriety and redemption. But at the moment, he was juiced on adrenaline alone, jubilantly inciting to riot. The fans were going absolutely bonkers.

"Redskins ball! Redskins ball!" they hollered.

This was not the dignified, deliberative process that the designers of instant replay envisioned.

Up in the press box, color commentator John Madden laughed and said, "Dexter Manley's trying to get the crowd to help that guy up in the booth!"

That guy up in the booth had already decided that Hill had had ample possession of the ball and then started losing control of it before his knee hit the ground, meaning it was a fumble, but . . . but . . . *had he then recovered it himself,* if only briefly, before hitting the ground? That would change everything. It was a Solomonic dilemma. Joe Gardi rewound the tape.

On TV sets across the country, the replay rolled again and again. Summerall and Madden were doing their best to fill airtime, speculating what might be going on in the booth, getting much of it wrong.

Summerall: "If he didn't have possession, it could be an incomplete pass!"

Madden: "You know that could be the other thing—is it a complete pass or incomplete pass? Is it a fumble or not a fumble?"

Summerall: "Was his knee down?"

Madden: "His knee *was* down, but did he have control of it?"

Summerall: "And the review continues!"

The delay was well past three minutes now, with no sign of ending. The officials on the field were standing around, glancing nervously up toward the booth, their hands pressing on their ear-pieces, as though this were a communication problem, as though everything would be better if they could just *hear* better. But there was nothing to hear from upstairs.

On the sidelines, Rams head coach John Robinson, a dour man ordinarily, was pacing and glowering. He was a bit comical looking in a thin parka and bright white Mickey Mouse–style gloves. If he had been a cartoon, lines of steam would have been radiating from his head.

Up in the press box, Madden realized something politically per-ilous was happening. The rotund former head coach—a superstar announcer known for his folksy, fumble-mouthed flamboyance—was a big fan of technology. He famously pioneered in the use of the Telestrator, which allowed broadcasters to scribble lines and circles over video. John Madden loved instant replay reviews. With the whole football world listening, he made his pitch.

"Instant replay is a vulnerable thing," Madden said, "and it's easy to criticize, and in this situation it's very easy for everyone to say, 'Do away with it.' But I don't think that's the answer. I think you have to stay with it, keep it. It's going to help football."

Uncharacteristically, Summerall stayed silent.

Madden and Summerall were the Oscar and Felix of an-nouncing teams. As always, Madden was in shirtsleeves, fore-arms bared. He looked as though he had sent his clothes to the rumplers. As always, Summerall was dressed impeccably in jacket and tie, which never seemed to wilt or wrinkle. Summerall *hated* delay. It offended him.

Minute three slouched into minute four and beyond, an unprecedented eternity. The CBS network had no idea what to do. Apparently, they feared cutting away to commercial lest they missed the decision. *No one was making any money on this.*

Unaccustomed to standing around in wind-whipped, 35-degree temperatures, the sweat-soaked players from Los Angeles were cursing and shivering. Up in the booth, Gardi watched one last time. Down on the field, the camera caught coach Robinson almost trembling with fury. Whatever momentum his team had achieved had been flushed down the toilet.

Up in the box, Gardi shut off the tape and spoke into his headset. It was a fumble, he'd decided. Redskins ball.

The fans went wild. In RFK Stadium, all was forgiven. Dexter Manley took a bow. But what about the experience for the TV viewers? What had just been done in postseason prime time to the industry of football?

In fact, the fiasco had exposed a second problem with instant replay, one the NFL hadn't really encountered before. It went beyond whether fans were impatient. It was that some players and coaches were livid. The delay affected momentum, literally and figuratively freezing the Rams players at a critical moment. Even if they'd *won* the call, their drive might well have still stalled.

Officially, the elapsed time had been four minutes and twenty seconds. Timing it themselves, some reporters had it at four minutes and forty seconds, but neither figure was quite right. Both counted from the moment that on-field officials announced they were going to instant replay. The actual delay from the end of the play—including the initial incorrect call, the consultation among officials, the realization they were deadlocked in disagreement, the call to Joe Gardi—was nearly six full minutes.

In the days that followed, the media was merciless. "This Play May Have Sealed the Fate of Instant Replay" was a headline in the *Los Angeles Times* on January 4, a few days before NFL executives were to meet—with replay delays number one on its agenda. "The decision was messy," wrote Mike Rabun of UPI, "and if instant replay expires, the events of last Sunday in Washington may be listed as the cause on the death certificate."

They were wrong. Joe Gardi's stubborn conscientiousness, his infuriating insistence on accuracy, may have saved instant replay review. The titans of football had been given the perfect template for what must never, ever happen again. They had something to work with.

It was by a single vote, but in January 1987 the team owners renewed instant replay for another year. The grand experiment lived on, but with certain revisions, begun immediately and continued over the years as technology developed.

Getting it fast became as important as getting it right. Calls would be made not from a little booth on the field but from a single office in New York, with multiple officials watching commodious high-definition screens. Cutting to commercial during the delay became routine. Review by instant replay would suffer some more setbacks, but it survived long enough so that the game would be unthinkable without it.

By the way:

The Redskins quickly and efficiently converted the Hill-Olkewicz turnover into a field goal against a rattled Rams defense, and won the game 19–7. Rams coach Robinson bitterly blamed the officiating for the loss, calling the delay "a damn disgrace." His center, Dennis Harrah, was more voluble: "Don't destroy the momentum of the game! Either way, get the call to us quick and don't take all day."

And in the next day's paper, *Washington Post* sportswriter Thomas Boswell ended his game story with a delicious double entendre. Referring to Redskins head coach Joe Gibbs, known for being a joyful Sunday school teacher, Boswell wrote: "Gibbs didn't do it alone yesterday at RFK. He had help from the man upstairs."

6:10 P.M., Winslow, Indiana

K ern Qualkenbush, the young Pentecostal pastor in this town of fewer than a thousand souls, was dressing for his Sunday-evening service when the doorbell rang. His wife, Velda, was at the kitchen sink, polishing off the dinner dishes. She would hear, not see, much of what happened next. Kern moved across the living room and answered the door.

It was a pretty room, dollhouse cute. Velda had a decorator's touch: sky-blue walls, rose-colored carpet, cream and blue leather furniture. The Qualkenbushes had built the house when they moved to Winslow to start their church a few years before. They loved that house, but would soon have to leave it for reasons they could have scarcely imagined on this evening. The reasons were at their front door.

Kern said hello to his neighbor Teana Ruppel, who had just turned sixteen, and her boyfriend David Hughes, who was twenty.

Teana was a high school freshman, a square girl with frizzy hair and an uncertain smile, as though she was always hiding a queasy secret. David was short, slight, and coarse-featured, with a feral, hunted look and an almost imperceptible hitch in his walk owing to a pin in one leg from a motorcycle accident. He was making eight to ten bucks an hour doing odd jobs while taking a course in diesel engine repair. He'd been fired from a previous job at an oil company after reporting three robberies and then not showing up when asked to take a polygraph test about exactly how the money went missing.

David struck people as meek and spineless, and the gun he always carried seemed compensatory, bouncing in a holster on his hip. It was a black-powder ball-and-cap .44-caliber muzzle-loader pistol, ungainly and imprecise, but at close range, a gun like that could tear a hole in your gut. He also favored leather biker jackets. He made people uneasy.

With their reddish hair, Teana and David made for a somewhat unwholesome-looking Raggedy Ann and Andy. Both were parishioners of Kern's, if reluctant ones. Teana came to services dutifully with her parents; David would drive up separately. He was not entirely welcome in the Ruppel home, but was stubborn in his courtship of Teana.

At the Qualkenbushes' door, Teana spoke first. "Have you seen my parents? They haven't been home since Friday."

"Since . . . *Friday?*" Kern repeated this, incredulous. That meant it was two days and counting. This was a couple with regular habits.

Gail and Mike Ruppel were new to Qualkenbush's small church, having joined the twenty-five-member congregation only in October. Gail, the more outgoing one, had decided her family needed spiritual guidance; she'd had a job in a liquor store and was worried that might be bad news for her soul. She was a brassy, imposing-looking woman—at five foot five, she was pushing two hundred pounds—and she took shit from no one. Mike was a mechanic who, like many of the men in Pike County, worked at a coal mine. Like David Hughes, he always carried a handgun, but without the ostentation; his was in his pocket, and it seldom if ever came out. Mike Ruppel was taciturn by nature but accessible and amiable when you knew him well. He was a man notable for having no apparent temper.

In their short time with the Qualkenbushes, Gail and Mike had become earnest churchgoers, attending services as often as three times a week. Just days before, they had agreed to be baptized, and Kern had performed the sacrament. The pastor had thought that was a fine sign of the seriousness of their intent to find the Lord, just as he thought it odd that the family had missed his service earlier on this Sunday.

Kern invited the young couple in and went through the obvious litany. Have you searched the house carefully? (Yes.) Had her parents left a note? (No.) Had they telephoned? (No.) Were their cars still there? (Yes. Not a good sign.)

There was an almost literary feel to this scene, a heightened sense of premonition. In the kitchen, Velda was listening intently to the monosyllabic, tooth-pulling conversation in the next room. She was a manager in human resources, a field that militates against snap judgments—you use your instincts, but only as informed by facts, supported by paper, defensible by logic. But Velda, at that moment, was going on gut alone. She'd gotten to know Gail Ruppel pretty well—the two women had worked together on a church-sponsored Toys for Tots program for the Christmas season. Gail was methodical and orderly. An unexplained disappearance was not like her. Moreover, Velda knew

there was trouble in the Ruppel household: Teana had been pester-
ing her parents to let her marry David—she was underage and
needed their signatures—and Gail and Mike were having none of it.

Three decades later, Velda Qualkenbush would remember the
moment in her kitchen vividly: "I felt my heart go up in my chest.
I knew in my spirit that Gail and Mike were gone and these two
people were responsible."

The whole conversation lasted no longer than five minutes.
The group decided they'd call in a missing persons report, and
Teana and her boyfriend left to return to the Ruppel house to
wait for the police. Minutes later, Kern decided to follow. He felt
a duty to offer pastoral support. Velda telephoned Teana to tell
her Kern was heading out the door and would soon be there.

Five minutes later, tires crunching wetly under a mantle of
new snow, Kern pulled into the gravel driveway of the Ruppels'
house. It was already dark, but when he killed the headlights, he
could make out a flicker of light dancing on the white-dusted
deck. David was coming around from the rear of his girlfriend's
house with a flashlight, checking the ground for . . . something.
Kern and David walked into the house. Just inside the front door,
Teana was on her knees, scrubbing the floor of the vestibule and
foyer. Beyond her, Kern could see the rest of the house—kitchen
and dining room to the left, living room to the right. At the rear
was a spiral staircase twirling up to Mike and Gail's loft bedroom.

This was a converted redbrick schoolhouse, last used for that
purpose in 1955. Mike had done some of the reconstruction himself. The Ruppels took pride in the house. Gail had furnished it
in unmatched antiques, items assembled piecemeal over time, as

though by someone with taste but not an abundance of money. If Gail had a decorating weakness it was for knickknacks; desktops and tabletops were overloaded with dolls and porcelain figurines and other homey kitsch.

Kern had been in the house before. It wasn't the clutter he was noticing. It was the disarray: mud on the kitchen floor, which Gail had always kept spotless. Sheets had been pulled off the beds. The house didn't exactly look ransacked, but it was not tidy. Gail enforced tidiness.

Teana looked up from where she was scrubbing the floor.

"Dog made a mess," she explained. Buttercup, the cocker spaniel puppy, was only five months old, and sometimes had accidents.

But Kern Qualkenbush saw no sign of dog mess.

TEANA STILL LIVES IN INDIANA, in a city that is a four-hour drive from where she grew up. On Facebook, she has a lively, jaunty, relentlessly upbeat presence. She has a different last name now, married at forty-seven to a woman named Annette. Teana's step-grandson Malachi visits a lot, a towheaded moppet who is adorable and, by all indications, adored.

Teana's Facebook profile shows a full-figured woman with a pleasant, pretty moon face. Scroll down her page, and you feel you know her. She favors dramatic lipstick. She's worked in animal rescue and for Avon cosmetics and now has a job with the Veterans Affairs office. She went to Ball State University. She is partial to pictures of cute animals. She is a friend of dog shelters and no big fan of dog breeders. She likes fragrant soaps and mo-cha peppermint iced coffee and *Grey's Anatomy* and funky hand-bags and spooky houses on Halloween. She is definitely not a fan of NFL players who kneel in protest during the National An-them. She happily displays those corny "Friends for 8 years" slide-show videos that Facebook makes available to pairs of users on the anniversaries of their friending.

Here's a picture of Teana smooching her wife. It's sweet and unencumbered. Here's a T-shirt she wants to buy. It says, "I never dreamed I'd grow up to be a perfect freakin' wife but here I am, killin' it."

She's a happy prankster, once videotaping what happened after she and Annette set a mousetrap and put it under the toilet lid so it would snap when Annette's visiting sister sat down. Sounds from inside bathroom: Snap! Pause. "Assholes!" Giggles from out-side: "We'd been waiting all night for you to go pee!" From inside, with resignation: "Assholes."

Unsurprisingly, there is no mention on Teana's Facebook page of the eight-year sentence she got in 1988 after pleading guilty to conspiracy in the murder of her parents. There is no mention of David Hughes, who was tried, convicted, and sentenced to two concurrent sixty-year prison terms for carrying out the murders, execution-style: five shots in Mike's head, ringing it like a crown of thorns, and two in Gail's head, front and back.

Reached by telephone, Teana agreed to answer some ques-tions so long as she was not quoted directly. She promised to talk longer, and fully on the record, in a face-to-face visit in a few days' time.

In the meantime: She said yes, she helped cover up her parents' killing, but only reluctantly, because she was terrified of David and was afraid that he would kill her, too, if she didn't help him. By prearrangement, she'd let him into the house on that Friday, but that was it. She was sitting at a kitchen counter, next to her mother, playing Connect Four, when David sneaked up behind them and assassinated Gail, to Teana's horror. She'd spent the next three days in December 1986 in a surreal blur, she said, not a participant so much as a hostage, trapped in a horror movie not of her own design. David had had a motive—he'd wanted her legally emancipated so they could be married—and maybe she and David had talked about it, but she couldn't believe David actually did it.

She was pretty matter-of-fact about this. Regret seems displaced by anger. For years, she said, she'd been sexually abused by her father; as a little girl, she says, her parents had lent her out to other adults for sex parties.

She was asked about something that had been briefly alluded to in a newspaper story, back in 1986: something about a note that she had written to her father on the day he was killed.

But Teana said she remembered nothing about a note. Then she said she had to get off the phone. And two days later, she telephoned to call off the visit. Her decision was final, she said, and there was no point in ever calling back.

MARK K. SULLIVAN STILL PRACTICES law in Indiana. In 1986 he was the chief prosecutor of Pike County, Indiana, which contains

Winslow, where the Qualkenbushes lived, and Ayrshire—the next town over—where the murder happened. Sullivan had brought the charges against both Teana Ruppel and David Hughes. He won Hughes's conviction after a two-week trial in October 1987.

Sullivan was told about what Teana had volunteered on the phone—about living in a horror movie, the surreal feel of it, the three-day blur; her fear of David and what he might do to her if she didn't go along with his plan.

There was a pause.

"You'll want to look at the case file," he said. "You'll want to read the trial transcript, all of it."

IT ARRIVED a few weeks later. It is 2,800 pages long, mostly a transcript of the trial of David Hughes. It begins, literally, with a flashback to December 28, 1986. The first prosecution witness was Kern Qualkenbush, and his testimony began with his door-bell ringing.

Once you start reading this document, it's hard to stop. You're back in 1986 in a small blue-collar county where it was tricky to impanel a completely impartial jury because most everyone seemed to know everyone else or work with everyone else or go to church with everyone else or be kin to everyone else. Eventually they found twelve people, but it wasn't easy.

Draw a line of longitude—north to south—bisecting the United States so that an identical number of people live to the east of it as live to the west of it. Now draw a line of latitude— east to west—so that an identical number of people live above and below it. The point that these two lines meet is considered the median center of population of the United States. The Census Bureau keeps track of changes in location of this statistical curiosity. As migration patterns have shifted over the last century, the median population center—a theoretical Middletown, the supposed demographic prototype of the United States—has been in the Northeast, glacially creeping southwest. It is currently located almost exactly at the old converted redbrick schoolhouse in Pike County, Indiana, in which Gail and Mike Ruppel were murdered in late December 1986.

The place isn't Middletown, exactly. It's a little too eccentric to be a prototype of anything.

The local patois is spare, direct, unpretentious, ungrammatical, and effective. Most witnesses—businessmen and -women, police officers, children, urban scavengers—tend to testify to what they "seen" and what they "done." In the transcript, it's mostly just the lawyers and forensic scientists who stay on the correct side of Strunk & White.

The area was built around rich five-foot-wide seams of bituminous coal that crisscrossed its hills underground. Aboveground, there is another type of seam, but a less generous one. Indiana is one of a handful of states that have more than one time zone, and in this state the divide is particularly confusing, snaking in and out through the western boundary like some ham-handed gerrymander. Ayrshire (locally pronounced "Assure"), where Teana lived with her family, was in the Eastern time zone, and Oakland City, just six miles away, where David lived with his family in their mobile home, was in the Central time zone. The dissonance could be disorienting. To arrange a business meeting or a date, you had to specify "your time," and "my time," which delivered a subtle sense of disconnect, even among friends and neighbors.

On the night of the Ruppels' disappearance, in fact, David and Teana were on a date, or so they told the police. Before they were officially interrogated on Monday, December 29, they were separated—customary police procedure where there is even a small possibility of collusion. And that is where, in their separate interviews in separate rooms in the Pike County jail, under questioning by two cops who seemed like dumb plodders and were anything but, their story began to unravel.

State police officers Larry Eck and Steve Chastain testified that Teana and David's accounts were consistent and coherent in the big details, the obvious facts you might think to rehearse: They left on a drive-around date at seven-thirty in the evening, they'd agreed, and returned at three in the morning to find the house empty. But Eck and Chastain kept prodding and weaseled out odd inconsistencies in the details of their date. They remembered different routes and different stops. They didn't even agree on which county they'd been in.

As the detectives parried with the couple, something significant was happening several miles away. A young man named Bobby McGowan, who worked at a turkey slaughterhouse, approached an old abandoned strip mine that locals sometimes used for illegal dumping. McGowan was scavenging for scrap metal.

When he got to the top of the pit and looked down, he testified, he saw an old refrigerator, tons of garbage, and what appeared to be a human arm and ear: "We got to looking real good and seen that they was two of them. The lady just had panties and socks and a shirt. The man had pants down to his knees and a shirt. The lady was on top, lying on top of the man."

The Ruppels' bodies had been half stripped, extinguishing all dignity, driven to this spot, and dumped over a retaining wall, falling forty feet into trash. Mike had gone over first, then Gail. When police arrived, they saw muddy tire tracks leading up to where the bodies would have been off-loaded. The tire tracks were distinctive and quite well preserved.

This discovery was surreptitiously fed to Eck and Chastain as they were interviewing Teana and David. For some time, they didn't disclose what they knew but kept up the questioning.

Tapes of these interviews were played for the jury. Eck and Chastain didn't do the good cop/bad cop routine; they were basically bad cop/bad cop. And they went after the inconsistencies relentlessly:

ECK, TO TEANA: You guys ain't even in the same vehicles, hardly. He got us going in one direction and you got us going in the other direction. You got us parking in one county, and he got us parking in another county. It just don't make good sense. Can you explain this?

TEANA: No.

ECK: Do you want us to find them?

TEANA: Yes.

ECK: Why?

TEANA: So we can go home and sleep in my bed and we can go on about our normal lives and people won't be asking me all these questions. I can eat some of her good cooking. Is that a good enough reason why?

ECK: Yep, it's a pretty good reason.

TEANA: I can do things with my dad. He can help me on my clock. I got to cut a piece of wood before I go back to school. See, I go back to school the fifth of next year. And I have to have a little piece of wood cut before I go back to school. Because I cut one of the sides wrong on the saw and I need a little sliver of wood and he said he'd help me. That way I could make an A.

ECK: Think we can find them?

TEANA: I hope so and pray so and if I have enough faith in God, you will.

It was slick and almost convincing. This was either an honest answer from a guileless, guiltless, scared child or a cold, manipulative act by a poised and ruthless young felon. Eck decided to try to break her. Didn't work.

ECK: They're not missing no more.

TEANA: You found them. Good! When do I get to see them?

ECK: Why do you think you can't see them?

TEANA: I don't know.

ECK: Where do you think they're at?

TEANA: I don't know.

ECK: Do you want to talk to your minister?

TEANA: No, I want to see my mom and dad.

ECK: Do you want to tell us about it? You got to tell us, Teana. We can't help you if you don't tell us.

TEANA: There ain't nothing to tell.

ECK: Yes there is. You know it and I know it. I only want the truth.

TEANA: I done told you the truth.

ECK: No, you haven't. You wish you had. See, there's a big difference between wishing that you tell the truth and telling the truth.

Later, Eck had Pastor Qualkenbush officially deliver the news to Teana. She went into a childish catatonia, asking for a teddy bear and calling for her mommy and her daddy.

Teana played her role remarkably well. David, not so much. He was the weaker and dumber conspirator, and the first to crack. It happened a few days later. In an interview in front of his family's trailer, he admitted to Eck and Chastain that he'd been drugged up and boozed up that night, and that he and Gail had had an argument over whether he should be allowed to take his gun on a date with her daughter, that she grabbed his arm, and that he told her to "shut the fuck up."

And then he volunteered something astonishing: He told police that Teana had twice asked him to kill her parents, but that he refused. Oddly, he said he might have been willing to threaten the Ruppels or even beat them up to make them let Teana marry him. But he would never kill them.

ECK: You couldn't handle him with a club.

DAVID: I dunno. He carries that gun all the time.

ECK: It would take a gun to handle him.

DAVID: Probably so.

DAVID: Could you have handled her without the gun?

DAVID: As big as she is, no.

Eck then asks him the main question one more time. Did he kill them? David wavered, and Eck and Chastain pounced. The exchange was bizarre and chilling.

DAVID: I doubt it, no.

ECK: You don't know, though. You don't know whether you killed them or not, do you? In your mind, you don't know.

DAVID: I think I didn't. As far as I know, I didn't. Teana said I didn't.

CHASTAIN: I believe I can see your heart beating back here. I can see you breathing. Just like you run a race. We're hitting pretty close to home, aren't we? Dave?

DAVID: Huh?

CHASTAIN: Did you hear me?

DAVID: What?

CHASTAIN: We're hitting pretty close to home, aren't we?

DAVID: No. You're not.

The officers asked one more time. Did he kill the Ruppels?

DAVID: Well, as far as I know, I didn't.

ECK: But you don't know for sure. How sure are you? You're not one hundred percent. Are you fifty percent sure?

DAVID: About ninety percent sure.

ECK: See, we want to know about that other ten . . .

David never quite admitted it. But at this point the officers felt they knew what had happened, how it happened, and why.

And David once again helped them by punching in with a case of the stupids.

Mike Ruppel had an inexpensive black plastic watch he loved; he loved it because he hated the alternative. He'd once had a nicer watch, a metal one, but when he was at work and accidentally scraped his arm against a short-circuiting wire, that metal watch damn near burned his wrist off. It was clear to his coworkers how much he liked his new piece-of-crap, nonconducting, nonfatal wristwatch. He wore it constantly.

Police found that watch in David Hughes's truck.

David also liked talking to the press, after his interrogation but before he was officially a suspect. It made him feel important. In an interview with Mike Bucsko, a local newspaper reporter, David described the exact position of the bodies when they were discovered and what they were wearing. These facts had not been publicly released. Hughes claimed they had been disclosed to him by a police official, but that guy took the stand and said nope, no way.

Police forensics and witness testimony would seal the case.

One man said he had seen the Ruppels' Chevy truck near the dump on the day of the murders. There were only a few people who could possibly have driven it there; the truck was rigged with two ignition switches, one of them hidden under the dash. You had to flip both for the car to start. Mike Ruppel had done it as a security measure so that no one but family would know how to start it up.

Plus, the tire tracks were a match. And someone had actually seen David driving away from the site. The coup de grace was the result of a sophisticated technology that Indiana police hardly ever used. Police decided to order a luminol test of the Ruppel home and flew an expert in from Chicago. Luminol is a chemical that is sprayed onto an area suspected to be a crime scene, under a black light. If luminol comes in contact with even invisible amounts of diluted blood, it glows an eerie electric blue for about thirty seconds, long enough to photograph the results.

The Ruppel house glowed like neon.

Prosecutor Sullivan remembers: "It was amazing! You could see where sponges had stopped as they tried to clean up. You could see a lot of blood that was cleaned. Then we used it on a bucket in the laundry room. We sprayed it and it glowed."

From the location of the blood, police concluded that Mike Ruppel had likely been shot in the foyer, right about where Teana was cleaning up the "dog mess." And that the rags and sponges used to mop up the gore were then taken to the laundry room and washed. Hardly something that, say, a robber would have done.

One witness testified to a shocking callousness shown by Teana after the killings. A relative of the Ruppels, he'd attended their funeral. He testified that he'd heard Teana excitedly say to David that they'd now have $85,000 in insurance money, a nice car, a nice motorcycle, and a nice house to live in: "She didn't act like there were coffins there at all."

Toward the end of the prosecution's case, Sullivan called two young witnesses to the stand. Both were friends and classmates of Teana's.

Sixteen-year-old Shawna Willis testified that she'd had a disturbing telephone call from Teana in the spring of 1986: "She just called me up and she just asked me, you know, what she should do, uh, just . . ."

SULLIVAN: Just what?

SHAWNA: Killing her parents. . . . She goes, what do you think I ought to do about it? I go, I wouldn't do it. She goes, why? I go, because you'll regret it for the rest of your life.

SULLIVAN: Did she indicate to you at the time who she was going to have kill her parents . . . David Hughes?

SHAWNA: Yeah.

Sullivan had one final question: "Is there, between David and Teana, is there one that dominates the other that you can see?"

"Her," Shawna said.

AND FINALLY, Sullivan called fifteen-year-old Jackie Rowe. Their colloquy was intense.

SULLIVAN: Jackie, can you recall a time when Teana indicated to you that she wanted harm to come to her parents?

JACKIE: It was at school in study hall.

SULLIVAN: What did she say?

JACKIE: She said she wanted to kill them.

SULLIVAN: Did she ask you to help?

JACKIE: Yes.

SULLIVAN: How?

JACKIE: She wanted me to come over and spend the night with her.

SULLIVAN: How was that going to help?

JACKIE: We were going to be gone. . . . we were going to leave the house.

SULLIVAN: Uh-huh.

JACKIE: And then we were going to come back.

SULLIVAN: Uh-huh.

JACKIE: And act surprised. That was . . .

SULLIVAN: Act surprised that her parents are dead?

JACKIE: Yes.

SULLIVAN: But actually it was going to be David Hughes coming in, killing them.

JACKIE: Yes.

SULLIVAN: How was he going to do it? Did Teana tell you?

JACKIE: Yes, he was going to come in from the woods. . . . Then he was gonna shoot her mother.

SULLIVAN: Did she, Teana, tell you where her mother was going to be shot?

JACKIE: The head.

SULLIVAN: Then what was going to happen?

JACKIE: They were going to wait for her dad.

SULLIVAN: Then what were they going to do to him?

JACKIE: The head, the same place.

Jackie said she forgot about that conversation not long after it happened, and Teana never again asked her to provide her an alibi. But that was more or less exactly how the crime was committed two months later. David Hughes approached the house

from the woods behind it and sneaked in through the door that
had been left open for him. He shot Gail in the back of the head.

Then he and Teana waited for Mike to come home from work,
around 10:30 P.M. According to police, they had a plan, and it
was diabolical.

Police found a small slip of paper in the couple's possession. It
had a big sticker at the top—a goofy, cartoonish heart—and a brief
message below. The message, a handwriting expert testified, was
written by Teana. It was the letter that, thirty years later, Teana
would say she had no recollection of, and then decide there would
be no more interviews.

The lines are stacked vertically. The longhand is all female
grade-school loopy. The spelling is inventive. It says:

Dad's
Clean out
the wood
berner ang
start a frir
Mom's in bed

The police theory, argued by Sullivan in his closing statement,
was that this note was written by Teana on the night of the murder. It was to be found by her father before he walked into the
house, which was warmed by a woodburning stove. The note was
telling him to clean out the wood burner and start a fire, meaning he'd have to fetch some firewood from a shed out front.

She did that, the prosecution believes, so that when Mike
Ruppel came back into the house, his arms would be loaded with

firewood. That meant he would be unable to draw his gun when he entered the foyer and David fired on him, sniper style, from a closet. That's where Mike fell. That's where the blood was.

WAS TEANA RUPPEL ever sexually molested by her father? Possibly, but many in Winslow doubt it; they suspect the allegation was either a ploy for sympathy or an invented rationale to bring herself to a state of mind where she could kill. During her interrogation, Teana did allege to police that her father had abused her, but the prosecutor told the jury he believes it was a lie. No corroboration was found. And even David Hughes—to whom Teana had given the same account—told the police he was skeptical of it. In Ayrshire, Mike Ruppel was generally respected as a good man and a loving, protective father.

What about the story of being lent out by both parents, for sex parties? Teana does not appear to have mentioned that alleged fact to anyone back in 1986. Maybe it was true and later became a repressed memory. Or maybe, like so many things from this splendid little liar, it was self-serving bullshit.

What had become clear to police not long into their investigation is that there were two conspirators but one ringleader—the smarter, more poised one. At one point, according to the tapes, they tried to flip David to get Teana:

LARRY ECK: Do you know what's going to happen when her attorney talks her into cooperating with us? Do you have any idea who is going to suffer whenever she tells the entire truth? Do you know who is going to suffer? Do you think she is going to suffer at sixteen? You know who's gonna suffer? Who did what she wanted to do to her parents. . . . You're gonna go down, and you're gonna go down hard.

But David never took the bait. He did not rat out his girlfriend, and he did go down hard.

Teana didn't rat out David, either. Despite Eck's prediction, she never cooperated with prosecutors. She testified briefly in David's trial and perjured herself with abandon: She said that neither she nor David was involved in the killing, and that she didn't know who did it.

Just months later, she would plead guilty.

But Eck was right about one thing: Teana was spared a stiffer sentence partially because she fired no shots, but more because of her age. It was not, however, because she was considered a victim of David or anyone else, or an unwilling participant.

AS MURDERS IN SMALL TOWNS tend to do, the Ruppel case rattled the Winslow area deeply. Shortly after the crime and before the arrests, people started talking. Some of it got crazy. In places like Winslow, gossip can make up for the absence of other entertainment.

Because Teana requested pine caskets with black roses for her parents' funeral, a rumor spread that there was an occult component to the crime. Townspeople started whispering about witches and pentagrams and devil worship.

Social scientists who study the spread of gossip, particularly following community trauma, say it is often a subconscious effort to control the narrative in a personally nonthreatening way. It's part of something called the attribution process, involving biased assimilation: People seek to attribute causes to events in ways that deliver reassurance or confirmation of their world view. If you want to feel, for example, that this sort of thing couldn't happen to you, you must distance yourself from the victims. They must have done something wrong, something that violates societal norms—and the more violative the better.

In the weeks after the murders, the rumor that took hold of Winslow went like this: That Kern Qualkenbush, the young pastor, was having an affair with Gail Ruppel, and to hush it up, he either committed or engineered her murder.

It was completely unfounded. It was preposterous on its face. Not even a small hint of any part of that ever surfaced. But the whispers spread to the point that Velda Qualkenbush herself heard it when she was shopping at the local grocery store. Her husband was an adulterer and a murderer.

Their congregation was already modestly sized, and the seeping poison whittled it down further. Pentecostal officials took note. They ordered Kern to close the church and reassigned him to another one. The new one was far enough away that the Qualkenbushes had to move away from the house they'd built and loved.

David Hughes served twenty-eight years in prison and was released on parole in 2015. Today he is not easily found. The Indiana parole office has his contact information and relayed a request for an interview. He declined, saying he wanted his privacy. He wanted to put this thing entirely behind him.

And then there is Teana.

She is also entitled to her privacy—and maybe to some compassion. She appears to be nothing like the person she once was. Public records indicate she has had some financial troubles, but no run-ins with the law. One of the first things she did after getting out of prison was to get a college degree. She is in a loving relationship for which she shows enormous gratitude. She seems to care deeply about abused and abandoned animals. She works for an organization that helps the most vulnerable people among us.

Imagine being Teana, trying to live with what you had done. You might well convince yourself that things that happened thirty years ago were more understandable, more excusable, and less malignant than they were. If she is a woman of conscience now, the self-deception might even be necessary for her to have any life at all, let alone a happy one. She seems like a joyful and fulfilled person now.

As of this writing, her most recent Facebook posts included links to two articles: how to stop your cat from peeing outside the litter box, and which Bible verses will best get you through the year.

6:15 P.M., Montego Bay, Jamaica

It was a kaleidoscopic sunset. Kaleidoscopic sunsets are the whole point of Jamaica, which is why the hotels have no trouble selling dead-of-winter wedding getaway packages. The choice is yours: Take your vows in front of a breathtaking vista on the beach or a breathtaking vista on the veranda. Bob Stevenson and Melody Marshall of Cherry Hill, New Jersey, picked the veranda. There were no wedding guests. The witnesses were hotel employees. The Reverend Terrence Gordon officiated. He came with the package.

The weather was ideal, the circumstances somewhat less so. The bride wore white, but the fabric was taut against her distended belly; no tailor on earth has the skills to hide a seven-month pregnancy on a petite woman. Because of a stiff wind she'd overdone it on the hair spray, which is why, in the photos, her formidable blond helmet is a little atilt, like a quarterback's on the sidelines. Also, she had a wicked sunburn. The rings were cheap onyx bands, a last-minute purchase from a vendor on the street.

The groom didn't dress up. Not his style. Bob Stevenson was an unschooled but intelligent man, a successful landlord and insurance executive with the bearing and body of a brute. His low forehead seemed Paleolithic. He'd done some amateur boxing, which showed in his cabbage face and in the way he carried himself, like a guy in a perpetual protective crouch. He could be romantic in safely distanced ways—Melody would get lots of flowers—but that was pretty much it. He didn't buy into modern ideas of the sensitive male partner, which is why he'd warned Melody not to expect him in the delivery room, whooshing and huffing with her like some candy-ass househusband, timing her contractions. Melody was fine with that. Her mom would be her coach.

With Bob Stevenson, what you saw was what you got, and what you got was unmodulated intensity. At work, he was suit and tie. Relaxed, he was *Goodfellas* lite—open shirts with dangly gold on black hair. He had a pinkie ring. His watch had gold braid. An eighth grade dropout, the product of a badly broken home, he'd once been a runaway who tried to rob a restaurant and wound up doing time in reform school. But then through prodigious work, he had pushed his way to the top of his various businesses. That appealed to Melody, whose first husband, in a brief marriage, had been a likable feckless partier—boozed, buzzed, and broke.

Bob may have been a mule, a hobnailed boots sort of guy, but Melody was no doormat. She knew you couldn't push him, but he had buttons, and you could push *them*. That's how this wedding happened: Melody had casually mentioned that even though they were living together and committed to each other, it looked as if the baby was going to wind up with her last name. Bob said . . . uh, what? Melody repeated that she supposed the baby was going to be named Marshall, not Stevenson, on account of that's the way it works when a lady is single. She was not *complaining*, she was just *observing.*

So here they were not many days later, in Jamaica, standing before the Reverend Terrence Gordon, saying their "I dos." A nice dinner followed, and then Melody and Robert Stevenson of Cherry Hill, New Jersey, and their unborn child, who would be a boy, went to bed.

ON MARCH 13, 1998, the Superior Court of New Jersey issued an order unprecedented in the state, and rare anywhere in the country. Contradicting two hundred years of case and common law, in which such a request was routinely granted, Judge William Cook denied a woman's petition to lift a restraining order against her husband. Because of the novelty of the ruling, Cook spent much of the ensuing pages justifying it. The facts of the case were so disturbing, he'd decided, that the state must in good conscience substitute its sober judgment for the dysfunctional one of a physically and emotionally abused woman. Or, as Cook put it,

> In the matter of Melody Stevenson, plaintiff, vs. Robert Stevenson, defendant
>
> Defendant was guilty of attempted criminal homicide, aggravated assault, terroristic threats, criminal restraint and burglary . . . These violations arose from a brutal, sadistic and prolonged attack by defendant on his wife during the late evening and early morning hours of October 29–30, 1997. The uncontroverted facts showed that during a drunken rage, defendant beat and tortured his wife so severely that she was critically injured, and had to be

medevac'd by emergency helicopter to the Cooper Hospital Trauma Unit in Camden.

Plaintiff, who appeared at the hearing with two black and severely swollen eyes, testified that on the late evening of October 29, 1997, defendant came into the marital bedroom, went into a total rage, punched plaintiff with both fists, held her down with his knees, kicked her in the back and ribs, and continued beating her there for approximately 25 minutes. Defendant then dragged her by her hair down the stairs and out of the house, and shoved her into his van, saying that they were going to go to a friend's house. Plaintiff was bleeding from her ears, nose and mouth. She got out of the van, ran to a neighbor's house and banged on the door. Defendant chased her, screaming he would kill her, and that he should have killed her before. She was "petrified." He caught up to her outside the neighbor's house, and choked her with both hands around her throat. He then dragged her down the street and pushed her back into the van. She escaped again and ran to another neighbor's house. At that point, defendant's vicious attack on his wife had been going on for 45 minutes. She went inside the neighbor's house and asked her neighbor to call the police, while she went into a powder room, closed the door, and tried to hide from defendant. Defendant went into the neighbor's house and proceeded to rip the powder room door off its hinges. The door landed on plaintiff. He dragged her out of that house, and back towards their house. Plaintiff grabbed onto trees along the way, trying to resist. He was furious because she had asked her neighbor to call the police. Finally, he let go of her, got into the van and left. She was badly injured and very scared. A neighbor came with a blanket and rendered first aid. She was rushed by ambulance to the Emergency Room of West Jersey Hospital. She had three large lumps on her head, two black eyes, blood running from her ears, and abrasions and lacerations all over her body. She also had trouble breathing. At the West Jersey Hospital Emergency Room, she was diagnosed as having head and lung injuries, and was in such critical condition that she had to be medevac'd by helicopter to the Cooper Hospital Trauma Center. She had a fractured skull, a concussion, four broken ribs, and a punctured lung (pneumothorax), in addition to the injuries noted above. She remained hospitalized at Cooper for several days, and was still under medical care at the time of the hearing on November 6, 1997.

Judge Cook refused to lift the restraining order. Pending Robert Stevenson's trial for the attempted murder of Melody Stevenson and lesser counts of applied mayhem, there would be no unsupervised contact between husband and wife. And that was that.

THAT WAS NOT THAT.

There are no adjectives that adequately describe just how unlikely were the events that followed. *Improbable* and *implausible* don't do it justice, but *impossible* is obviously wrong. *Stevenson v. Stevenson* did not play out as a cautionary tale about domestic violence or substance abuse. It would not become a case study on the virtues of judicial activism. It would offer no sustainable lessons for victim advocates. It would encapsulate no easy universalizing themes. There was just this: In the end, against immeasurable odds, *Stevenson v. Stevenson* became a love story, with a jaw-dropping finale.

THEIR RELATIONSHIP BEGAN on the telephone. He sold cars in Philly; she sold insurance twenty miles away in Voorhees, New Jersey. Sometimes his client needed to be issued an on-the-spot, short-term policy to drive a car off the lot. Melody was good at that, a maestro of the quick fix. Eventually she and Bob met at her office one Saturday afternoon to discuss business. They'd flirted some on the phone, so Melody was a bit excited. But she also was a bit wary—there was enough of a whiff of danger in this guy that she arranged for a friend to be with her. Not long afterward they were a couple, and two years after that, after a little bulge appeared and a little wifely noodge occurred, the couple went to Jamaica.

On the night of the assault in 1997, the ten-year marriage of Melody and Bob Stevenson was about as gangrenous as a relationship could get. Interviewed separately many years later for this book, neither could adequately explain how so much mistrust had developed in so relatively short a time. But by 1997, Melody was furtively talking to a divorce lawyer, and she'd recently made the mistake of doing it on the phone when Bob could overhear. It had gotten him angry, but it had also gotten him scared. He was afraid that in the rancor, leveraged by what he saw as an institutional bias toward women in domestic cases, his wife would take their son.

Bob Stevenson had never been generous at showing affection in conventional ways. He didn't believe in cooing, he believed in action, so he would lavish his intensity on people he cared about.

In the case of his only child, the blond, cherub-cheeked little boy born two and a half months after that night in Jamaica, it meant sharing his passion for competitive sports.

There is no point in learning a sport, he'd informed a four-year-old Bobby, if you weren't going to be better at it than anyone else. And to be better than everyone else, you needed to put in the hours. At five, Bobby was already playing roller hockey and ice hockey, a sport Bob Stevenson favored because its junior league coaches were similarly driven. Dad did not subscribe to what he saw as the namby-pamby scourge of many American youth leagues: inclusion. He hated the theory that everyone gets to play, and that, win or lose, everyone wins. Losers lose, Bob believed. So Bobby Stevenson played and practiced hockey full tilt, driven by his father onto the ice most mornings at six A.M., before school. There are kids for whom this would amount to parental abuse, but Bobby seldom even rolled an eye. He loved the time with his father, and he loved the game.

He was also good at it. Bob Stevenson was no expert in hockey, but he understood the imperatives and subtleties of sports. Bobby skated well and he had good hands—he could control a puck and fire off an authoritative pass or shot on goal. These are valuable but teachable skills, improvable through practice. The innate gift the boy seemed to have—good at five, better at eight, amazing at ten—was an ability to see the whole ice, to anticipate vectors and angles of incidence and angles of reflection, to know who is where and moving at what speed relative to him. It's called having eyes, and it's an almost mystical quality, prized across all sports.

John McPhee's 1965 biography of a young Bill Bradley, the

Princeton basketball great who would become a U.S. senator and presidential candidate, was titled *A Sense of Where You Are,* to underscore this subtle essential ability. Bradley was never the best pure shooter or the fastest runner or the most tentacled defender, but he rose above most others because he knew who he was and where he was. He played to his strengths and kept his focus, in sports and later in life. Bobby had this. In the months and years after the attack, it would help rescue him.

That bad night started out fine. Father and son went to a Philadelphia Flyers game against the St. Louis Blues. Bobby was excited because his favorite player, Brett Hull, played for the Blues, who won, 3–2. By the time they got home, though, Bob Stevenson was stewing. Part was the sweetness of the night, dourly measured against the possibility that there wouldn't be many more like it. And there was something else.

After putting his son to bed, Bob went to check on a recording device he had secretly set up in the house, monitoring their home phone. He'd bought it and hooked it up after overhearing Melody's call to the lawyer. It was a scummy thing to do, but this was a marriage lacking trust in all directions, and Bob was, at that point in his life, a kind of scummy guy—angry and vindictive and controlling; to him, it seemed, marriage was indistinguishable from ownership.

He played back the recording. On it was a conversation between Melody and a man, but not a lawyer. It was a guy who had pills—Percocet—that Melody was arranging to buy. Years later, Melody and Bob would disagree on the extent of her drug problem—he says it was disabling; she says it was sporadic and mostly harmless—but she definitely had an appetite for an illegal buzz, and Bob disapproved, and she knew it. They'd had words over it before, and Melody had made solemn promises.

You can speculate about what would have happened if Bob had confronted his wife immediately. His temper was incendiary, and he was not beyond violence. Outside the home, he'd brawled; inside, there had been confrontations and altercations and, according to the courts, minor incidents of violence, though Bob and Melody both deny the latter. The fact is, had Bob approached his wife right away that night, there likely would have been a hellish scene, but not much else. Instead, he gathered up his anger and resentment and feelings of betrayal and took them to a neighborhood saloon, to marinate.

Bob Stevenson pursued drinking the way he pursued most things: never, ever halfheartedly. So he usually didn't drink at all. But when he did, it was with a competitive frenzy.

The man who returned to 117 Thornhill Road an hour and a half later was a savage in a feral rage.

WHEN POLICE ARRIVED, Bob Stevenson was on his front porch, his eyes resolute, his fists raw. He was headed out of the house, not to turn himself in but to find the man with the Percocet and make him pay. The arrest was without incident.

Bobby Stevenson went to stay with his grandparents. When he was finally allowed to see his mom in the hospital—when her wounds had healed enough so she merely looked busted up, not pulverized—he told her that he had slept through the entire night. He still says that. Maybe it's true, or maybe it's a manufactured memory, a necessary painkiller.

The Stevensons separated. Bob got out on bail. Not long before he was to go on trial, he'd heard from a friend of his, a man who had watched him in the boxing ring; the friend said he'd been interviewed by authorities and that they wanted him to testify that Bob's fists were lethal weapons. That is the moment Stevenson understood he'd be cut no slack at all, that the state was going to seek a maximum penalty, which could be twenty years. That is also the moment Bob Stevenson decided to flee.

He obtained a phony ID, based on a birth certificate poached from a friend whose brother had died in childhood. In the fall of 1998, he jumped bail and headed west. As soon as he crossed the Jersey state line, he became a federal fugitive.

These actions were perhaps predictable. Bob was not a cautious person, nor was he overly concerned with the letter of the law. What is somewhat harder to fathom was what happened next. Seven months later, at midnight, alert for tails, Melody trundled Bobby into the car to head out west, to live under an assumed name with the man who had beaten her half to death.

MELODY STEVENSON IS STILL a petite blonde. She still lives with Bob in a cheerful Colonial home not far from Cherry Hill. He manages a nearby gym.

At fifty-five, her face is thinner now, more angular than it was on the beach in Jamaica. Back then she'd had the bangly look of a mafia moll, cute but tough, with lots of makeup and big, feathered platinum hair. The ostentation is gone. She's no-nonsense now—unfussy shoulder-length hair, gym clothes, and lots of sinew.

One of the first things she tells you is "I was never a battered wife."

She means, not stereotypically.

"I was never a pathetic, helpless victim," she says, as the courts
and many of her friends and neighbors assumed. She was not,
she says, cowed into defending a man who terrified her nor was
she making excuses for him. He didn't terrify her, either before
or after. She didn't have that common battered-woman delusion
that he was omniscient or omnipresent. She didn't have Stock-
holm syndrome. She didn't blame herself for what he did, except
a little.

She knows how those last three words sound, but the truth as
Melody Stevenson sees it is that you can't look at their awful night
the way the courts did, as though it had just *happened,* stripped
of context, without antecedent, without motive. The truth, as she
sees it, is not that her husband inexplicably got drunk one day,
went batshit, and did something horrible. The truth, as she sees
it, requires a much longer sentence with several dependent
clauses. She had reneged on a pledge that was important to him
because he feared her use of drugs would imperil the family and
hasten a divorce he didn't want because, as a child of divorce, he
knew what it can do to children. When he caught her in a lie
about something that had gnawed at him, a promise she'd made
that he expected her to keep, he was justifiably furious. And *then*
he got drunk and went batshit and did something horrible. The
difference doesn't remotely excuse his actions, she acknowledges,
but it helps explain what happened afterward.

With the attack in some perspective, she could look at it as
part of a timeline of failures—some hers, some his—in a mar-

riage destined for dissolution at the expense of her son. She could understand how Bob's fear and fury had overwhelmed his sanity, Melody says, and she realized to her surprise that she was sadder for her husband than she was angry at him, even when she was still in her hospital bed.

"I was sad for all of us, but mostly for him. I knew his life was ruined. And I knew immediately—I knew *immediately*—that he would never do it again because of how ashamed he was. He was so ashamed.

"I *knew* that and I *said* that, but the court wouldn't accept it. They treated me like a dumdum, like I had nothing of value to say, like I wasn't a person. Hello, I was a grown woman, and I was not a stupid woman. It was mortifying."

At least five times she tried to get that restraining order lifted. Each time it was denied. The criminal justice system itself, Melody said, was more responsible for her flight than any other single factor. That's because its main victim, as she saw it, was Bobby.

"I wanted Bobby to be back in his father's life because it was really important for both of them, and the court made it impossible."

The restrictions were understandable but extraordinary. Bob Stevenson could not go near his own house. He was prohibited not only from seeing Melody but also from seeing Bobby, unless chaperoned by both grandfathers. Visits were wooden and awkward for everyone.

"It wasn't until I couldn't be with my husband that I realized how much I wanted to be with my husband," Melody says.

So things took this profoundly ironic turn. Bob and Melody Stevenson found themselves slowly drawn back together, their

leprous marriage beginning to heal over shared outrage at an implacable enemy, the government that was trying to protect her
from him. In spite of the restraining order, husband and wife
secretly met a few times alone. At times, with her acquiescence,
he stayed overnight. It all felt surprisingly normal, except for the
sedition of it. That part simply felt good. It was the very beginning of the Escape Plan. The Escape Plan was complicated, but
it was mostly about Bobby.

Bob would leave when his trial loomed too close. Publicly,
Melody would be shocked, shocked by his flight. Mother and son
would wait out the school year until Bobby completed sixth
grade, as Bob the fugitive scouted the country for a place to live.
Their only criterion was that it be a healthy distance from New
Jersey and that it have a world-class youth hockey league.

Hockey snakes through this story insistently, and even if you
do not know where this all is headed, the investment of time and
commitment may seem strange. It shouldn't, even on the surface:
Hockey gave Bob and Melody Stevenson a pivot point around
which to rebuild their marriage. The one thing they shared with
equal passion, unequivocal and without baggage, was love for
their son and concern for his well-being. Their son was all about
hockey, so hockey became an easy, convenient common goal. In
their lives, Melody says, hockey had already replaced religion;
now it was a perfectly logical source of comfort in troubled times.

On the night they chose for their escape, Melody and Bobby
drove to Baltimore, where they met Bob in a parking lot down by
the piers, near a crab shack, and headed west together in their
van. They were a family once more, if a deeply wary, hunted one.

————

BOB HAS THICKENED SOME SINCE his wedding day, but he runs a gym and makes use of it compulsively, so his triceps have biceps and his lats have pecs. He's still got all his hair, and that Cro-Magnon forehead still suggests a brute, something he is no longer. He also doesn't drink anymore. He also doesn't cut himself much slack.

"I didn't deserve my family," he says.

Melody says her husband's spirit is broken now, that he never regained his old swagger. This is hard to reconcile with the beefy, taciturn, seemingly self-confident guy you're talking to. But the guy you're talking to has this squint, with a duck of the head, which he does when forced to revisit what he did. Contrition is not a natural state for him, nor is humility. This takes a long time to come out: "Only two people had the power to forgive me, and they forgave me."

Then: "I didn't have any right to expect that or to deserve that."

Finally: "I got lucky. I could have lost my son and my wife, they both could have walked away, and no one including me would have blamed them."

When alone on the run, Bob had checked out Canada but in the end settled on Redondo Beach, California, which had maybe the second-best American youth hockey program after Cherry Hill. By the time Melody and Bobby got out there, the family had a new last name—Ryan, chosen by Bob on a whim, after seeing *Saving Private Ryan*. The title character, of course, was the object of a manhunt, though a particularly benevolent one.

Focused as always, Bobby learned his new identity flawlessly and simply accommodated himself to the fugitive lifestyle. On car rides, it became his job to look for tails, write down license numbers of cars that seemed to be following too closely. If they felt heat, if Bob had to split again, he would.

Bobby stuck to his story, even after some of his new teammates recognized him. They pointed to his picture in a publication about America's junior hockey leagues, where he was identified as Bobby Stevenson, a star from New Jersey. "I'm Bobby Ryan," he answered, stone-faced.

"Some parents suspected," Melody says dryly. "Some parents *knew*. They didn't ask questions."

Things went well for about a year.

Four forty-five A.M. is an important time of day in law enforcement. It's the consensus best moment for a SWAT raid that's mostly likely to find everyone asleep: It's too late even for night owls and too early even for early risers. So it was 4:45 on a February morning in 2000 when a twenty-member team of federal marshals showed up at the Ryan house and broke in the door. They had automatic weapons and riot shields. This time it was nothing Bobby could sleep through. He was in his pullout bed, downstairs, where they entered. He watched as the feds stormed upstairs to find his father.

"It was the worst thing you can imagine," Melody says. "Bobby is down there surrounded by men with guns. I am screaming, 'MY SON! MY SON!' But they're storming up the stairs and I can't get past them. I just wanted to hold him and comfort him and I couldn't."

No hockey parent had informed on them. No one had informed

on them. Bob had made the mistake of using an old credit card to try to rent a video at Blockbuster. In retrospect, he says, he should have suspected something when the card was declined. Turns out it had been on a federal crime database.

IN NEW JERSEY, Bob Ryan pleaded guilty and got a five-year sentence, which you could call lenient given the gravity of the crime, compounded by his jumping bail. Or you could call it harsh given his contrition, and husband-wife reconciliation, and maybe common sense.

Melody stayed in California. She moved to a cheaper home in a cheaper town. She had a job at a hockey rink and took another at an airline, both for the extra bucks and so she could get discounts on airfare for Bobby—when your team has elite talent, you need to move great distances to find worthy opponents. Bobby skated during the day while Melody worked at the rink. Then dinner and homeschooling, from Melody. Then she'd leave for her second job. She did not get an abundance of sleep.

Five difficult years passed. At sixteen, Bobby played right wing for the Owen Sound Attack, a minor league team in central Canada. The team paid for a home so Melody could join her son and continue his schooling.

By that time Melody had decided to keep the name Stevenson. Bob and Bobby opted for Ryan. Bob did his time uneventfully and got out on parole in the summer of 2005, and almost immediately requested permission to leave the state for a few days. Considering the circumstances, the request was granted, which is how Bob Ryan came to be in the ballroom of the Westin

Hotel in Ottawa, Ontario, Canada, on July 30, for the National Hockey League Entry Draft. It was there that the general manager of the Mighty Ducks of Anaheim selected Bobby Ryan with second overall pick, right after Canadian phenom Sidney Crosby.

There are photos from draft day. Bobby was six foot two, with a pink, plump face, barely looking his age, which was eighteen. He was taller than his father and towered over his mom, both of who look indescribably proud. This benign picture would get into the Jersey newspapers, which was not good. Yes, Bob had been cleared to travel, but that restraining order was still in place, so he was not permitted to be near Melody. They popped his parole for that, and put him under house arrest for the next eighteen months.

"It was worth it," Bob says.

IF YOU ARE a pro hockey fan, you may or may not have heard about Bobby Ryan's past, but you likely know of his career, which has been splendid. At the 2010 Winter Olympics in Vancouver he scored America's first goal, then helped lead the team to the silver medal. In Anaheim he became a face of the franchise, a fan favorite who starred in some slick, funny videos setting up a supposed rivalry between Ryan and Ducks teammate Ryan Getzlaf. Getzlaf's Canadian squad had won the gold against the American silver in those 2010 Olympics, and in these videos Getzlaf keeps joyfully rubbing that fact in Ryan's face.

Ryan's face has matured. Today he is singularly handsome; all that's left of childhood is a faint sibilance—a trace of a little-kid lisp—and vulnerable, liquid light blue eyes. He's a wealthy young man. In 2014 he was traded by the Ducks to the Ottawa Senators, where he signed a $50 million, seven-year contract extension.

Bobby speaks only infrequently about his parents' difficulties and his change of identity and his short, frantic life on the run. He doesn't like to speculate about whether these things might have added certain skills to his repertoire. He doesn't like to revisit all of this very much at all. He declined to speak for this book.

From an early age he had more drama and trauma thrown at him than most people experience in a lifetime. If you are going to survive drama and trauma, you need to develop the ability to separate things in your brain, which Bobby did. That's a very good tool to develop intensity of focus.

The Bobby Ryan highlight reel is spectacular. He is a master of the deke feint, the casual juggle of the puck that leaves defenders looking like dopes. There is his unassisted, Maradona-like drive to the net during a play-off game against the Nashville Predators, where he spins a defender dizzy, using the man's own body as a pick against the goalie, and slaps the puck home. There is his "broken bat home run," where he scores the tying goal against the Dallas Stars with seconds to go in the third period on a shot that breaks his stick in two in his hands. The resulting wobbly half shot imparts English onto the puck, which takes a bouncing journey toward the net, knuckleballing between defenders, as though it had eyes.

These are all the early skills on display: stick-handling, shot-making, a sense of where you are. But there is something else, and you see it time and again.

After bearing witness to, and somehow assimilating, the

mauling of his mother by his father, during his family's escape and fugitive life, adopting a new identity and sticking with it, lying when necessary and coming to terms with that, watching your father arrested and hustled out of your home, and finding a way to accommodate that, too; watching your mother struggle to survive, juggling time and money she didn't have to somehow keep things going, learning to make decisions on the fly, taking what comes and improvising based on available options, however sparse they might be—after all these things, Bobby Ryan learned to use resourcefulness as a weapon, and he learned calm in the face of chaos. On the ice, he seems preternaturally composed, seldom surprised, never at a loss for what to do, even where there is no precedent and no script.

IT IS December 12, 2010, at 17:26 of the second period. Bobby's Ducks are hosting the Minnesota Wild, and leading 4–2. The action begins in the left corner near the Wild's goal.

The Wild's bad-boy center, Mikko Koivu, loses the puck, and along with it, his stick, which slides away. Calculating that retrieving the wood would leave the goal underprotected for too long, Koivu instead turns and follows the puck until it is momentarily corralled by Bobby Ryan maybe fifteen feet in front of the goal, which is not good for Koivu's team. In an instant, Koivu senses a way to solve both his problems at once. It is unconventional. He reaches out with his left hand and grabs Ryan's stick.

ANNOUNCER ONE: Koivu just stripped the stick away from Bobby Ryan!

ANNOUNCER TWO: Is he using it?

ANNOUNCER ONE: He's using it!

It is piracy. It is perfidy. It is grand theft—a stickup, if you will. Neither announcer has ever seen it before. It should be a penalty of some sort, but the officials missed it. The now-uncontrolled puck goes skittering away from the net, back toward the right corner, near the boards. Koivu skates in pursuit, using Ryan's stick.

What now? They don't teach this one at the academy. Stickless, Ryan also follows the puck into the corner where he battles Koivu and another Wild defender for it, using only his skate blades. He does a frantic dance, imprisoning the puck between his feet, while shouldering away the others. Somehow he wins this lopsided fight, kicking the puck out toward a teammate. Now the Ducks are in control. They pass the puck out to the left, to coordinate an assault on the net.

Lingering behind, Ryan spots Koivu's stick on the ice and picks it up. The feel isn't perfect—Koivu uses a lefty's stick, Ryan a righty's, so the curvature is out of whack, but this is very much an improvised, make-do, DIY moment. The action is now thirty feet away from Ryan, to the left of the net, but Ryan holds back, to the right, standing there alone, poised for . . . something.

He seems out of the action until his teammate Toni Lydman rockets a shot toward the net. Bobby's positioning on the ice had anticipated this: vectors, angle of incidence, angle of reflection. The shot ricochets off goalie Nicklas Backstrom and right at Ryan, who flicks it at a sharp angle past the helpless Backstrom and into the net. All done with Koivu's repurposed, all-wrong, retaliatory counter-purloined, lefty stick.

For a moment, it looks as though the officials are going to nullify the goal, because it has been scored with unauthorized equipment. But there doesn't seem to be any precedent for that, or for any of it, really, or any basis on which to make a ruling. In the absence of laws, common sense and fairness prevail. The goal stands.

IN MAY OF 2015, the Stevenson-Ryans are preparing for Bobby's wedding, which is to be out west. A big problem involves the family's Siberian huskies. Bob is so attached to them, Melody explains so he won't board them and is very particular about dog-sitters. It's almost funny, she says. They are working on it. He's also a softie for the cats who live at the gym.

Melody still has her cheap wedding band from Jamaica, bought on December 28, 1986. Bob long ago lost track of his ring. He's not big on mementos.

Melody is. For a wedding present, she is sewing Bobby a quilt from scraps taken from all his hockey uniforms, starting when he was five, playing for the Thunderbirds in Cherry Hill.

So if this is, in the end, a love story, why has this marriage endured? Why do they love each other still?

Bob?

"I'm not gonna answer that," he says. "I don't talk about that sort of stuff. Ask Melody."

Melody? Why does Bob love you? He won't tell me.

There is a long pause, then a sigh, then a half laugh. "He won't tell me, either."

Why do you love him?

She hesitates only a second. "The only way I can explain it is this," she says. "You know how when you go on a first date, sometimes, with the right person, you feel little butterflies, and your heart skips a beat? I never lost that feeling with Bob. I never lost that feeling, even after that night. If I had lost it back then, maybe I would have left him. I tried to lose it. I fought that feeling. I didn't want to have it anymore, but it never went away. I don't know if it's selfish of me, but it's just a fact. I wanted that. I still want that. And it's still there."

7:45 P.M., JFK Airport, New York City

Children were staring. Parents were peeking. The fifty-odd people milling together in the departures area here seemed just a little . . . off. It was not that some were speaking Russian—this was, after all, the international terminal. It's that this crowd seemed not so much Third World as Old World. Many were dressed in sturdy, unattractive clothing, and a little too much of it, like 1910s immigrants at Ellis Island. For the few men who were bewhiskered, it was in one of two styles: Marx or Rasputin. Nearly everyone wore a woolen muffler around the neck, as though it were part of a dress code. Both men and women had positioned themselves beneath big cylindrical Cossack-style fur hats.

Just a little . . . off.

As it turned out, their story was compelling, not comic. These were unwitting political pawns during the final momentous, pitiful last days of the Cold War.

All fifty were Russian émigrés who, years after coming to the United States in search of freedom and plenty, had chosen to return to the Soviet Union. Many had become U.S. citizens. This was not the ordinary direction of immigration between the Soviet Union and the United States—it was essentially a rare reverse commute—and it was no accident it was happening all at once, the largest one-day repatriation of Russians from the U.S. in anyone's memory. The flight would be briefly delayed when Aeroflot realized it needed a bigger plane.

For years, the Soviet Union had been denying the vast majority of return-home requests from those who had emigrated to the West. Shrewdly—cynically?—the Soviet government had now decided to honor most of these requests on the same day, with prearranged transportation, which meant there would be a long line of people disillusioned by life in America, all together in one place waiting for the same flight, and all available to the U.S. media, who had been tipped off and were there to witness this unusual scene and dutifully record the kvetches. Many of these returnees were Jewish.

It was a double propaganda bonanza for the Soviets. First, it suggested that America was not the Shangri-la it was widely rumored to be—that to Russians accustomed to a certain way of life, the United States could be inhospitable and disappointing, even terrifying. Second, it demonstrated that Russia was serious about glasnost, Mikhail Gorbachev's social reform policy relaxing Soviet-era limits on personal freedoms. In the past, émigrés to the United States had been regarded as turncoats. The fifty at the airport were, at least publicly, being welcomed home warmly.

So yes, it was something of a manufactured event. These people represented a minuscule proportion of Russians who had come to the United States; virtually all of the thirty-five thousand who had arrived here since 1981 had chosen to stay. But those facts didn't complicate the news reports of the weekend of December 28. For the Russians, as they say, the optics were great. As was the audio.

"I'm really anxious to get back," Taras Kordonsky told *The New York Times* at the airport. "I felt immediately I didn't belong here. I felt so negative emotionally, so homesick."

"America for Americans, Russia for Russians," Vladimir Troshinsky succinctly informed the Associated Press. He'd worked in the United States as a taxi driver and auto mechanic, but said he wanted to be a chemical engineer and felt he had a better chance at an education in Russia.

The AP quoted a limo driver named Alexander Cherkasets complaining that life in New York was "harsh," with too much greed, crime, and poverty.

The Soviets seized on this sentiment and ran with it. Aleksei Zhvakin, vice consul for the Soviet embassy, told the media in a sonorous voice that the émigrés were "afraid of destroying their children." The United States is too violent and too permissive, he said: Russian parents "don't want their children to be criminals." Soviet radio in the United States concurred. The people who were returning, said the announcer, could not bear "the ruthless competition, the spirit of money-making, crime and drug addiction."

It may have been managed news, but it was *effectively* managed news. In the ongoing game of propaganda points, the Soviet Union had just raked in a pile of red chips.

Lost in the crowd at the airport was a colorful family of four. Valery Klever and his wife, Lidiya, were with their two children, chestnut-haired daughter Karina, who was sixteen, and two-year-old son Nikita, a winsome tousle-haired blond.

Even at first glance, the Klever family seemed nothing like the homogenized Cleavers from the 1950s sitcom *Leave It to Beaver.* Valery was pale-skinned, projecting a dignified melancholy. He wore a drab trench coat like McGruff the Crime Dog and one of those Rasputin beards that tapered down a half foot beneath his chin. No one could mistake Valery Klever for a local. His wife, part Greek, part Ukrainian, was darker of skin, and similarly somber of mien. The baby was a baby. But daughter Karina seemed from another world altogether, even at first glance. She wore faded jeans and a fashionably sloppy top; she'd been in the United States since she was eight years old, and it showed. She was an American teenager.

The Klevers were not interviewed in New York. Whatever their story was, they would carry it back with them to Moscow.

As the fifty émigrés trundled toward their flight, you couldn't help but notice something. Disillusioned though they may have been, they clearly understood there were trade-offs in what they were doing, that a different, more austere life awaited. Many were burdened with packages—electronics and other luxuries purchased in New York and in short supply in Russia. Taras Kordonsky, the homesick man who felt he didn't belong here, carried a bass guitar. One woman had an electric typewriter and a videocassette recorder. These people were heading home voluntarily, but hardly naively.

Packages thumping against knees and thighs and walkway walls, they shuffled forward toward their plane and into their new, old lives.

———

TWELVE HOURS LATER the group was in Moscow's Sheremetyevo International Airport. In New York, the Soviet government had not been in charge, and things did not seem choreographed. Not so now. This was unapologetically stage-managed.

As the plane unloaded, a harried-looking silver-haired man in a platinum-colored suit and tie stood in the terminal with a megaphone, barking orders. Beside him, to get this all on record, was a woman wrestling with a bulky reel-to-reel tape recorder— all but obsolete in 1980s America, but apparently still state of the art in Soviet Russia. Even before they went through customs, the émigrés were shepherded into a room filled with Western news correspondents. The returning Russians were urged: Talk, talk.

They talked. The first passenger off the plane was Rebecca Kotsap. She was crying.

"There's nothing more important than your motherland," she said, her voice breaking. "I kiss my native soil with happiness." She said that in America she had cowered in fear of crime. "We cannot live there. It's a foreign people, a foreign language, a foreign life."

These were mostly blue-collar, working-class people for whom English was a second or third language, but they spoke it with poetic sparseness. A sad-eyed man with one of those Karl Marx beards, holding a three-year-old child in a gaily colored clown-face hat, told CBS with a shrug, in a heavy accent but without even a momentary break in cadence: "I miss my mother, my relatives, my friends, my culture, my city."

The Soviets were adept at propaganda, and propaganda was

deemed a legitimate tool of the state, but American news media felt manipulated and defensively swept themselves into the spin business as well. The CBS segment ended with correspondent Wyatt Andrews pointing out that international travel between the United States and Russia had historically been a one-way street. When the Russians decided to go back home, he said, the American government didn't hassle them or move to block their departure. A lesson the Soviets never intended to deliver, Andrews dryly and accurately noted, was that "the émigrés had to use the freedom of America in order to leave it."

It was here in the terminal that the American media found the Klever family and first began to puzzle out who they were. Valery—the melancholic father with the Rasputin beard—was part of a midcentury underground artistic movement in Russia called Nonkonformizm, a word that needs no translation. When Klever had been driven into exile in 1977 along with other painters, he was as famous among Russian artists as he was reviled by Communist party apparatchiks.

Under Soviet repression, Klever's work had been exhibited mostly in secret, advertised by hushed word of mouth, often displayed in the homes of like-minded dissidents. Sometimes his pieces were confiscated. Once, famously, they were literally bulldozed.

When Klever left Russia, his work was mostly in oil or watercolor or charcoal on paper; his painting style was mainly an amalgam of the influential artists he admired: Picasso, Braque, Léger, and Chagall. But the artist he most resembled, perhaps, was not a painter but a writer from the 1930s: Mikhail Bulgakov, author of novels that savaged the Soviet government effectively but obliquely, through parable, metaphor, and allegory. In Bulgakov's best-known work, *The Master and Margarita,* people aren't "dis-appeared," they *literally* disappear—*poof!*—in the middle of the street, and no one seems to think there is anything unusual about it, because it is the way of life. It was unsubtle, but also plausibly deniable.

In Klever's painting titled *No Trespassing,* a man whose head is wrapped in linen, like a mummy—he is both muzzled and blinded by his bandages—lovingly holds a naked woman. They are behind the picket fence that surrounds their home, on which they have placed a NO TRESPASSING sign. But the fence has an eye in it. Message: Any effort at privacy in such a world is futile. Any effort at individualism will be in vain; all men's faces are made to look the same, and all are silenced.

Some of Klever's art is more opaque but no less dark. A mother in a headscarf has four eyes. She stands disconsolately at the feet of a soldier who is also mummified—blinded and gagged. He holds a samovar. Upon a cross is a severed hand, punctured as from a crucifixion. Eventually Klever would explain to would-be buyers that this was retelling an incident he had experienced when in the Red Army, where good morale was considered patrio-tism, depression was seen as a weakness of resolve, and suicide on the battlefield was deemed a crime against the state. Soldiers who took their own lives were treated as "deserters," Klever said, and were buried at night, in secrecy, often near the enemy dead.

Klever remembered a mother's arriving at his platoon to ask about her missing son. Those multiple eyeballs suggested her confusion and agony. Klever's fellow soldiers initially told her that her son had died but, following policy, did not tell her it was sui-cide or where he was buried. Afterward, the soldiers covertly erected a cross over his body—defying the government's edicts against the practice of religion—and brewed tea at his grave in a ceremony of respect.

There was other Klever art that was not opaque at all: Joseph Stalin grinning grotesquely, with blood dripping from a tooth.

In the airport, the Klevers were interviewed by *The New York Times*'s Moscow correspondent Bill Keller, who would eventually become the newspaper's executive editor. Considering their background, the Klevers' explanation for their departure from America was surprisingly prosaic: They couldn't make a go of it financially in a country where economic success depended not on talent so much as self-marketing. Yes, they'd been persecuted when in Russia, they said, but they hoped that glasnost would resolve all that.

The family was willing to renounce its American citizenship, Lidiya Klever said, a statement perhaps more directed at her Russian handlers nearby than at the American press.

Mordantly, Valery Klever said that in the United States, it was dog-eat-dog. "What kind of freedom is there? It's tough freedom, you have to worry about your life and your apartment, your bills every month, everything. A man has to become a wolf there to survive," he said. His wife added: "Every month, every day, I was waiting for the next dollar to pay bills."

But the best ten seconds of screen time belonged to Karina, the pretty sixteen-year-old. She affected a modified pout and eye roll, familiar and not entirely repellent to every parent of American teenagers. Karina's aim was to decry Western materialism and superficiality (though she seems to have managed to find the time to apply lipstick before letting the cameras approach). Positioned beside her baby brother, in a riveting, eloquent sound bite,

Karina Klever said this about her life in high school, in perfect, unaccented English:

"They say that you can be with this group if you have eight pair of jeans. I say that I don't have eight pair of jeans. I say I don't even if I do, because I don't want people to know me for my pants."

They were Jordache's.

KARINA KLEVER IS NOW FORTY-NINE. She has lived in the United States for more than thirty years. She owns a million-dollar five-bedroom house in the L.A. suburb of Thousand Oaks, a home she shares with her mother and Elijah, her son from a long-ago marriage. Elijah is a sound engineer—Karina converted a walk-in closet to a sound studio for him. Her brother, the baby Nikita, has legally changed his name to Nik and directs short feature films and commercials. Karina owns her own company, Klever Compliance. She is a highly sought-after consultant in IT management, with a six-figure income. She also administers a website, kleverart.com, which exhibits and sells her late father's paintings. She is very much an American.

To understand how she got to this life, and why, you have to go back to 1986 to revisit from the inside out the confounding, deeply misinformed final days of the Cold War. Some of it touches directly on the events of Sunday, December 28.

IN 1986, in relations between the Americans and the Soviets, no one really knew what the hell was going on. Nothing was quite as it seemed to be.

Gorbachev and Reagan held each other in wary respect, but there was one enormous bone of contention upon which each man was intransigent—the Strategic Defense Initiative, nicknamed Star Wars. Star Wars was Reagan's pet project, with the ambitious, arguably fanciful goal of establishing a land- and satellite-based defensive shield that could shoot down incoming ballistic missiles before they reached their targets. Reagan insisted that the United States be allowed to continue to develop the program for the next ten years; Gorbachev was amenable in theory, but only in theory. He insisted that this program be limited to laboratory work—in effect, that the United States could not build and test prototypes. Neither man would budge, and the summit broke up without any agreement at all—not on missiles or any of the other issues Reagan had hoped to slap on the table: human rights, the Soviet intervention in Afghanistan, and emigration of Jews and dissidents.

The whole thing stank of failure. The participants seemed defeated. Their body language was revealing, and something they made little effort to hide. In the most widely published photograph from Reykjavík, Reagan and Gorbachev walk side by side. Reagan is in a white coat. His Soviet counterpart is in a black coat. Both are frowning, looking not at each other but gloomily at the ground.

Both men and their staffs claimed there had been incremental progress, but to many this seemed like wan, transparent face-saving. In the media, the event was generally interpreted as a blown opportunity. A dud.

As it happens, it was anything but. Obscured by the dispiriting atmosphere, something remarkable had occurred. During a trade of proposals to rescue the talks, both leaders had offered escalating disarmament concessions that went beyond anything many had thought possible. Reagan had broached the eventual goal of bilateral elimination of all nuclear weapons, and Gorbachev agreed. After the stench of failure had lifted, this realization led to a realignment of possibilities and priorities for both countries. In less than a year, it would result in the Intermediate-Range Nuclear Forces Treaty, which led to the destruction of thousands of missiles. It is considered a historic breakthrough. No dud.

In late December, determined to persuade the world that glasnost was real, Gorbachev released Andrei Sakharov from his seven-year exile in the heavily policed city of Gorky. There the dapper, dignified political dissident had lived with his wife under constant surveillance and harassment—prevented from traveling, prohibited from speaking publicly. (None of this was new for Sakharov—it was merely more draconian than what he was used to. When Sakharov won the Nobel Peace Prize in 1975, the Soviets did not allow him to leave the country to attend the ceremonies in Oslo.) His release in late December 1986 was instant, international news.

Sakharov had been an ingenious nuclear physicist, instrumental in the development of the Soviet hydrogen bomb. In the late 1950s, aghast at what his work had wrought and also at the repression of free speech by the Soviet government, Sakharov became an activist for disarmament and human rights. In the United States, he was lionized—in 1983, Reagan declared May 21 National Andrei Sakharov Day.

And so three years later—on this Sunday, December 28, 1986—it came as something of a shock when ABC aired an interview with the newly released dissident. Speaking with authority in both his roles as a physicist and antinuclear activist, Sakharov essentially said he thought that Star Wars was an idiot idea, an enormous waste of time and resources that, if built, could easily be circumvented by Soviet science. He added, almost as an afterthought, that because of ill health he would no longer have a leadership role in the human rights movement.

What? Reagan was angry and unnerved. Many in the media were skeptical. Had there been a corrupt deal? Had the great man traded his integrity for his freedom? Sakharov was actually asked about this several times and denied it . . . *but of course he would.* What was really going on?

What was really going on was that Sakharov was still a man of honor and conscience. There had been no deal, as became clear by the scientist's subsequent unalloyed criticisms of the Soviet Union. What he'd said about Star Wars was simply the truth, evident to anyone with the facts and training to understand them: It *was* an idiot idea, financially and technologically. Without ceremony, the program that had torpedoed an international summit was abandoned by the United States not long afterward, after having lost most political support.

And Sakharov *was* in ill health—he'd be dead in less than three years, at sixty-eight.

AS THE SAKHAROV INTERVIEW was being edited for broadcast at the ABC studios in New York, the ultimate in Cold War incompetence was bumbling out in a room at a Holiday Inn near Heathrow Airport in London. There, a polygrapher from the U.S. Naval

Criminal Investigative Service was interrogating a slight, frightened, naive young Native American U.S. Marine sergeant named Clayton Lonetree. Temperamentally, the twenty-five-year-old from St. Paul, Minnesota, seemed dull-witted, servile, and emotionally immature—somewhere between a schmendrick and a tool. He was also a depressive and an aspiring alcoholic. An eventual psychological study of him, conducted by the government after his case was over, concluded that "his capacity to feel is greater than his rational capability." And: "He displays an unconventional thought process that is rich in fantasy."

This was the man being grilled at the Holiday Inn. Lonetree had been a security officer in the U.S embassy in Moscow, and on this day, he stood accused of espionage: passing classified information to the KGB. He'd allegedly done most of it through an intermediary named Violetta Seina, a tall, dark-eyed, sultry Russian beauty who worked in the embassy as a translator and who had contacts with the KGB. She had seduced Lonetree in what people in the spy trade colorfully call a "honey trap."

All of that was basically true. In the hotel room, Lonetree was admitting it, and further volunteered that the KGB had paid him $3,500 for his work. He'd done it, he said, because he was lonely and lovesick and vulnerable, and mostly because he was caught up in the intense, international drama of the thing. Temperamentally, he remained an adolescent.

But his inquisitor had a big problem: There had been recent security breaches within the American spy network. Some had dreadful consequences. The Soviet Union had apprehended and executed several Russian informants who had been valuable assets for the United States.

The United States obviously harbored a mole somewhere, with access to the most sensitive of data, but investigators had gotten nowhere in trying to ferret out who he was. Was Lonetree their man? Maybe, but the timorous sergeant was admitting to no such thing. The betrayals he acknowledged were mostly paltry. The documents he said he'd handed over to his Soviet contacts were items like the floor plan of the U.S. embassy and embassy telephone directories. Some of the stuff was technically classified but of no practical value to the Russians. He also said he had given documents to the KGB when he was briefly stationed in Vienna. None of it was big-deal stuff. None of it was likely to get people killed.

Lonetree was nearing the end of the third frustrating day of interrogation, and he still wasn't budging. The questioners decided they would have to push harder. It would be a consequential decision.

According to journalist Rodney Barker in his 1996 book on the case, *Dancing with the Devil: Sex, Espionage, and the U.S. Marines*, here is how the subsequent questioning went:

> "Come on, Clayton. If you don't cooperate, we are going to burn your ass. We know you are holding back. Now tell me the truth."
>
> Lonetree answered that he had been telling the truth.
>
> "Well, tell us more."
>
> "There IS no more."
>
> "Talk to us, Clayton. Come on, talk to us."
>
> "What do you want to hear?"
>
> "Say something. Say anything. Say that the walls are green, whatever. Just talk to me."

"Do you want me to lie to you?"

"Okay, make something up. Tell me a lie."

Tell me a lie. It was a controversial challenge from a polygrapher to a suspect, and a potentially perilous one. The idea is that if you get a person talking more volubly, sometimes inventions lead to the inadvertent spilling of truth. "Tell me a lie" may sometimes work. Here it didn't.

The suggestible and ingratiating young sergeant apparently tried to accommodate his interrogator: He said he had penetrated highly classified parts of the embassy, brought KBG agents in at night, and let them page through files. He said he had retrieved highly classified information and turned it over to Violetta and her "Uncle Sasha," who was a KGB agent. The sergeant confessed to other heinous actions by saying yes, and even elaborating, when his interrogators suggested other crimes of which he might be guilty. Significantly, he wept, which was taken as an indelible suggestion of remorse. Most likely, what had actually happened was that this high-strung, emotionally stunted man prone to histrionics had become overwhelmed by his own fantasies. But some of the investigators believed they had their mole. They'd cracked the case! Lonetree was court-martialed and sentenced to thirty years in prison, and the big spy case was apparently closed. Unless it wasn't.

It wasn't. What eventually became clear was that although Lonetree had committed espionage, it was of the relatively benign kind he'd volunteered before he was urged to lie. Afterward, he had confessed to having entered embassy areas to which he simply had no access while giving "tours" to KGB agents, tours that never happened. He fingered a co-conspirator, a Corporal Arnold Bracy, and though both Bracy and Lonetree admitted to these supposed crimes under relentless questioning, Bracy immediately recanted his statement, saying he'd been coerced. Further investigation proved Lonetree and Bracy had never been together with an opportunity to do what they were accused of.

It just didn't fly. Charges against Bracy were dropped, but initially no one seemed to wonder if Lonetree's sentence deserved some rethinking. Eventually the American government stumbled on the right man: a crafty, incorrigible, Milquetoast-like CIA counterintelligence double agent named Aldrich Ames. Ames had turned over names. People had been executed.

An extensive follow-up investigation conducted by the Naval Criminal Investigative Service after Lonetree's sentencing concluded that though the sergeant had turned over some materials to the KGB, "he did not commit the much further-reaching espionage activities alleged." Lonetree's sentence was cut in half and he was released after serving nine years.

Did the rush to judgment on Lonetree leave the U.S. intelligence services complacent, confident that the bigger case had been solved? Some in the spy trade think so, and that the error gifted Ames with six more years of deadly treachery before he was caught.

That's what 1986 was like in Russian-American relations: a series of misunderstandings, misinterpretations, misrepresentations, misapprehensions, missed opportunities, and misguided hopes, a year that ended with the Klever family's return to Russia in earnest search of a better life.

―――――

"IT WAS A MISTAKE," Karina Klever says today, echoing precisely what her father said upon his family's return to the United States after only five and a half months in Leningrad.

The Klevers' experience wasn't atypical. The Soviet government would eventually confirm that by 1988, at least fifteen of the original fifty repatriates who'd left the United States with such fanfare had quietly returned. And those figures were incomplete—the actual total may have been closer to half. Among the returnees was Alexander Cherkasets, the limo driver who'd said at the airport that life in the U.S. was too "harsh," filled with poverty and crime. His turnaround wasn't quite as quick as that of the Klevers. He was back in the United States in sixteen months. That was about the average.

What on earth had happened?

KARINA KLEVER STILL BEARS the no-nonsense air of defiance that was evident at Sheremetyevo Airport, when as a sixteen-year-old she was bitching about the need to stockpile Jordache jeans in order to be socially accepted. Today she's six feet tall, with lush shoulder-length hair that she wears swept up when she is at work, the better to command respect from the rooms full of men she advises. She loves the United States, but still finds some things infuriating: the same sort of trivial materialisms that bothered her as a girl, but have now matured into issues of adulthood. She's mostly an American, but retains a bit of the Old World in her, too.

"I'm extremely socially inept here," she says, laughing. "I can stand up and create IT environments for multimillion-dollar global companies, but I can't do chitter-chatter noise. I don't like that the first twenty minutes of a business meeting is talking about last night's sitcoms, or how someone bought a fancy whiz-bang car. It's not an efficient use of time, but, you know, I let it go."

She laughs. She's wrestling with a fundamental paradox.

"I don't mean to be insulting. I just don't get a lot of what Americans find important. I don't think the Kardashians should be part of my life."

No nonsense. No frills. No showing off. Karina Klever, stylish American, has never even gotten her ears pierced.

The Klevers had no choice about leaving the Soviet Union the first time, in 1977: They were kicked out by the government, along with other artistic dissidents. A planeload of a hundred-odd political pains in the ass were told, Karina recalls, that they could get dropped off at their choice of any of three cities: Jerusalem, Vienna, or Paris. The Klevers chose Vienna. It took two years to wend their way over the Atlantic, to L.A., to Maine, to upstate New York, and finally, to Flatbush, Brooklyn.

The departure from Russia that first time had been bittersweet and complicated. Yes, the Klevers were uprooted against their will, separated from everything they knew, and they were uprooted for patently unjust reasons. No, Karina would never again see her beloved maternal grandmother, a physician. Requests to visit, as the old woman lay dying, were denied by the Soviets. But leaving Russia had brought relief as well. Few in the West, Klever says now, knew the sorts of outrages that disobedient artists had to endure. Some of those outrages even reached a six-year-old, quite directly.

At six, Karina Klever slept in the bottom drawer of a dresser, acting as a human shield—or, more precisely, a human decoy. The idea was that her presence might dissuade any KGB agents who entered the apartment from pushing aside the dresser, behind which was a false wall, behind which was a trove of her father's artwork. There *were* raids, but they never found the art.

Life in Soviet Russia, Klever says, was as threadbare and politically stifling as the rest of the world generally understood, but aggravated for some families, such as hers, by the constant threat of arrest, punishment, or deportation. Mostly, she said, the system did not even remotely prepare them for what they would find in the United States.

"The Soviet Union infantilized people," she says. "The government issued you things, they gave you a place to live, they gave you whatever they felt you needed. You became entitled, dependent, compliant, and complacent. You were kind of on perpetual welfare—your basics are taken care of, but you are not well off. You learned to accept that. You remained a child. When my parents arrived here in 1979, my father was forty and my mother was thirty, and they didn't know to put money in the bank, they didn't know what real estate was. The adjustment was apocalyptic. It gave them a feeling of cultural incompetence."

Plus, their source of income withered. Nobody wanted original subversive paintings decrying Russian totalitarianism, even by an artist who was famous in Europe.

"People wanted $29.99 posters of seascapes or flowers or an ocean scene," Karina says, laughing. "Art can be about where you find your serenity. Americans tend to find it in nonstressful, feelgood things. Russians are very different. Russians take their stress with them and hold it close to their chest, like a badge. It delivers pride. Russians want Stalin, dripping blood from a tooth."

So in the United States, the family was going broke. Lidiya Klever, ever resourceful, sewed clothing for Karina from curtains and draperies. This did not exactly help her fit in at school.

The worst part, Karina says, was when her classmates accused her of wanting to kill them.

It would happen fairly regularly, she says, particularly in L.A. around 1980, after nuclear readiness drills—during the very last days of those silly duck-and-cover exercises in the classroom. Teachers rolled out TV sets that displayed a cartoon image of a nuclear missile leaving the Soviet Union and then showed the children how to hide under desks and tables to avoid incineration.

"Those are the days I got punched," Klever says. "Sticks to the legs, skin scratched, hair pulled out. I was called a commie. I was the girl who didn't speak English well—maybe I had a nuclear weapon up my sleeve. I was nine."

When the Gorbachev government started making noises about academic and artistic freedom, the Klever family applied to the Soviet Union for visas to return. For one thing, they had dozens of paintings stashed in the homes of fellow dissidents, paintings they wanted to recover. For another . . . maybe things had really changed in the last nine years. It took a while for the visas to be approved, until a whole planeload of returnees was ready to go.

WHAT THE KLEVERS found when they got back was bewildering. In some ways, things had changed profoundly. Restrictions on art and personal freedoms had been loosened, but a feeling of institutional dry rot remained, and, oddly, it seemed to have intensified. It hadn't—it's just that at this point, there was a comparison to draw.

As promised, the Klevers had been issued an apartment in Leningrad . . . which they had to share with another family. It was a large apartment, but the whole arrangement—enforced lack of privacy—echoed the sort of famously shabby, make-do subsistence accommodations of life in a shtetl.

For the returnees, there were creaky remnants of Cold War repression that were hard to understand and impossible to justify: Restrictions on travel remained intact, even within the country. Having the right papers remained essential. For some, having lived in the United States remained a stain on your work papers; despite having returned with a warm welcome, some of these people were denied jobs because they were deemed to be "traitors." Jobs were scarce. Good jobs were scarcer.

The Russian economy remained a jury-rigged affair, but somehow now it felt more ratty and shopworn than before. In the United States the Klevers had gotten Americanized in ways they didn't even realize. The family had gotten a lingering taste— sometimes literally—of what capitalism could provide.

"In the United States in 1986," Karina Klever says, "if you wanted fresh watermelon at two o'clock in the morning in January, you could go out and get fresh watermelon at two o'clock in the morning in January. In Russia, in 1986, if you had fish but you wanted peas, you had to hope you could find a neighbor who had peas but wanted fish.

"Once we went to a friend's house, and I remember this exchange, which seemed so normal to them: The sister came over, we were standing in the kitchen, and she said she'd give me three cans of peas for my two bags of beans. That was the state of the economy."

In the space of less than a year, the Klevers had witnessed a collision of two philosophies of life. One was hard to navigate: It was outwardly implacable and heartless, and demanded extraordinary personal accountability—but it mostly worked. The other was outwardly devoted to social comity and shared bounty, offering people a protective cocoon—but the whole system was in extremis, on life support.

The United States offered opportunity that seemed absent in Russia. A practical woman, Lidiya Klever found herself thinking like a hesitant but hopeful entrepreneur—thinking like an American, pushed by fear and hope—wondering about taking IT classes, getting a job in a cutting-edge industry, becoming the breadwinner for the family. The United States could make that happen. (And this is in the end what happened. Karina would follow her mother into the IT field and get pretty adept at it.)

So, Karina, that is why your family went back? Because the economy wasn't working?

"Not really. We might have stayed. There were things about Russia we loved."

Was it still about artistic freedom?

"Not really. That was changing."

Well, what was it about?

"It was mostly that the Soviet government refused to make us citizens unless we renounced our American citizenship. They forced us to make a choice.

"So we did."

Forced to make a choice—and able to make a choice—they made a choice. When you think about it, this was pretty much exactly how the Cold War ended.

8:35 P.M., Great Neck, Long Island

The place was named Lakeville Manor, though there was no lake and nothing you'd even generously call a manor. It was a pickup joint with a bar and a dance floor. It billed itself as a singles club, but that was a fib, too, since many of its patrons were looking but not single.

Sharon Sultan Goldstein got there before her date, Gambler Steve, which is what she called him, but not to his face because he didn't know she knew he had a gambling problem, one that made him both profligate and cheap at the same time. Gambler Steve hadn't picked her up at home, insisting instead that they meet at the manor, most likely so she'd have to pay her own cover charge (twelve bucks, cash only). Gambler Steve was a piece of work.

Sharon was not interested in Gambler Steve, but he was a convenient elbow to use while trawling for other men. She was thirty-nine, in the middle of a frenzied, undignified expedition for a husband. In the previous two weeks she'd had twelve dates with ten different men, a sprint that began the day after her ex-husband's wedding. If you don't understand this on some level, you've likely never been divorced, middle-aged, and female.

Sharon's ex was famous for being an asshole, but in a good way. He was an accountant with an odd hobby: He liked to crash celebrity parties, which is like crashing weddings but with much higher visibility. He'd insinuated himself into photos in newspapers and magazines, in fancy clothes, at famous venues, in the Waldorf Astoria, at the World Series, on reviewing stands, near people like Jimmy Carter, Ed Koch, Gerald Ford, Morgan Fairchild, and Hal Linden, the guy who played *Barney Miller*. In the captions under pictures of crowds, he was often identified as "(unidentified)," until he finally got busted by a TV station and gave an interview to *Life* magazine about being a notorious celebrity mooch. He was a live wire, crackling, 24/7. Sharon didn't fall out of love with him so much as run out of the energy required for his maintenance. Now he was getting married again and she was getting desperate.

So she'd paid her way into Lakeville Manor and, as usual, was moving against the flow of mingle, the river of polyester holding drinks. That way she could bump into whomever she wanted to bump into, and also see trouble coming and avoid it, and whoa, who was this guy?

Sharon noticed four things about him right away. He was tall, and she liked tall. He was broad-shouldered, which appealed to her. He dressed well, which stood out in this crowd. And he had moist, generous, sultry lips. Mick Jagger lips. Jean-Paul Belmondo lips. She liked those, a lot.

Stephen Cutler was forty-four, dark, intense, and laconic, a twice-divorced, ambitious ladies' man. He was not the kind of guy to get pinned down, but Sharon didn't know that yet, of course. She also didn't know those shoulders were flattered a bit by that suit she admired.

Steve had arrived just minutes before with a guy friend, and one of the first people he laid eyes on was a woman he'd briefly dated, bedded, and then dumped. Moments later, he saw another one with whom he had the same history. Dodging daggers, he was about to turn and head for the door when he saw this ringlet-haired blonde, moving against traffic, frankly appraising him. She looked like Dyan Cannon.

Sharon was small and Jewish in a way that didn't look Jewish, *exactly* like Dyan Cannon, née Friesen, who had convincingly played a shiksa in the 1969 wife-swappy farce *Bob & Carol & Ted & Alice*. Sharon had those same curls, those same bedroom eyes. Steve Cutler was Jewish and was looking for a Jewish woman, but for the moment he didn't know he'd found one. For the moment, he didn't care.

Sharon owned and ran a nanny-hiring agency on Long Island. Steve had done a little of everything—some retail, some real estate. Most recently, he'd been managing a lumberyard. His real skill was that he radiated self-confidence, and he knew how to use that to make money, and women.

Steve threw out a goofy line—"funny meeting you here"— and offered to buy Sharon a drink. She allowed this. He had bourbon and Coke, which wasn't enough to repel her. She had dry white wine. And then she whispered, "You'd better work fast, because my date just walked in the door."

So they exchanged names and phone numbers. He promised to call her the next day and take her out for dinner. This furtive transaction had just been completed when Gambler Steve oiled his way across the floor and gave Steve Cutler the stink-eye, so Steve beat it out of there. One of the last things he heard before walking out the door was a woman asking him, "Why didn't you call me?"

And that was that, for December 28, 1986, the day Sharon met Stephen. They had been together all of five minutes.

ON MONDAY THE TWENTY-NINTH, Steve didn't call. So at four P.M. Sharon phoned him. Shy, she was not. "Are you gonna take me out or what?" she asked, Lawn Gyland in every syllable. Steve said, "Yeah, I guess, sure," and he did. They went to Manhattan for a date at a club owned by a friend of his. She found the veal tough but the conversation tender and witty. Then he drove her home and managed one kiss on her couch before he fell asleep with his head in her lap. After a time, she extricated her lap from his head, but let him finish the night asleep on the couch.

On Tuesday night, the thirtieth, Steve took his new girl to his office Christmas party at a big catering hall. She wore a little black dress. By midevening, when they posed for snapshots, her face was rosy and glistening. His hair was likably mussed, a damp banglet on his forehead, his suit still immaculate, a ruffled hand-kerchief in his jacket pocket. He dressed snappy. They looked happy. They were quite pickled.

"We love each other, don't we?" Sharon asked suddenly.

Steve considered this. "Yeah," he said.

"Then why don't we get engaged?" You know, just floating it out there.

Steve said that sounded like a swell idea. So what if their in-timacy, thus far, had been confined to a kiss or three?

"Well, why don't we TELL everyone?" Sharon suggested.

So Steve stood up, as best he could, and called for silence, and announced that he and the lovely woman swaying by his side had just gotten engaged. Applause! Christmas party became engagement party.

More than one coworker took Steve aside that night and— nudge, wink—complimented him on his strategy for making sure the rest of the evening played out nicely.

If anything actually happened that night, neither Steve nor Sharon remembers it. They do remember the next day vividly. Wednesday the thirty-first, late afternoon on New Year's Eve. It was when Steve showed up at Sharon's house and moved in.

They had talked it over and decided that this, too, was a good idea. So Steve arrived in his car, with belongings. Sharon was a little wary about this—to tell the truth, she hadn't even remembered exactly, *precisely* what Steve looked like, what with the whirlwind pace of what could only charitably be called a courtship, and she did not entirely trust the judgment of her previously inebriated self—so she stood there holding the remote to the garage door as he drove up, ready to close it quick if he looked predatory or less appealing than she'd thought or unpleasant in any unremembered way. The garage door remained open. So he drove in, then moved in, which is the first time Stephen learned Sharon had children, two *very* suspicious preadolescent sons. The subject somehow had not yet come up. The boys had been with their father for the weekend.

And that was the stupid, impulsive, poorly considered, alcohol-fueled, nakedly libidinous, romantically ill-omened manner in which the year 1986 closed itself out at 3448 Bertha Drive, Baldwin Harbor, Long Island.

———

2014, BETHESDA, MARYLAND.

They walk into the diner together. He's leaning into her, using her as a crutch, because he's thrown his back out again. They choose a table on a raised floor near the front window, but then decide it will be quieter in the back, nicer to talk, for this interview. They are sixty-six and seventy-one.

She's Sharon Sultan Cutler now. Improbably, they've been together ever since they met on that Sunday and gave new meaning to the term *speed dating*. They're both semiretired. She blogs nostalgia about the boomer generation; he sells mattresses part time at Macy's. They live in Chicago, and are in Maryland to visit her son Eric. They're doing just fine.

Sharon sits, smiles, and suggests that none of any of this might have happened if she hadn't telephoned the big schlub the next afternoon, after hearing nothing from him all day.

"I might've gotten around to it," protests the schlub.

"Ha!" opines Sharon.

So what made you ask Steve to propose marriage and then announce it, in one fell swoop, in front of a room full of strangers?

"Well, it was a big decision. I wanted him to be involved a little."

"*Nice* of you," he says.

This is a Greek place that offers feta-heavy breakfast options, but Steve and Sharon stick with American basics. Easier on the digestion.

So, why did she decide to keep the garage door open that New Year's Eve?

"He looked okay," she says. Turning to him: "You had some hair, still."

"It's true," he says. "And you had a waistline."

She surveys her middle. "Now it's a wasteland."

So how did it go with your sons when this *guy* shows up with his stuff?

"I said, 'This is Steve, and he's living here with us.' It went fine."

"It went *fine?*" Steve says, slack jawed, a forkful poised in the air.

Sharon nods. It went fine. Next question, please.

"Eric took all the clothes out of your dresser," Steve says dryly, "and threw them on the middle of the floor."

Eric was ten.

"Okay, he was a little upset."

"Uh-*huh.*"

"You know, he and Jeffrey thought you were a homosexual."

Jeffrey was eight.

"What, just because I polished my fingernails?"

"You carried a purse."

"It was a bag," he says, with dignity. "A man's shoulder bag."

"It was a purse."

This is their lingua franca, the DNA of their relationship, and it has been for thirty years. It's a competitive mélange of teasing, baiting, noodging, ruthless editing of each other, all leavened with a jubilantly fatalistic sense of humor. If anything can go wrong, it will, and you deal.

So, if he hadn't fallen asleep, would he have gotten lucky that second night?

"Oh, yes," he says.

"I'm pretty sure no," she says.

"Oh, yes," he says.

When did you know this was the right woman, Steve?

"Right away."

Why?

"I owned a boat at the time, and she had a dock," he says.

Sharon scowls and tsks, with a faint blush.

Stephen shrugs. Facts are facts. He's a salesman—he's not in the metaphor business.

After he and his boat moved in, Steve stayed home for a full month, to make sure Eric and Jeffrey had no choice but to get used to him. It was a process.

"The master bedroom had one of those folding doors," Steve remembers. "You could just push in the middle and it would open. And the kids were used to doing that, which was not good. So the first thing I do, the very first thing? Remember I'm in the lumber business. I install a solid-core door that it would take a blast to get through, with three-inch heavy-duty piano hinges and a lock."

Sharon's eyes twinkle. Apparently, that took care of the privacy problem.

Sharon and Steve lived together for ten years before they got married.

"I was throwing out hints," she says. "I got a wedding cake topper, a little bride and groom, and I kept hiding it in places where I knew he'd go—a sock drawer, the refrigerator." Steve pointedly never took the hint. He wanted it, but he wanted it on his terms.

What's the point of a straightforward wedding? What's the fun in that? Where was the opportunity for mischief?

"Finally we got married on May third, 1997," she says.

"May fifth," he says.

"We argue about it all the time," she says. "May third? May fifth? Believe me, I'd know the date of my own wedding"—she looks up archly over her glasses at Steve—"*but I had nothing to do with it.*"

Steve had decided that her wedding would come as a surprise. A double-barreled, boomerang, switcheroo surprise. So he told her they'd been invited to a black-tie party thrown by his boss, to show off his new boat. There was chamber music and a comedian emcee, and suddenly it became a surprise fiftieth birthday party for Sharon, which explained all her friends being there, and the funny, roasty testimonials, but then things started getting really strange, particularly when the comedian came back out in a Groucho Marx outfit, and then when the plucked rubber duck dropped down from the ceiling when she got induced to say the magic word, which was *marriage*. The comedian turned out to be a famous singing rabbi, David Benedict, the same one who had married *The Nanny* to her millionaire boss on TV. Cantor Benedict was the go-to guy for schmaltz, so of course Steve had gone to him.

"That was a year before . . ." Sharon starts, then stops.

"Fourteen months," Steve says.

"We got through it," Sharon says.

They not only finish each other's sentences, they seem five moves ahead. They are the Fischer-Kasparov of bicker.

You wait for whatever punch line is coming. Instead, Steve is talking about why he went to identify the body.

"I didn't want her to have to."

On July Fourth, 1998, Sharon's younger son, Jeffrey, died in a freak accident on a Jet Ski. He was twenty. They got through it somehow, as you do, together.

"I gave her space to grieve," Steve says. "She wanted to talk, I let her talk. I didn't cut her off," he says, and she laughs a little, and then he laughs a little. In this particular relationship, that was no small concession.

"Also," she says, "you handled the media."

There was front-page publicity, and CNN came to the house, because it was a holiday death, and because there was a waterway safety bill being debated in Congress, and because, Sharon notes sardonically, these were the suburbs, not the inner city, and "he was a nice-looking blond Jewish boy."

There is no subject, even this, about which humor is entirely absent.

"In those weeks and months afterward, I did whatever I could to make her life easier," Steve says. "That was my job. We needed a new car, so I took her to a Subaru dealer. It was a really good car at a reasonable price. She got in the car, drove it four feet, and said, 'It's okay.' We passed a Lexus dealer on the way back. She said, 'Let's stop there.' So she gets into the Lexus RX 300, drives it four feet, and she says 'This is the one.' It was twice as much money!"

He sounds aggrieved. The nerve of her. Then a shrug.

"So we got the Lexus. She wanted it in white, and they didn't have white, but they had red, so . . ."

Just the slightest pause.

"I took a train to a New Jersey dealership, where they had a white one, and drove it home to her."

"We had his-and-hers cancer," she says.

Hers was breast cancer, in 2001. They got it all after the third surgery, but at that point Steve had quit his job to care for her, and they ran into financial troubles.

"The only thing I absolutely never wanted to do was sell cars," Steve says. "But we had to survive, so I took a job at a Toyota dealership."

"He was very good," she says.

"I became an elite salesperson in record time," he says.

Things go wrong. You deal.

He was at the dealership, standing at the urinal, when he noticed a little pink. A little pink is a lot bad, sometimes. The diagnosis, when it came, was dreadful.

"Mantle cell lymphoma," he says. "In the bloodstream."

"Not a common cancer," she says.

"Eighty percent mortality rate," he says.

"Sharon did some research and came up with a doctor at the University of Miami who was doing a study . . ." he says.

"A clinical trial," she amends.

"I was in for the fight of my life," he says. "Two months high-intensity chemo in the hospital . . ."

"Four months," she amends.

"I couldn't walk, and at one point I lost control of my bodily functions," he says. "I lost my hair, I looked like hell and felt even worse."

"He asked the doctor what would happen if this doesn't work," she says.

"The doctor told me, 'You die.'"

"As sick as he was," she says, "he snuck out of the hospital to take me to a steak dinner for my birthday."

"McCormick and Schmick's," he says.

The treatment worked. He's been in remission for nine years.

HOW DO YOU RECONCILE this strong and happy relationship, this forever relationship, with the absurdly impulsive way it started? What are the odds, really, of this sort of thing working out?

There is a Yiddish word, *beshert,* which describes something that seemed foreordained. Kismet, for Jews. You can go there, if you believe in such things. Or maybe it was about the power of urgency—maybe these two people found each other at exactly the right moment in their lives, when a lonely end game seemed foreseeable, when it made sense to expend real effort in making this endure. Or maybe it was something else entirely.

Ask them, here at the diner, and you don't get much help.

"The women I had dated had always wanted more relationship than I was willing to give out," he says.

"He was always on the six-month plan with women," she says. "He wouldn't commit."

"Well," he says, staring her down, "I wasn't willing to commit to something I didn't really want."

This is as close as they come to saying they love each other. And it is at this precise moment that there is a squeal and a loud bang outside, in the street.

Outside, a young woman who is having a very bad morning has lost control of her car, veered across oncoming traffic and sideswiped a bus. Then she hits the gas instead of the brake, jumps the curb, and plows into the diner. The wall crumples but holds. The window shatters, and inside the restaurant, glass flies at eye level. The driver sits stunned behind the wheel, as white as her airbag.

"Goodness," Sharon says.

"Wait, that's . . ." Steve says, looking over.

"It is. It's exactly where," Sharon says.

It's exactly where they'd been sitting before they decided to move.

Life together has been like that for Sharon and Steve, right from the beginning. Crazy. Full of adventure. Hard to believe, if you didn't know it was true. Above all, pretty lucky, considering. Maybe that's what it is. Maybe they're just two very lucky people.

11:55 P.M., Oakland, California

Steam hovered above the crowd. The walls were damp and then some; water was beading up and, in places, running in slender, ropy rivulets down to the soggy floor.

As a concert venue, the Henry J. Kaiser Convention Center was . . . unconventional. The acoustics and amenities were more than adequate, but the ventilation was bizarre. With a full house and bodies swaying and grinding in the aisles and walkways, moisture condensed on cool surfaces. There was an invigorating melodrama to it—depending on your mood, you could say those walls were sweating or weeping.

With only 5,500 seats, the Kaiser Center was funky and appealingly intimate for an arena, though it couldn't host really big acts. But it never had trouble landing the Grateful Dead, who were onstage tonight. In 1986—twenty-one years after the band coalesced in Palo Alto as a quirky acid-folk-rock quintet inclined to improvisation—the Dead played to audiences that were only moderately large but fanatically loyal.

Deadheads were yoked to one another by a devotion to a group of gifted counterculture musicians who made nothing easy for their listeners. Their songs were not tidily structured—often lacking hummable hooks, and strewn with extemporized, desultory, seemingly interminable instrumental riffs. To be a Dead fan, you needed musical sophistication but also a degree of forbearance. In concert, the band would barely pause between numbers. Instead, they oozed musically—seamlessly—from one song to the next, as though they were unaware there was an audience at all. They seemed almost to disdain and begrudge applause, hurrying past it as fast as they could.

Some people saw all of this as contempt for the fans. Deadheads saw it as a measure of respect: They were being welcomed into a rarefied club of pure musical artistry. There may have been a tinge of elitism to this, but it surely brought people together. Each concert became a communal experience. To call the Dead a *cult* band wasn't fair. They were much more than a fad. They were a *worshiped* band.

On this night, just shy of midnight, the Dead had been onstage for well over an hour. People were dancing. The walls were doing their thing. The band was nearing the end of its night. Jerry Garcia, the Dead's genial, gnarly-bearded front man, oozed from "The Other One"—an allegorical tribute to chemically altered states of consciousness—and into "Black Peter," one of the Dead's iconic songs. "Black Peter" was a dirge—a mournful piece about the banality of death.

In the audience, to the right of the stage, halfway up in the balcony, Dave Taylor and Steve Christie leaned forward. The two teenagers had a sense of the drama of what might be coming, and they were right.

Almost six months earlier, on July 12, Dave and Steve— eighteen and seventeen, respectively, and Deadheads both—had made the two-day drive from their homes in Seattle to Ventura, California, to take in a Dead concert. When they got to the Ventura County Fairgrounds, they were turned away, informed that the show was canceled because Garcia was sick. Bummer.

The announcement had been circumspect and incomplete.

"When we learned the truth, we were devastated," Taylor says today.

In fact, Garcia was dying.

THE GRATEFUL DEAD didn't just embrace the drug culture—they bear-hugged it. For years, the band's sound engineer was Augustus Owsley Stanley III (nickname: "Bear"), who sidelined as a clandestine chemist, a discipline he learned with the help of his girlfriend, a chem major at Berkeley. The grandson of a U.S. senator and a subject of Tom Wolfe's era-defining book *The Electric Kool-Aid Acid Test,* Owsley Stanley produced some of the purest LSD ever made and distributed tens of thousands of doses, including to his band. But the Grateful Dead didn't stop at acid. Several of its members, including Garcia, dipped in and out of addictions to cocaine and heroin.

Oddly—on some level, it must have been a cultural embarrassment for him—Jerry Garcia's near-death experience was not caused by recreational drugs. It had the most plebeian etiology: a toothache. Garcia had had a mouth abscess, ignored it for too long, got sicker, went for treatment, and fell into a deep coma. Part of the problem was his generally lamentable state of health—he was an overweight forty-four-year-old stoner with diabetes he was ignoring.

Also, the doctors had allegedly given him intravenous Valium, to which he was allergic. He nearly flatlined. For a time he was on a ventilator, unable to breathe on his own. He did not regain consciousness for four days.

When he recovered, Garcia said he'd lived through some odd semiconscious experiences. As recounted in Dennis McNally's excellent biography of the Dead, *A Long Strange Trip,* Garcia told friends, apparently quite seriously: "I started feeling like the vegetable kingdom was speaking to me. It was communicating to me in comic dialect in iambic pentameter."

And: "My main experience was one of furious activity and tremendous struggle in a sort of futuristic, space-ship vehicle with insectoid presence. After I came out of my coma, I had this image of myself as these little hunks of protoplasm that were stuck together kind of like stamps with perforations that you could snap off. They were run through with neoprene tubing, and there were these insects that looked like cockroaches which were like message units that were kind of like my bloodstream."

A long strange trip, indeed.

The back-to-life Garcia was lucid, entertaining, needy, grateful, and musically inept. He had lost a lot, including the ability to play the guitar, especially in concert with other musicians, especially the ability to pick up cues. Evidently some of his synaptic connections had suffered a serious jolt to their well-being. He was screwed up and needed help.

Garcia told McNally, "It took a while before I really had a sense of how music worked." Those subtle skills were coaxed back, over time, by his friend Merl Saunders, the blues and rock keyboardist.

The two men started by playing simple blues riffs and gradually expanded their complexity. Garcia recovered his abilities and stayed chemically clean, at least relatively, and at least for a while.

It was an ongoing struggle: Garcia had always had a seemingly inextinguishable weakness for a buzz.

Is there some sort of unholy alliance between artistic creativity and the susceptibility to substance abuse? It seems so, intuitively, by the numbers of musicians and artists and writers who famously succumb. But brain scientists have so far been unable to find any such link—drink and drugs, it turns out, are temptations for a large subset of people at all levels of intelligence, inventiveness, and achievement. It's just that creative people tend to be well-known people, and so their struggles and relapses and deaths make the news. We hear about them, and not the millions of others. We hear about people like Nikki Sixx.

Minutes before the Grateful Dead were taking the stage in Oakland, five hundred and fifty miles down the California coast, in Van Nuys, Sixx was scribbling in a diary about his ongoing descent into madness. He was the bassist and songwriter for Mötley Crüe, a heavy metal band as musically different from the Dead as possible in the world of eighties rock. But Sixx closely resembled Garcia in at least two ways: his fame, and his history with hard drugs. He had been using heroin and freebasing cocaine for months, and he was an out-of-control paranoiac.

Decades later, Sixx's diary would become a book titled *The Heroin Diaries.* This was his entry for December 28, 1986:

> 9:40 p.m. After I binged last night—or was it tonight—I was convinced yet again that there were people coming to get me. It was

more than just shadows and voices, more than just fantasies . . . it was real, and I was scared to the core. . . . I try to keep it all together but then I gave in to the madness and became one with my insanity.

I always end up in the closet in my bedroom. Let me tell you about that place, my closet. It's more than a closet—it's a haven for me. It's where I keep my dope and where I keep my gun, I know when I'm in there I'm safe, at least until I get too high. I can't be out in the house—there are too many windows and I know I'm being watched. Right now it seems impossible that cops are peering in from the trees outside or people are looking at me through the peephole at the front door. But when the drugs kick in I can't control my mind. Today, last night feels like a lifetime ago. But the sick thing is I could do it again tonight.

"The only way to bring myself down quicker," he later added in retrospect, was heroin: "Heroin would make the madness go away; it was the easy solution. It seemed to make sense at the time."

Nikki Sixx was losing his mind on the very night Jerry Garcia was trying to fully recapture his.

Garcia and the Dead had gone back on tour in mid-December, and though it was clear to his friends and to his audiences that Garcia was healthier, his performances were initially listless. He'd lost something.

The song into which Jerry Garcia glided at a few minutes to midnight on December 28, 1986—with Dave Taylor and Steve Christie in the balcony, leaning in—was one that Garcia had written in 1969 with lyricist Robert Hunter. Hunter is reportedly the great-great-grandson of the Scottish poet Robert Burns; if true, he shared some of his illustrious ancestor's existential melancholy. "Black Peter" has 1960s overtones of racial injustice, but mostly it is about death. Peter is on his deathbed, surrounded by friends who are trying, and apparently failing, to console him. They offer only platitudes. In fact, they seem to morbidly enjoy the drama of his impending death. As it turns out, Black Peter survives at least another day—another day indistinguishable from the previous, filled with awkwardness and banalities and the inability to meaningfully communicate.

This was the Dead's fifth concert since Garcia returned to the stage. Once before on this comeback tour he had played "Black Peter." It had been on December 17 and McNally, the band's biographer, was watching.

Jerry Garcia had had an unusual relationship with lyrics. He was an instrumentalist, not a lyricist. He understood how words and music went together, but to him, the lyrics were almost secondary and largely structural—a textured way to carry the tune. On that first night, the night of the seventeenth, with "Black Peter," McNally saw Garcia transform.

The song begins,

> *All of my friends come to see me last night*
> *I was laying in my bed and dying.*

"He almost physically stumbled," McNally recalls today. "There was this ripple of emotion that went through him."

It was as though Garcia was really hearing the lyrics for the first time, McNally says: "It was startling. He was startled. My eyes were glued to him."

That concert, in toto, was only okay. There were musical lapses. Garcia's attention wandered. His reconnection to music, and his epiphany about words, was an ongoing process for him. By Sunday, December 28, he had evidently figured it out.

So here he was, again swinging into "Black Peter." As customary, Garcia was on the far right of the stage. He wore his customary purple T-shirt. His floppy shock of white hair, boinging with the beat, almost glowed under the lights.

> *All of my friends come to see me last night*
> *I was laying in my bed and . . .*

Garcia swallowed the next word. There is a surviving video of this concert, and *dying* nearly disappears. Jerry Garcia was literally internalizing it.

"You could hear a pin drop," Steve Christie remembers. The crowd was transfixed.

Garcia moved on with the song:

> *Fever roll up to a hundred and five*
> *Roll on up*
> *Gonna roll back down*
> *One more day*
> *I find myself alive . . .*

That last line was being wailed out by the man who almost died, and then came back to his friends: There were five thousand of them here this day, and they loved him, and there was nothing banal about it.

The Grateful Dead audiences usually stayed respectfully quiet during numbers. But at this moment, at that line, in this song, the crowd erupted. People cheered, whooped, almost drowning out the next few words, which speculate that Peter might be dead the next day.

Steve Christie remembers the moment vividly. "It was superb, amazing," Christie says. "It actually delivered a sense of release and of relief." Garcia was going to be okay.

Altogether, it was a smoldering set. The timing and the transfers were perfect. Not a misstep anywhere. Not a false note. Not a tepid moment. Not a line delivered without emotion.

"The band was on fire that night," says Christie.

JUSTIN KREUTZMANN IS the son of Bill Kreutzmann, the Grateful Dead's longtime drummer. Justin is now a filmmaker and video director, specializing in musical documentaries.

In 1986, when he was sixteen, Justin often traveled with his father, and he remembers being backstage after the late December show in Oakland—almost certainly the 28th—in the greenroom, with the band. The band members, sweaty and elated, were gobbling food and drink.

Garcia, Kreutzmann said, was electric, someone filled with a newfound sense of awe.

"Jerry was saying, 'God, I never realized what a great band this is. I haven't been listening for years.'" Kreutzmann laughs. "It's like he had finally become a Deadhead."

———

BY THAT POINT, midnight had passed. The twenty-eighth day of the twelfth month of the year was done. Eva Baisey had gotten her new heart and Todd Thrane had lost his life trying to save babies, and baby Michael Green had been burned beyond recognition and Cara Knott had been pulled, dead, from a culvert and Ed Koch had been booed by his loyal constituents and the Confederate flag was marched home and someone had stolen the weather vane and Terry Dolan and Joel Resnicoff had died of AIDS and Brad Wilson had somehow survived his helicopter crash and the football replay had gone on and on and on and little Heather Hamilton had saved the princess. The day would quickly fade into imperfect memory. The events of a single day are hard to hold on to in the relentless flow of time, the most powerful and mysterious force of all. Everything moves on.

JERRY GARCIA MOVED ON, too. He was a changed man for a while. His sense of awe remained for a while. His physical and musical rebirth led to a period considered the creative and commercial pinnacle of the Grateful Dead. In the next few years, the band produced some of their most successful and iconic albums, and released their only Top Forty hit, "Touch of Grey." They toured with Dylan. They had to move from their beloved Kaiser Center bandbox to a larger venue, to accommodate larger crowds.

In 1987, Ben & Jerry's made Jerry Garcia a household name across all cultures and lifestyles in America—grandmas in Everyburg, U.S.A.!—by debuting the Cherry Garcia flavor; it became one of the company's all-time best-sellers. Jerry did radio commercials for Levi's jeans.

The money came, too. When the band's guitarist Bob Weir was asked how financial success was changing his life, he told his interviewer, "You know those occasional pistachio nuts that are really tough to open? Now I just throw them out."

For some time, Garcia enjoyed not only the unaccustomed wealth, but good health as well—and remained mostly clean. His estranged wife, Carolyn "Mountain Girl" Garcia—a former Merry Prankster who had helped nurse Garcia through recovery, stayed around to talk him through his new life. She lives in Eugene, Oregon, now.

"I thought he had come back too soon," she says today, "but Jerry was driven. Ever have a dog chase a ball till it gets exhausted, but the next opportunity keeps coming up, and he takes it? That was Jerry.

"But the whole thing did force him to be straight. It improved his personality for a while. For a while, he had to think about his survival, rather than just living day to day. It was a really sweet time."

AS IT HAPPENS, on this very day—December 28, 1986—a small essay appeared in the Sunday magazine of the *Miami Herald*. It was written by a man who, several years earlier, had somehow walked away from a seemingly unsurvivable car accident.

He was on foot. Five feet away, a small car was pancaked by an out-of-control, ten-ton truck. That little car had not rolled over him—it had *bounced* over him. He was nearly without injury.

His essay discussed how this experience had affected him:

The nighttime sky shimmered with mystery and grandeur. A man could get lost in it, out there in the blackness in his back yard, sitting cross-legged on the hood of his car, captivated and humbled, oblivious to the bitter cold.

A raw tomato, eaten like a McIntosh, was the finest meal a man could want. How could I have not noticed its pebbly sour-sweet perfection before?

A stranger's cigarette butt, hurled from a car window at night, became a thing of beauty, exploding on the road in a tiny, magnificent fire shower.

A man can taste water, if he tries.

A man can taste a woman without touching her, if he tries.

It lasted several weeks, this sense of wonderment. Then it began to weaken.

I tried desperately to hold on to it, but there was no use. It slipped away. And—God help me—never returned.

IT WOULD SLIP away for Jerry, too.

Mountain Girl doesn't know exactly when it began—"Jerry didn't let his family see his debaucheries," she says sadly—but by at least 1990, it was clear he was on a personal downslide, and the end became inevitable.

By July 1995, Garcia was again in the thrall of heroin. He checked into the Betty Ford Center in Rancho Mirage, California, but checked himself out again two weeks later—to celebrate his fifty-third birthday with family and friends. Apparently he didn't feel his recovery was complete and reentered treatment at a different facility, Serenity Knolls, in Marin County. It was there, just before dawn on Wednesday, August 9, that a clinic counselor found him in his bed. The heart of the Grateful Dead had succumbed to a coronary, apparently in his sleep.

At the time, his then-wife Deborah told the world that Jerry had died with a smile on his face. She hadn't been there, of course. Maybe it was true, or maybe it was wishful thinking, or maybe it was just something you say to comfort people. But it presented an interesting idea, for discussion purposes.

Back in 1965, Jerry Garcia had chosen the name for his band, borrowing the term from a folktale common to many cultures: An unfortunate soul who dies too poor to afford burial faces an eternity of torment, but a generous stranger shows up and pays for a proper interment. The spirit of the deceased is so thankful that he returns to earth to reward his benefactor. It is a tale of redemption and resurrection. And of course, gratitude.

It's not clear whether Garcia knew the entirety of that story, at least initially: He'd later said that he'd seen the term in a dictionary, and was thunderstruck by the power of the collision of those two particular words.

It's quite a collision. We are all serving time on death row; only the length of our stay is indeterminate. Dead people, walking. If our lives are to be fulfilling, we must be grateful for the experience alone.

Those who have had a brush with death and survive, who have come nakedly face-to-face with their own mortality, get a visceral glimpse at that truth. It is terrifying and humbling; it changes perceptions and priorities and delivers awe. But denial tends to quickly take hold again—we navigate our terrors through denial—and we return to the mundane: our old habits, our take-for-granted thinking. Each moment becomes once again just another in a series of unremarkable moments, instead of a soul-searing blast of the inexpressible wonder of being.

Acknowledgments

I conducted more than five hundred interviews for this book over six years. Many of the interviews were face-to-face. Some were on the phone, and some were face-to-face *and* on the phone, via Skype. This was all in an effort to triangulate or rectangulate (or further polygonize) people's disparate and sometimes conflicting recollections into a coherent narrative of the events of a single day thirty-plus years in the past. That meant reaching people, and often reaching them again, challenging them on details, sometimes requesting proof, almost always hassling them about minutiae. Alas, some of these people and their stories didn't make it into what you are reading. I apologize to them, thank them for their cooperation, and cringe in fear of their online vituperation, which will be warranted.

I know there are mistakes in this book; I just don't know what they are. Any work, however conscientious, that partially relies on people's memories (and an often incomplete historical record) is going to get some things wrong. I believe these instances have been minimized through the help of some amazingly skillful backstops. I have had the assistance of one of the world's greatest librarian-researchers, Julie Tate, who, in the *Washington Post* newsroom, is more associated with Pulitzer Prizes than Joseph Pulitzer is. And I am lucky enough to count among my closest friends the world's funniest copy editor, Pat Myers. Pat doesn't just find illiteracies, which are unfortunately all too common in my work, and she doesn't just correct errors and fix grammar and syntax and word usage and such. She brings to her work an encyclopedic knowledge of wildly eclectic subject matters: say, seventeenth-century Flemish art, NFL football, the classification of goldenrod species, Judaic history, cooking with garlic, and so forth. Pat negotiated her services to me in exchange for a nice dinner. (So she's not a great businesswoman. That's not why I love her.)

I relied, at least initially, on hundreds of contemporaneous newspaper and TV accounts, and because of my love and respect for journalism, I will not reveal here the disturbingly high percentage of them that had serious errors of fact; the expression *the first rough draft of history,* commonly used to refer to journalism, should emphasize *rough.* Many of these pieces, however, were extraordinarily well researched and crafted, not the least of which was Steve Salerno's excellent coverage in the *Los Angeles Times* of the events following the murder of Cara Knott. Among the many books I relied on for research material, two were particularly helpful: *Getting to Ellen,* by Ellen Krug, and *Badge of Betrayal,* by Joe Cantlupe and Lisa Petrillo.

I am particularly indebted to my friend and colleague David Von Drehle for his wisdom and guidance, and specifically for a profound observation of his that I flat-out stole. He won't remember it, which is just as well.

I thank Chris Manteuffel for the chapter I did not write.

I am grateful for able research by Arlene Reidy. Celia Ampel contributed valuable reporting suggestions. At Dutton, Katie Zaborsky and Cassidy Sachs provided intelligent, sensitive editing. Also I am indebted to Rachel Manteuffel, for her Herculean efforts, mostly successful, to keep me sane and focused during the dreadfully overlong time it took me to complete this book—four years past the contracted deadline. My capable literary agent, Gail Ross, was more than essential in these tricky matters.

Speaking of four years overdue, if you are an author you know how startling it is to have a publisher with the forbearance, confidence, and sheer decency to make allowances they were not required to make. I was lucky enough to have not one but two of this rare breed of intellectual *mensch*: David Rosenthal, now of Houghton Mifflin, who initially purchased the book and ushered it through much of the initial writing, and John Parsley, of Dutton, who took it over seamlessly, and continued showing extraordinary patience, encouragement, and support.

And finally, there is the awkward matter of Tom Shroder. Tom is my good friend and villainous nemesis. He has been my principal editor at the *Post* and has edited most of my books. He has the sensitivity of a corduroy condom. (In my columns I have bestowed on him the sobriquet "Tom the Butcher.") Here is his modus operandi: He will receive my latest chapter, which he knew was written by a man under enormous pressure, in iffy health, fighting personal demons, losing brain cells by the thousands per day, out of time and energy, sapped of will, exhausted by anxiety, defeated by life, pathetically succumbing to it all.

Tom will weigh all these things, carefully consider his human duties to me as loyal friend, and inform me that I have botched everything and need to have a rewritten chapter to him by Monday at the latest, and it had better address his problems or there will be Hell to Pay.

I absolutely hate Tom and fully intend never to talk to him again—until I need him, which will be soon, because, damn, he is the best.

Bibliography

Barker, Rodney. *Dancing with the Devil: Sex, Espionage, and the U.S. Marines: The Clayton Lonetree Story.* Simon & Schuster, 1996.

Cantlupe, Joe, and Petrillo, Lisa. *Badge of Betrayal: The Devastating True Story of a Rogue Cop Turned Murderer.* Avon Books, 1991.

Dolan, John T. (Terry), and Fossedal, Greg. *Reagan: A President Succeeds.* Publisher's Proof Copy. Conservative Press Inc., 1983.

Geherin, David. *John D. MacDonald.* Frederick Ungar Publishing Co., 1982.

Green, Brian. *The Fabric of the Cosmos: Space, Time, and the Texture of Reality.* Alfred A. Knopf, 2004.

Greenfield, Robert. *Dark Star: An Oral Biography of Jerry Garcia.* Plexus Publishing, 1996.

Headley, Lake, and Hoffman, William. *The Court-Martial of Clayton Lonetree.* Henry Holt & Co., 1989.

Hinckley, Jack, and Hinckley, Jo Ann. *Breaking Points.* Zondervan Publishing, 1985.

Hoffman, David E. *The Dead Hand: The Untold Story of the Cold War Arms Race and Its Dangerous Legacy.* Random House, 2009.

Hynes, Charles J., and Drury, Bob. *Incident at Howard Beach: The Case for Murder.* G. P. Putnam's Sons, 1990.

Jackson, Blair. *Garcia: An American Life.* Penguin Books, 1999.

Kirklin, James K., Young, James B., and McGiffin, David C. *Heart Transplantation.* Churchill Livingstone, 2002.

Koch, Edward I. *All the Best: Letters from a Feisty Mayor.* Simon & Schuster, 1990.

Krug, Ellen. *Getting to Ellen: A Memoir about Love, Honesty and Gender Change.* Stepladder Press, 2013.

McNally, Dennis. *A Long Strange Trip: The Inside History of the Grateful Dead.* Broadway Books, 2002.

Merrill, Hugh. *The Red Hot Typewriter: The Life and Times of John D. MacDonald.* St. Martin's Press, 2000.

Richardson, Peter. *No Simple Highway: A Cultural History of the Grateful Dead.* St. Martin's Press, 2015.

Sixx, Nikki. *The Heroin Diaries: A Year in the Life of a Shattered Rock Star.* Simon & Schuster, 2007.

About the Author

G ene Weingarten is a feature writer and syndicated humor columnist for *The Washington Post*. He is the only person to have twice won the Pulitzer Prize for feature writing. His previous books include *The Hypochondriac's Guide to Life. And Death*; *Old Dogs*; and *The Fiddler in the Subway*, a collection of his best-known work. With Horace LaBadie and cartoonist David Clark, he writes *Barney & Clyde*, a syndicated newspaper comic strip.